D1525097

OPERATION THUNDERCLAP AND THE BLACK MARCH

OPERATION THUNDERCLAP

AND THE

BLACK MARCH

Two World War II Stories
from the Unstoppable
91st Bomb Group

RICHARD ALLISON

CASEMATE
Philadelphia & Oxford

Published in the United States of America and Great Britain in 2014 by
CASEMATE PUBLISHERS
908 Darby Road, Havertown, PA 19083
and
10 Hythe Bridge Street, Oxford, OX1 2EW

ISBN 978-1-61200-265-1
Digital Edition: ISBN 978-1-61200-266-8

Cataloging-in-publication data is available from the Library of Congress and
the British Library.

10 9 8 7 6 5 4 3 2 1

Printed and bound in the United States of America.

For a complete list of Casemate titles please contact:

CASEMATE PUBLISHERS (US)
Telephone (610) 853-9131, Fax (610) 853-9146
E-mail: casemate@casematepublishing.com

CASEMATE PUBLISHERS (UK)
Telephone (01865) 241249, Fax (01865) 794449
E-mail: casemate-uk@casematepublishing.co.uk

Contents

ACKNOWLEDGMENTS 7

FOREWORD *May 15, 1945* 11

One Training 1943-44 19

Two The Bishop Crew Formation and Deployment 35

Three 91st Bomb Group—Bassingbourn 49

Four The "Oil Campaign" 61

Five Tragedy for the Bishop Crew 69

Six Paul's POW Odyssey Begins 89

Seven USAAF Heavy Bomber Policy—
Operation Thunderclap 105

Eight *The Black March* Begins 123

Nine *Operation Thunderclap* Continues 139

Ten Swinemünde to Halle, Nazi Germany 147

Eleven The Left Echelon 155

Twelve A Red Army Horseman 167

Thirteen Watching The Soviet Army Sweep 177

Epilogue Conversations with Addison Bartush
and Paul Lynch 193

NOTES 215

SELECTED BIBLIOGRAPHY 227

INDEX 229

ABOUT THE AUTHOR 240

To Susan, Shawn Elizabeth and Nate, with love.

Acknowledgments

My gratitude goes out to my friend and former trust client Addison Bartush who in 2008 indicated willingness for me to interview him about his military career with the U.S. Army Air Forces in World War II. Addison provided me with a large box that contained letters from his parents, siblings and friends, USAAF school graduation commemorative pamphlets, photographs, sewing kits, technical flying manuals, uniform patches, Army shoelaces, a wartime newsletter from *1st Air Division Headquarters*, and (most notably) 28 yellowed and crumbly publications of the *Stars and Stripes* newspaper, each containing a write up on a mission flown by him. Missing however, were letters that Addison wrote home to his parents, brothers and sister. This turned out not to be a problem, however, for Addison's memory of his World War II service was excellent. In my extensive personal interviews with Addison he was able to fill in all the blanks. In my gratitude to Addison, I wish to especially thank him for his service to country. I happened to be born during World War II and have lived a good life in a free America since then—thanks, Addison.

I wish to convey my special thanks to Addison's crewmate, Paul Lynch, for permitting me to use excerpts appearing in quotations from his 1998, 34-page personal memoir about his World War II experience entitled *The Great Warrior*, and also for allowing me to extensively interview him through telephone and email exchanges; for carefully reviewing his story about World War II for accuracy and for providing valuable and timely input at all times. Paul asked me in 2011 if I would write about his POW experience, and I decided to do it and also combine it with Addison's story. Paul is co-author of much of each chapter that pertains to him. Many of the images appearing in this book are used with Paul's permission. I likewise thank Paul for his military service in both a national and personal sense.

Recognition should be given to the resource book entitled *The Ragged Irregulars of Bassingbourn: The 91st Bombardment Group in World War II.* Written by Marion H. Havelaar and William N. Hess and published in 1995, this work contains, in addition to the war-story narrative, a number of detailed and highly useful appendices. It has a listing of every combat mission the 91st ever completed, scrubbed, cancelled or aborted, the history and name of every aircraft flown by it, and a 28-page "Roll of Honor"—the 91st Bomb Group's casualty list by name and date—killed in action, wounded in action, prisoner of war, survived ditching and other categories. This reference work proved to be invaluable in reconstructing who, what, when and where of the air combat records of Addison Bartush and Paul Lynch. The Havelaar family was most generous in granting excerpt permissions and authorization to re- produce images from this important historical work.

Thanks go the 91st Bomb Group Memorial Association for maintaining on their website a plethora of historical information about World War II operations of the Bomb Group including daily reports of squadron activities. I highly recommend the Memorial Association's website, www. 91stbombgroup.com, to all readers who are interested in learning about the glorious history of the USAAF 91st Bomb Group. This website is outstanding. Particular appreciation goes to its President, Mick Hanou, who assisted in the final edit of my book.

I am grateful for author John Meurs, who wrote *Not Home for Christmas: A Day in the Life of the Mighty Eighth,* a work that devotes a chapter to each of 34 heavy bombers from the Eighth Air Force lost on November 26, 1944, one of which was *The Wild Hare* with Paul Lynch and eight others aboard. *Not Home for Christmas* enabled me to flesh out personal particulars for a number of members of this bomber's crew, which contributed to the presentation of this story. For the account of the downing of *The Wild Hare* I relied primarily upon information furnished to me by Paul Lynch and also from other attributed sources.

Gratefulness is expressed to Hillsdale College for publishing *Imprimis* (Latin meaning "in the first place") its no-charge national speech digest. Scholarly presentations delivered at this college's many seminar and lecture programs are made available to the public through this publication. One such paper, given in 1988 by Nikolai Tolstoy entitled *"Forced Repatriation to the Soviet Union: The Secret Betrayal,"* proved invaluable to me in understanding and putting forward a point of view on the relationship existing between the United States and Soviet Union immediately following the cessation of hostilities in World War II. Not only is Hillsdale College to be commended for its "subscription free upon request" policy, but also its blanket openness rule granting permission to reprint presentations in whole or in part.

I am indebted to my longtime friend and fellow writer Michael Goodell who edited my manuscript. Last but not least, I wish to thank my brother Mark Allison for his invaluable assistance as my primary editor and agent. Mark put in long hours improving my writing, fact-checking, working on images, dealing with publishing houses, and took on a whole host of other responsibilities. I honestly could not have done this writing project without his encouragement and backing.

RA, 2014

Foreword May 15, 1945

First Lieutenant Addison Bartush's voice was being drowned out by the unmistakable scream of a Pratt and Whitney-powered P-47 flying overhead. "To go dancing with the four 'M's," he yelled in answer to his friend's question. "At the Terrace Room of the Statler Hotel . . . Mary, Mary, Marilyn and Marion!"

Addison sat at a table in the Officers Club at Bassingbourn USAAF Air Station, about 40 miles north of London, where he served as a second pilot flying B-17s in the 91st Bomb Group of the mighty Eighth Air Force. The 91st completed its last mission of the war on April 25 and the Nazis surrendered unconditionally on May 8. The celebration on base had continued uninterrupted since then, and this day would be no exception. It was a time for the survivors to celebrate their hard-won victory and to rejoice at their own good fortune. It was a time to decompress and to dream about going home. It was a time to reflect upon their recent experiences that, over time, would become indelible memories, and it was also a time to think about the friends they had lost.

The P-47 roaring overhead was called the Thunderbolt, but just as often it was referred to by its ignominious nickname, the "Jug," as it looked like one. In a dive, the P-47 was magnificent and fast. This particular plane was used by the 91st to locate their bomb group in relation to other bomb groups forming up for missions over Nazi Germany. Today it had been liberated for a joy ride by one of the B-17 pilots who had 20 hours experience flying one.

Slowly sipping his beer, Addison was not the least bit distracted by the racket outside. It had taken the better part of a month for it to finally sink in that he had flown 31 combat missions and would not have to fly number 32. He no longer had to suit up every fourth or fifth day in the very early morning. He no longer had to endure a somber breakfast followed by a tense mission briefing. Now he could relax and enjoy his morning cigarette rather than just suck one down for a quick preflight fix. Even the Officers Club was more fun now. Germany was "kaput"—destroyed. His gladiatorial lifestyle was now in remission. Although he might get dragged into the war against Japan, he was able to set those worries aside for the time being and bask in the satisfaction of a job well done. The nervous feeling he carried in the pit of his stomach was now subsiding.

Addison looked around the room packed with celebrants—men parked at the curved, polished wooden bar or seated at the tables; practically every table was filled. Cards were being shuffled and dice were shaken in a cup. It was early evening, getting towards sundown and a fair amount of scotch and beer had been consumed. "I'm lucky to be at Bassingbourn," Addison thought. "The Savoy Hotel of air bases!"

Addison thought of his last strategic mission, the attack on that airfield in Pilsen, Czechoslovakia, on April 25, the last mission of the war for the Eighth Air Force. It had really scared him. The war was supposed to be about over, but there he was flying through the most ferocious flak field he had ever seen. The first pilots in his squadron, the 324th, including his own first pilot, had disobeyed orders to make a second pass at the target area and turned back for home.

This episode seemed like a bad dream. Most of his combat experiences were bad dreams, Addison reflected. He had seen things from a viewpoint almost five miles high, and even from that altitude some of what he saw shocked him. "Dresden," he uttered under his breath.

His thoughts switched back to dancing at the Statler Hotel in Detroit. He would proudly wear his summer khaki uniform with jacket and tie. Above his left breast pocket would be his silver USAAF wings and an Air Medal with a number of oak leaf clusters, each cluster denoting five combat missions performed. In 1943 when he left the company of those young ladies, the four 'M's, he had been a fraternity boy. In 1944 when he briefly saw them again on home leave he was a newly minted flight officer, proud but nervous about the future. Now he was returning as someone else entirely, and he felt good about the changes. The war had aged him well beyond his 23 years. Now he was a first lieutenant and a combat veteran. He had accomplished something.

After the chuckles about his many girlfriends subsided, Addison's thoughts shifted again, as they often did that day. He remembered that horrible event of November 26, 1944 when German fighters shot down a B-17 that carried six of the crewmen that he had trained with in Gulfport, Mississippi, along with three veteran airmen. He himself had flown his first combat mission only the day before. When this happened a few parachutes had been spotted, but not knowing who may have survived, the USAAF listed the entire crew of nine as missing in action.

Of his six buddies from the Gulfport days, he now knew, both from official sources and letters from family members, that two had been killed, three had been taken prisoner and that one, the tail gunner, was still not accounted for. All he could do in the immediate aftermath of that tragedy was to commiserate with his other two Gulfport crewmembers who, like him, were not assigned to fly that fatal mission. A devout Catholic, Addison also prayed with Father Ragan, a chaplain at the base, who had been wonderful to him throughout his time at Bassingbourn. Addison knew that top turret gunner Charles Cumings and radioman John Kendall were dead and did not hold out much hope for the missing tail-gunner, Owen Monkman. Six months on a MIA list with no International Red Cross change in status was not a positive circumstance for Owen. Addison also appreciated that a B-17 tail-gunner had the least chance of any crewman of evacuating a stricken bomber. With only a few chutes spotted, chances were that Owen's was not one of them.

And of his POW buddies?

The two officers, First Lieutenant Dave Bishop, his pilot, and Flight Officer Robert J. "RJ" Miller, his navigator, were said to be in the Stalag Luft I, a large POW camp for commissioned officers, near Barth, northern Germany. The news reported that the Red Army had liberated Stalag Luft I on May 1 without shots being fired. Addison was mindful that a U.S. and British airlift to this camp was in progress at this very moment. Hopefully he would be reunited soon with Dave and RJ, or at least be notified of their safe return to U.S. military control.

Where POW waist-gunner Sergeant Paul Lynch might be at that time was unknown. Paul had been shipped to an NCO POW camp in northern Poland in December, but there had been press reports that in early February the camp had been closed and that most of its occupants were put on a forced march through Nazi Germany. Both the International Red Cross and Paul's family were in the dark as to Paul's status since this march began. On the move, Paul could not mail out letters or postcards as he did from the POW camp.

Addison remembered one thing about Paul that would serve him well if he was still alive: the guy was resourceful. At Gulfport, when their bombardier unexpectedly dropped out late in the B-17 crew training, the three remaining officers picked Paul out of six enlisted crewmen for training on the Norden bombsight. Paul was a quick learner and physically strong. Over several months Paul demonstrated time and again the ability to make sound decisions. If any one could make that march, Addison thought, it would be Paul. "Thank God that the shooting is now over," Addison reflected, thinking that if Paul were still alive this circumstance would help him.

A number of Addison's friends and associates had perished during his time at Bassingbourn. He was immensely grateful for his own survival, but contemplated from time to time, "Why me?" He looked slowly around the room at the faces of his fellow celebrants and knew instinctively that everyone present had recently asked himself the same question. There had been close calls, lots of them, and all here had shared the risks.

Again, "Why me?" he asked.

The sound of the P-47 came back again, even louder than before. "Pull up!" someone shouted from the bar inside in response to the deafening noise. That yell was followed immediately by a loud crash outside.

"My God!" Addison screamed.

Major James Griffin, the well-liked operations officer of the 324th squadron, went down near the intersection of the two runways at the Bassingbourn airfield while attempting a low altitude roll. He became the last casualty of the 91st Bomb Group in Europe in 1945.

———

For three months Sergeant Paul Lynch had been on a continuous march; he reckoned that he had lost about a third of his body weight, but had no way of knowing this other than the fact that his filthy, itchy, lice-infested wool uniform hung off him like a loose bag. He smelled and looked horrible; his hair and beard were unkempt and matted by dirt—caked hard by the smoke of many evening fires and the dried-up perspiration that had accumulated after three months of slogging through snow and mud and sleeping in barns. He knew he looked like a wild beast, but there wasn't much he could do about it.

On May 12 his trek across Europe had finally ended, and for the past three days he had been billeted in a dormitory of what had been a technical school before the war. Paul was now in the custody of the Red Army and received regular meals, but he knew it would be some time before he recovered from the effects of slow, persistent starvation. And try as he might he could not significantly improve his personal hygiene, as there were no baths or showers available and no change of clothing.

The last three afternoons and nights had been horrible. He had never witnessed anything like them in his life. This was not the world that he had been raised in. When would the horror end?

The U.S. Army was nearby, just a few miles away. The war was over. When would he be permitted to go home?

Paul remembered back to the day in early October 1943 in Leominster, Massachusetts, when he walked to the bus stop with his kid brother, Bruce, on his way to his induction at Fort Devens. Bruce was 11 years old and he looked up to his 18-year-old brother with envy and pride for the "adventure" that Paul was about to begin. "Some adventure," Paul muttered to himself, followed moments later by a defiant "I'm alive!" In the quiet of fading daylight, he then offered, "Thank you, God, for letting me live. If I ever return to my family, I vow to put this whole episode forever behind me."

Paul had accomplished something remarkable. Along with three other American airmen, on April 22 he escaped his Nazi captors and made his way through the battle line to be liberated by advancing Soviet forces. Now, in supposed peacetime, he and approximately 160 other Americans, all former POWs of the Nazis, were held in a Soviet-administered collection center for U.S. servicemen in the city of Riesa, Germany, anxiously awaiting repatriation.

Paul looked out a dormitory window at the balcony of an apartment house across the street. He dreaded the advance of the day as he knew that was when the drinking of vodka would start up in earnest. He felt truly sorry for his former enemy. Would he witness again what he saw before?

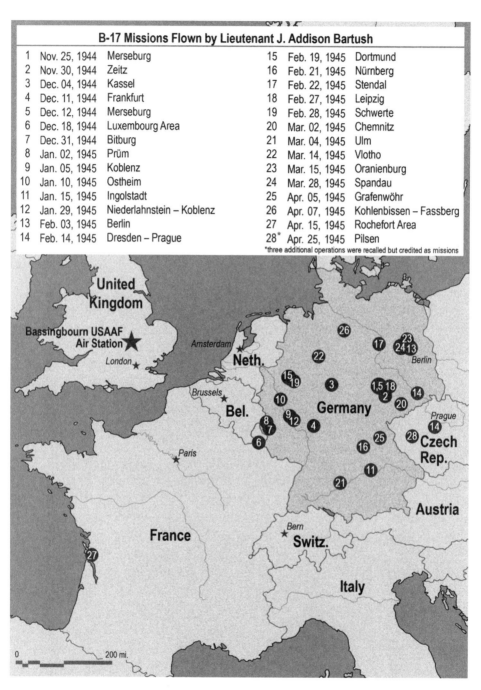

B-17 Missions Flown by Lieutenant J. Addison Bartush

#	Date	Target	#	Date	Target
1	Nov. 25, 1944	Merseburg	15	Feb. 19, 1945	Dortmund
2	Nov. 30, 1944	Zeitz	16	Feb. 21, 1945	Nürnberg
3	Dec. 04, 1944	Kassel	17	Feb. 22, 1945	Stendal
4	Dec. 11, 1944	Frankfurt	18	Feb. 27, 1945	Leipzig
5	Dec. 12, 1944	Merseburg	19	Feb. 28, 1945	Schwerte
6	Dec. 18, 1944	Luxembourg Area	20	Mar. 02, 1945	Chemnitz
7	Dec. 31, 1944	Bitburg	21	Mar. 04, 1945	Ulm
8	Jan. 02, 1945	Prüm	22	Mar. 14, 1945	Vlotho
9	Jan. 05, 1945	Koblenz	23	Mar. 15, 1945	Oranienburg
10	Jan. 10, 1945	Ostheim	24	Mar. 28, 1945	Spandau
11	Jan. 15, 1945	Ingolstadt	25	Apr. 05, 1945	Grafenwöhr
12	Jan. 29, 1945	Niederlahnstein – Koblenz	26	Apr. 07, 1945	Kohlenbissen – Fassberg
13	Feb. 03, 1945	Berlin	27	Apr. 15, 1945	Rochefort Area
14	Feb. 14, 1945	Dresden – Prague	28*	Apr. 25, 1945	Pilsen

*three additional operations were recalled but credited as missions

Map showing the location of the 91st Bomb Group in England and the targets attacked by Lieutenant Bartush.—Map by Mark Allison

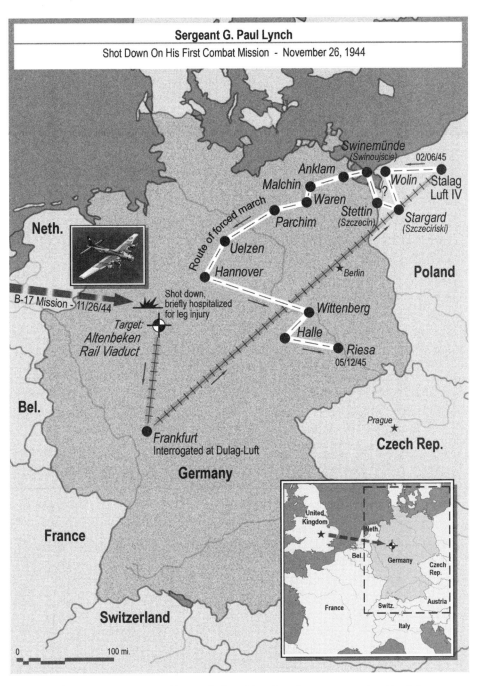

Sergeant G. Paul Lynch
Shot Down On His First Combat Mission - November 26, 1944

Swinemünde
(Swinoujście)   02/06/45

Anklam

Malchin   Wolin   Stalag
                                      Luft IV
Waren
Route of forced march   Stettin   ?
Parchim   (Szczecin)   Stargard
                                 (Szczeciński)

Neth.

Uelzen

Hannover   *Berlin   Poland

B-17 Mission - 11/26/44

Shot down,
briefly hospitalized
for leg injury   Wittenberg

Target:
Altenbeken   Halle
Rail Viaduct
                              Riesa
                              05/12/45

Bel.

Frankfurt   Prague
Interrogated at Dulag-Luft   *

                              Czech Rep.

Germany

France

Switzerland

0   100 mi.

Inset map:
United Kingdom
Neth.
Bel.   Germany
France Czech Rep.
Switz. Austria
Italy

Map showing Sergeant Lynch's travels from his point of capture near the Altenbeken target site to his repatriation to U.S. control six months later.—Map by Mark Allison

CHAPTER ONE

Training, 1943–44

"**P**ull wings in, Cadet!"

"Yes, Sir!" Addison Bartush, age 21, responded smartly to his friend's order. Smiling, Addison snapped to exaggerated attention, making his chest large and his waist as narrow as he could.

"Shoulders back, elbows to your sides!" his would-be commander added for emphasis. In a few minutes Addison and his friend would form up with other cadets and stand at attention for real; they would march as a company to their graduation ceremony at Army Air Forces Southeast Training Center Pre-Flight School (Pilot). This day at Maxwell Field, Alabama, not far from Montgomery, was beastly hot; it was late September 1943 and Addison was about to be promoted to corporal. Maxwell Army Airfield was named for Lt. William Maxwell, an Army aviator and Alabama native who died heroically in a 1920 plane crash in the Philippines. It was a gigantic airbase. Addison's school was just one of several located there.

The previous February, Addison was in Detroit. With the war effort in full swing, he knew he was about to be drafted if he did not first volunteer for service. He chose the Army Air Forces for its promise of adventure. In the ensuing months his reality had been anything but adventurous. He had survived eight weeks of regular Army boot camp in Miami, Florida, another eight weeks in the College Pilot Training Program at the University of Pittsburgh, a month of physical and mental examinations in Nashville, Tennessee to determine his suitability to serve as a pilot, navigator or bombardier (where he was selected for pilot training), followed by two months in the heat at Maxwell, the "West Point of Alabama," where incoming "plebes" wore white gloves and had to ask permission to speak to an upperclassman. A total of seven months had passed since Addison had taken his oath but he had not yet even looked inside an airplane save for one short flight in a Piper Cub back at Butler, Pennsylvania during which he was given the controls for a few joyous minutes to see what it felt like to fly.

Addison now thought: And this was the U.S. Army Air Forces? "At this rate the war will be over before I get into it," he despaired. He was bone tired of his textbook work at Maxwell—studying the mechanics and physics of flight, the science of deflection shooting and similar stuff. The classrooms were so hot one could barely stay awake. And when he was not in class or studying, he was doing physical training, drill marching or undergoing picayune personnel and barracks inspections.

Addison gazed a last time at his wooden barracks and thought of eight men packed into a room built size-wise to accommodate only two. Sleeping in skivvies and on stacked bunk beds with only a small electric fan or two to push around the hot, moist air, this stark accommodation was a world apart from what Addison experienced growing up. He would not miss it.

Oh, to fly an airplane.

But Addison's friend was not yet finished with him: "Ride the beam, Cadet Bartush!" he screamed.

This time Addison ignored his friend, who, in the spirit of irrational exuberance, blurted out the school honor code for no reason whatsoever. Quivering cadets had been required to recite this code and other school jingles, mostly during their first week; this was done in the presence of up-perclassmen or officers. The practice was not an endearing memory for Addison, or for that matter anyone else who had experienced it.

An Aviation Cadet will not lie, cheat or steal, nor allow any other Aviation Cadet to remain in the Cadet Corps who is guilty of the same, Sir!

"You're annoying me," Addison pleaded. "Stop!"

Grinning wider, the young man pressed on, reciting the cadet mission statement: "Strong bodies, stout hearts, alert minds and a liking for the air and its adventures . . . Sir!"

Addison looked at the parade ground and was thankful that today would be his last performance at this command. He remembered the weekends when for one night only the cadets were free to drink beer at a nearby hotel and dance with the locals. This habit grew old fast and some of the cadets started referring to their dance partners as "cadet widows," a euphemism for young ladies known by several classes of aviation cadets. The problem was that there was little, if anything, wholesome to do in the vicinity of the base other than perhaps enjoy a milkshake at a soda pop stand located on base at the USO.

Addison longed for the company of college coeds—specifically the ones he hoped might be waiting for him back in Detroit. At the time of his enlistment, he had completed one and a half years at the University of Detroit, majoring in business administration, and that had qualified him for consideration in the air cadet program. The two months at the University of Pittsburgh was so the government might review his academic performance in college courses selected for him and not by him.

Addison thought again of the weekend parade ground reviews that were usually scheduled for the morning after the night before. Being hung-over was not a good idea for these events and Addison quickly learned to regulate the amount of beer he consumed. The sun would beat down mercilessly while cadets braced in ranks and waited endlessly for the two specific orders to be issued: "Shoulder arms!" and "Forward march!" The marchers would then advance and turn to pass in front of the reviewing stand, ending up in the barracks area where the ordeal concluded.

Addison never fainted but once came close. An alert cadet standing behind him grabbed him on the way down. With great concentration Addison managed to straighten himself up and remain conscious until the magic words finally barked out.

"Keep knees unlocked," Addison mouthed to himself on that occasion. "Move just a tiny bit but don't let them see it. Shift weight from one foot to the other, but imperceptibly. Mix up the breathing: faster, slower, deeper . . . stimulate those capillaries!"

Standing at attention was supposed to build character, Addison had been told. Ha! More like building broken skulls, he knew. He had witnessed a number of cadets collapse, and some indeed hit the concrete hard. Insufficient blood-flow to the brain, he appreciated. With enough time standing motionless, gravity would always win. Dehydration in the hot Alabama sunshine combined with the previous night's alcohol consumption was an effective one-two punch to hasten the process.

"Ride the beam, Cadet! Eyes forward!"

Addison remembered knife and fork school. He had been chagrined (but wisely kept his mouth shut) when he "learned" in the classroom that the fork and napkin were always placed on the left side and that in America one always placed chewable food in one's mouth with a fork held in one's right hand, prongs pointed upwards. "Every U.S. officer must be a gentleman," his instructor emphasized, "and do this properly." What Addison didn't let on was that he and his siblings were well aware of these rules, having been raised in circumstances where this was always done properly.

Although Addison's father started out from modest means, he went on to build a successful business and became a major player in the dairy products industry. Addison and his siblings had grown up in affluence, but their parents, who passed down the lessons of honest dealings and hard work to their children, had not overly pampered them. During the summer months the Bartush boys were expected to do their share, laboring long factory hours at an ice cream plant.

"I said: Ride the beam, Cadet! Eyes forward!" his friend barked to Addison's annoyance.

"Yes Sir, General Spoony, Sir!" Addison answered.

The best advice that Addison had found in his current military situation had come, surprisingly, from the man responsible for practically everything that happened to him at pre-flight school. The school commandant, Major Mark C. Bane, Jr. had written a pocket booklet for pilot-hopefuls at Maxwell Field. In it, he wrote:

> *In all the phases of your cadet life, be sincere, but not too serious. Remember that a sense of humor, while officially it must be restrained, is indispensable to you as individuals.*

From this booklet Addison learned the different ways at Maxwell Field to address the subject of stupidity: first, either directly by title ("Mr. Dowilly, Mr. Dumbjohn and Mr. Dumbsquat") or alternatively, indirectly by comparison, in like, "Dumb as a Dodo Bird." He also learned that a "Dawn Patroller" was a cadet who had the habit of arising before reveille (a practice frowned upon) and that the word "Spoony" was a derogatory term denoting a cadet who was always "neat and meticulous."

And a "Hot Pilot?"

"One exceptionally adept at flying in his own opinion."

"Gigs," depending on the number accumulated, could lead to a "Tour," that is, a solo punishment march during what would otherwise be precious free time. Addison remembered the cause of one of his tours: an inspector kicked his second pair of shoes out of alignment to give Addison that extra requisite gig needed for his "tour award."

You're in the Army now, you're not behind a plow . . .

Oh, did Addison and every other cadet long for a home-cooked meal, the loving smile of parents, the mischief of siblings, the laughter of friends and the element of civilian freedom that used to be. Major Bane, to his credit, did offer to the cadets a method whereby they might express disrespect without being *officially* disrespectful. The word "serious" stood for all things important, the Major wrote, and the word "seri*ass*" the exact opposite. By a slight inflection in one's voice one could dissent! It was best to be discreet, however, when doing this.

"It will be good to graduate," Addison remarked to his snickering friend. They both had had enough of the West Point of Alabama and looked forward to actually start flying. "This place is seri*ass*," he added.

––––––––

At the approximate time Addison started primary flight school, Paul Lynch, recently turned 18, enlisted in the USAAF, and like Addison, he did it for the promise of adventure and the sure knowledge that if he did not volunteer, the draft would take him anyway and he might end up in the infantry, where the next meal and clean clothes were not always assured things. Also, Paul thought that his chances for survival might be better in the air than on the ground. Someone he knew from his hometown of Leominster, Massachusetts had been killed in the infantry in Africa, and this weighed on his decision to join what was referred to in his 1943 high school yearbook as the "Army Air Corps." Of the nine male graduates shown on the open page spread where Paul's portrait appeared, three indicated a preference for the U.S. Army, two the Marines, two the Air Corps, and one, the class president, "Naval Aviation Cadet." Only one young man listed "Undecided."

The almost equal number of female graduates shown on the same pages identified various colleges (including nearby Wellesley) and preferences for careers in nursing, office work, teaching and business. One young lady, Barbara A. Landers, expressed an intention to join the United States Marine Corps following graduation.

Paul had been an average student at Leominster High School and his extracurricular activities were the Speech Club and *Magnet*, the school newspaper, where he acted as a typesetter. Paul's father, Roger owned a small print shop in town and Paul worked there for three hours every afternoon following school, often doing messy jobs or other tedious tasks. "This will motivate you in later life," Roger Lynch told his son. "You will hate factory work." The Lynch family lived in a well-maintained wooden frame home painted crisp white and located at 59 Grand Street. Leominster exuded New England charm and was the birthplace, in 1774, of John Chapman, later to become known as Johnny Appleseed. Paul was the oldest of four children and his family was staunch Methodist.

Although Paul had not put forward much of an academic effort in high school, he did excel in one senior year subject. With the war on, the high school administration applied for and received accreditation approval for physics teacher "Bucky" Bucknell to teach a course in aeronautics to a special class of male students—those interested in entering the air services. Mr. Bucknell had a reputation for being a challenging teacher, and at first Paul was not sure that he wanted to sign up for what would surely be a difficult elective. He did, however, and Mr. Bucknell quickly realized that Paul had the ability to grasp scientific concepts. More important, for perhaps the first time in his life, Paul Lynch wanted to learn. It was Mr. Bucknell, Paul would appreciate years later, who put him on a track ultimately leading to a PhD degree in biochemistry and physiology from an Ivy League university.

Also in his senior year Paul signed up to participate in the Army Air Forces Cadet program administered in Manchester, New Hampshire, hoping this would bolster his chances for becoming a USAAF pilot. There were a few openings for young men without any college experience, but not many. Still, ambition had crept into the life of Paul Lynch. Turning 18 in late September, he was proud to sign the contract as an Army Air Forces Cadet; only one other graduate from his high school had been accepted into the program. Two weeks later, at an extended family dinner, Paul was honored with the gift of a watch. The following day he walked to the bus stop with his kid brother Bruce in tow to wish him goodbye.

In World War II millions of young Americans went through a family farewell such as Paul Lynch experienced. Of those, approximately 418,000 would not return. On the day that Paul left home, October 4, 1943, SS-Reichsführer Heinrich Himmler harangued his Group Leaders in Posen, occupied Poland. He talked about a cruelty that eventually would embroil Paul. An audio recording of his diatribe contained this:

Whether the other races live in comfort or perish of hunger interests me only in so far as we need them as slaves . . . Whether or not 10,000 Russian women collapse from exhaustion while digging a tank ditch interests me only in so far as the tank ditch is completed for Germany."[1]

———

Following his stint in Pre-Flight School at Maxwell, Addison had to succeed at three flying schools that spanned, in the aggregate, a period of seven more months, following which he would be given 15 days home leave—the only leave he would receive before deployment to the war. Each school was roughly the same number of weeks. The schools were known as primary flight school, basic flight school and advanced flight training (twin engine).

By the fall of 1943, the USAAF trained pilots in scores of airfields located across the United States. It was a real advantage for the U.S. to be able to do this without enemy interference; moreover the terrain of North America offered great diversity for different flying conditions.

Addison was sent to Fletcher Airfield in Clarksdale, "Missippy" as he referred to the State, mimicking the vernacular of the locals, for primary flight training. Upon his arrival, he was pleased to learn that the rumor he had heard about the instructors being civilian was true. The Army had contracted out the training. Addison said: "We had a couple of sergeants and only one lieutenant. The focus was all on flying and it was fun!"

The airplane that Addison would learn to fly was the Fairchild PT-19 "Cornell" Trainer, a two-seat, open cockpit monoplane that sported the affectionate nickname "Cradle of Heroes" for having first borne so many cadets who went on to achieve so much in the field of U.S. military aviation. Addison was proud of the fact that he never flew a biplane and that he qualified to fly solo after only eight hours of flight instruction. He found out that qualifying for a solo flight was different than actually experiencing the task at hand, however, and whatever notions Addison may have held about his first solo flight during his months of anticipation did not pan out on the big day itself. The three basic components of flight occupied his mind: a successful takeoff, a stable flight, and a safe landing. For the first time these were all his alone to control. Terrified, he survived without incident. He adjusted his apprehensions though, and fondly remembered subsequent solo flights: "Flying really gets in one's blood," he effused. "It's infectious."

Shortly afterwards, Addison received a letter from a favorite uncle, who wrote: "Your dad told me you had a solo. No doubt it was quite a thrill to be up in that vast sky all alone, no one around to bump into; in other words you were experiencing that phrase, the sky is the limit."

When Addison arrived at Fletcher Airfield, a man named A.K. Schaefer, who lived in nearby Clarksdale, contacted him. Mr. Schaefer was a producer of cottonseed oil who did business with Addison's father. What followed was a series of invitations to Addison for home cooked meals served with true Southern hospitality. Mr. and Mrs. Schaefer and Addison would remain friends for life.

"The instructors told us in case we needed to make a forced landing to fly down in line with the cotton rows and not to cross them, otherwise we might flip the plane over." While Addison was at Fletcher Field a tragedy happened to another cadet—not a crash—he was killed while turning over the prop of a PT-19.

Addison's basic flight training took place at nearby Greenville, Mississippi, a distance of only 75 miles from Clarksdale, and he learned upon arrival that Greenville was a seri*ass* place. "It was all military," he bemoaned. An official publication of the airfield went by the name *The Cadet Rudder— Regulations and Information*, and its author lacked the light touch of Major Bane. "Military discipline is intelligent, willing, and cheerful obedience to the will of the leader," this pamphlet for enlisted cadets started.

"Cadets returning from the flight line or ground school will march in formation, and in no case will the formation consist of less than ten men, unless ordered by an officer." The *Rudder* went on to explain exactly how marching was to be accomplished: "Eyes will be kept straight to the front and off the ground. There will be no talking. Body will be held erect with shoulders square . . . arms . . . will swing three inches. . . . Cadets will refrain from having hands in pocket at any time."

The officers, being officers, were exempt from this.

Addison knew that when it came to judging flying skills, officer and cadet students would be on equal footing. Basic school airplanes had a canopy and a radio, and the emphasis was on navigation. Using only a map, trainees were ordered to fly to some town or other location and from there, to proceed to another spot. When destinations along the route were reached, the pilot would radio to a ground observer who would visually confirm the plane's position using binoculars and log in the time. "Railroad tracks came in real handy," Addison commented. Basic school also involved flying at night, and this scared Addison but he got through it.

At the successful conclusion of this school Addison was asked his preference for an airplane model. He responded stating he wanted a B-25—the sleek Mitchell 2-engine bomber. Off to twin-engine school he went at George Field, Lawrenceville, Illinois, where he learned to fly the Beech AT-10 "Wichita," also known as the "Beaverboard Bomber" due to the fact that the majority of the airplane was made of sheets of pressed wood, including, interestingly, its gas tank. This was done to conserve strategic materials for real bombers. The little bomber sported oversized radial engines and a stubby-looking nose. "Both engines should operate at the same speed," Addison noted. "Otherwise, there'll be vibrations. Not good."

As his course completion date approached, the USAAF informed Addison, to his disappointment, that he would be designated as a second pilot and would be promoted to flight officer, but would not be commissioned as a second lieutenant. This smarted. Many graduates in his class received full commissions, not the warrant appointment that he received. He was also informed that he would train on the B-17 Flying Fortress instead of the B-25 he had requested. "One takes what one gets" he wisely philosophized about his military flight training. "I had my silver wings." Addison had survived the culling-down process; the washout percentage for the aviation cadet pilot program was approximately 40% at that time.

Addison was consoled in a letter from one of the four 'M's. Mary B. wrote: "Co-Pilot of a B-17 sounds very impressive Ad, but it won't be long I'm sure before you are 'first pilot.' "

On April 15, 1944, some 14 months after enlisting, Addison was awarded his silver wings at a ceremony attended by his parents and 12-year-old sister, Mary Cay. His family had to have been bursting with pride. He was the first Bartush so distinguished. His graduation book, *Wingspan 44-D*, contained this:

> *We find it thrilling to graduate as a full-fledged member of the hardest hitting team on earth, but none of us will have a feeling of satisfaction until our enemies have been blasted into submission.*

After 14 months of military service, newly minted pilot Addison Bartush now had a short-term objective that was even more important to him than flying in a B-17. He was about to embark on that coveted 15-day leave.

His immediate plan was to get to the Terrace Room at the Statler Hotel, the best hotel in beautiful downtown Detroit, Michigan, one of the richest cities in the world. It was a luxurious place with fine dining and dancing to the music of premier bands. Would Pancho and his Sambas be performing? Addison enjoyed both dancing and Latin music, but he did not particularly enjoy dancing to the Brazilian-style music that Pancho played, and he hoped that a different band would be booked then at the hotel. In a pinch, however, Pancho would do just fine. "All I wanted was dumbsquat pleasure," Addison confessed. U.S. Army Air Forces regulations required him to wear his uniform at all times when outside his home of residence, and this Addison would do with pride.

———

Paul Lynch contracted into the aviation cadet program at Fort Devens, Massachusetts and in between the paperwork processing there played in a pickup game of touch football that turned ugly. One of the players on the opposing team had been a member of the University of Iowa football squad and was determined to demonstrate his ability. "We were just as determined not to back off," Paul recounted about this incident.

Boot camp for Paul would be at Biloxi, Mississippi, which was some 60 hours distant by rail. At stops along the way, local citizens, the USO and the Salvation Army provided free coffee, donuts and other refreshments. Paul was touched by this kindness and patriotic support.

As Paul viewed countryside he had never seen, it was late 1943. The

U.S. Army in the western Pacific under the command of Gen. MacArthur was making slow progress against the Japanese on the island of New Guinea. Africa and Sicily had been cleared of the Germans, and Italy was about to become a new battleground. The Soviet Union's Red Army advanced onwards towards Kiev, having defeated the Germans at the enormous battle of Kursk the previous July. The Soviets still had approximately 1,000 miles to go before they reached Berlin, however, and the Americans and the British would not land at Normandy for another eight months. In either direction, east or west, there was plenty of war left for Paul Lynch to join in on.

Paul took his training at Keesler Field and lived in a tent city, four men per tent. The weather was mild at first until a hurricane hit, flooding the entire base including Paul's tent. "We paddled around and then it got muddy," he recollected. It was not long before Paul joined others in referring to Keesler as the "S—hole of the universe." The only diversion from mindless marching and reviews was the across-the-street WAC barracks. In the evenings, which ladies might leave their shades up?

It was Keesler Field that the playwright Neil Simon later immortalized in his play *Biloxi Blues*. His famous one-liner, "You need three promotions to be an asshole," fit Paul's circumstances to a tee. At Keesler there were plenty of drill sergeants who had more than their requisite three.

Paul, like Addison, witnessed men collapse on the tarmac. The ambulances that picked them up were referred to as meat wagons. Recruits were shown graphic films about the effects of venereal disease; shocking films depicting grossly afflicted male and female genitalia. The disturbing images and strong warnings made an impression on Paul, who reflected on his sheltered existence growing up in small-town Massachusetts.

World War II exposed tens of millions of young adults to behavior previously unknown to them. True to his religious upbringing, Paul did not succumb to temptation. But no one who participated in the war, succumbing or not, would come out of it "naïve."

Another thing significant to Paul's experience at Keesler was something that he was intentionally not exposed to. All the time he was there, he never once saw what today is referred to as an African-American, and back then, a Negro, in uniform. And yet, there were 7,000 African-American soldier-airmen training on the other side of the Keesler Airfield when Paul was there.[2] Not only did he not see them on or off base, Paul didn't even know they were there. It was not until 1948 when President Harry Truman integrated the U.S. Armed Forces by Executive Order that this segregation policy ceased to exist.

As luck would have it, Paul got a cushy assignment while at Keesler. At a beer party at the PX one night a sergeant came up to him and asked, "How would you like to ride the jeep tomorrow during the parade?" Paul jumped at the chance to avoid standing outside at review in the hot sun. For the rest of his stay at Keesler Paul got to ride each week as part of an elite "Camouflage Unit." "Our only job was to keep the jeep clean," Paul joked.

Paul's basic training at Keesler ended in a disappointment for him, somewhat akin to Addison's, but with more impact. Only two members of his 200-man unit were selected to continue on in the air cadet program, and he was not one of them. "One had a commercial pilot's license," Paul observed. Paul believed that at this juncture, the U.S. Army Air Forces had more air cadets than needed.

Paul learned that he would proceed to Buckley Field, near Denver, and then on to Las Vegas to learn about B-17s and how to operate the M2 Browning .50 caliber machine gun. "I was pleased to discover I would be going to Europe," he said. No one told him this but he deduced it (undoubtedly Addison did as well) from the fact that that was the war theater where practically all the B-17s operated. Paul explained: "I had absolutely no desire to fly long distances over water. I once almost drowned as a kid." The prospect of being in Great Britain appealed to Paul also.

At Buckley Field Paul learned how to release a Sperry Ball Turret (it weighed more than 1,000 lbs. and in an emergency situation it might need to be jettisoned), to arm and safely dispose of bombs that might become hung up, and to clean and service machine guns. "Week-end passes were offered for good grades," Paul reported, "and I got 'em!" On one occasion he skied at Berthoud Pass, elevation 11,300' and on another hiked near there. For Paul, this was a far cry from the rolling country of the eastern woodlands. On weekends Paul and his buddies shunned the local saloons and honkytonks in favor of the Park Lane Hotel, the Statler-like establishment of downtown Denver. They wanted to meet nice girls, he explained.

Once on a Sunday morning, Paul and his friends headed off base to a church service, where en route, prostitutes solicited them by calling down to them from the open windows of their establishment. "This bothered me,"

Paul recollected tongue-in-cheek, "as my mother taught that Sunday is a day of rest." When they arrived at the church, one that they had not attended before, they discovered that they had walked into a fever-pitched hallelujah revival! All in all, it was a surreal day, Paul reflected—the stuff good memories are made of, particularly for young men new to a larger world.

In World War II the USAAF trained 300,000 gunners, "more than any other specialty except aircraft maintenance,"[3] and the schools were in remote areas where bullets and shell casings could drop harmlessly on what was then considered desert wasteland (today environmental concerns would be raised by such an activity).

At Las Vegas Paul began by shooting skeet on the ground and quickly ended up in the waist of a B-17, shooting the powerful M2 Browning machine gun that had a muzzle velocity of 3,050 feet per second, an effective range of 2,000 yards (more than a mile) and could fire at a rate of 500 rounds a minute.[4] "We shot at a sleeve towed by another aircraft," Paul said. Each student's bullets were colored differently and the color would rub off on a target sleeve, enabling the instructors to determine those students who scored hits. Sleeves were towed at a distance of 500 to 1,000 yards. Piloting a tow plane was dangerous work and women sometimes performed it. "They feared being accidently hit," Paul indicated. "Some trainees did not seem to know what they were doing."

Paul was taught to lead his opponent, that is, to let the enemy fly into his stream of bullets, and also to fire in short bursts. The gun sights had rings around them that the gunner could use to lead an attacker—two rings for longer distance, one ring for more close in. Shooting accurately was very much a judgmental matter, Paul learned, and there was not much time to react.

At a survival course Paul was instructed on how to use a parachute. He was told not to open a chute too soon because of air turbulence behind the B-17; that the wash of the props and the large airplane body might spill the air out of the parachute. "Count to ten before pulling your rip-chord," he heard. Also, "If enemy fighters are in the air, wait on the rip-chord until you can distinguish tree branches below." No practice parachute jumps were made.

Paul visited Las Vegas only once and was not impressed. It had gambling centers, yes, but was yet to be improved by the gangster Bugsy Siegel. He enjoyed seeing nearby Boulder Dam, however.

Paul's next assignment would be at Gulfport, Mississippi, where he would become part of a B-17 crew. It was August 1944.

———

The co-pilot detachment Addison went to following home leave was at Buckingham Army Air Field, Fort Myers, Florida. In short order he was flying almost daily. The airplane that he flew, the B-17 "Flying Fortress," was one of the most famous and extensively used combat airplanes to come out of World War II. The Flying Fortress had a service ceiling of 35,600 feet, a maximum speed of 287 mph (although Addison would dispute this) and could deliver a 5,000 lb. bomb load to targets as far as 800 miles away. Its large rudder/tail assembly and long wingspan, at almost 104 feet, made for stable flight. Moreover, the B-17 looked as a propeller driven heavy bomber should: a thin, rounded, tapered fuselage, proportionally large airfoils and four enormous Wright "Cyclone" turbo-supercharged radial engines—each capable of producing 1,200 hp.

It was the B-17's reputation for absorbing battle damage, however that made her special. Newsreel after newsreel depicted incredibly torn, twisted, holed and seemingly unflyable B-17s successfully limping back to home base. "Built tough," a great deal of credit also belonged to the expert ground crews that superbly maintained this aircraft. The American public fell in love with "The Fort." So did Addison Bartush.

The B-24 airmen became jealous of the B-17 crews, and started calling the B-17 the "Hollywood Bomber," because it appeared in so many newsreels and movies about the war. In retaliation, the B-17 airman started referring to the stumpy looking B-24 not as the "Liberator," its proper name, but rather the "Flying Boxcar."

Addison quickly learned that there was more to being a B-17 co-pilot than simply being available to take over command of the aircraft if something happened to the pilot. The co-pilot had a host of duties: pre-flight checks, starting and warm-up duties, pre-take-off and take-off duties, in-flight responsibilities, landing functions and a detailed report to be completed after landing. A co-pilot under instruction wrote a poem entitled *Lament of a Co-Pilot* and Addison agreed with what it said.

To start right engine—procedures the same;

Just use the checklist—don't trust your brain.

When Addison was a veteran combat second pilot this checklist proved exceptionally handy on one memorable occasion. His squadron was grooming him for first pilot status, and one afternoon out of the blue on a day that he had no assigned flying duty, the word came down that he was to immediately take up a B-17 by himself, that is, without any crew including a co-pilot. "The problem," Addison confessed, grinning like a red-faced Cheshire cat, "was I had had a beer." It was the checklist that saved him.

Addison learned formation flying while at Buckingham. He also had some time to sightsee the Fort Myers area, where Henry Ford and Thomas Edison had winter estates. Addison enjoyed the wild aspect of the lands and waters. "It was beautiful," he said.

It was at this duty station that Addison received an interesting communication from Shedd-Bartush Foods, Inc., the new name of his father's ever-expanding company. An uncle who worked at the company wrote:

Dear Addison,
Enclosed is a new Air Travel Card showing the change in company name.
Also enclosed are instructions in connection with the use of this card. Kindly
return your old card which was given to you just before you left Detroit . . .

The instructions explained that any charges would be billed to Shedd-Bartush Foods for payment and that airlines were not to accept cash from Addison for his purchase of tickets. This card enabled Addison to travel anywhere in the world on 16 different, named, commercial airlines.

Joseph Addison Bartush, his full name, was not an average Joe, so to speak. "My problem," Addison chuckled, "was that during the war I couldn't go anywhere!"

It was August 1944 and Addison was ordered back to "Missippy," only this time to the Gulfport Army Airfield—to a Combat Crew Placement Pool there.

———

"Pleased to meet you," Addison said, extending a hand. "My name is Addison Bartush. I will be your co-pilot."

"Paul Lynch, Sir, and I'll be one of your waist gunners." As the two men sized each other up in the briefing room, Paul reflected that maybe this was a good start. Addison had not introduced himself as Flight Officer Bartush.

CHAPTER TWO

The Bishop Crew Formation and Deployment

"Men," Addison said, addressing eight of his fellow crew-mates, "I've learned that one of the cadets that I got to know at the University of Pittsburgh, Dave Bishop, is now a first pilot and under orders to report to Gulfport. He is expected to arrive in a day or two. Dave hails from South Carolina, and I have put in a request that he be asked to consider commanding our aircrew."

When Addison announced this no one in the room raised questions. In the very short time the "team" had been together, Addison had come across as a seemingly reasonable, even likable second-in-command and all sensed it was preferable to have him request someone that he knew and had confidence in to command them rather than risk what might be had if the USAAF made the selection. Almost immediately after Dave Bishop arrived in Gulfport he accepted the position. The "Bishop Crew," as it would be known, had a full complement.

Members of the Bishop Crew came from all over the United States, and like other crews consisting of only 18-to-21-year-olds, some members were more mature, capable and gregarious than others. Not everyone was without an Achilles heel, and disagreements could and did erupt. However, part of the purpose of the time at Gulfport was to iron all of this out. Each man had been trained in a specialty and at Gulfport they were supposed to learn how to mesh their skills together in order to operate as a team.

Flight officer/navigator Robert J. "RJ" Miller grew up in Nevada, Missouri, a small town that had been almost completely burned down by Union militiamen during the Civil War. He was painfully thin, a chain-smoker and easygoing. "We had confidence he could do the job," Paul said, and Addison echoed that sentiment. Miller let it be known from day one that he wished to be addressed by his nickname, "RJ."

Flight officer/bombardier Raymond Peacock, from Utah, was the only member of the crew to sport a mustache. Pleasant to work with and seemingly competent, a personal situation came up for him towards the end of his stay at Gulfport that precluded him from deploying overseas with the Bishop Crew. The most the USAAF would do for Peacock, however, was to defer deployment for a short period. This action left the Bishop Crew without a bombardier.

Sergeant John S. Kendall, the radio operator from Vermont, had droopy eyelids growing up that earned him the nickname "Sleepy." According to Paul Lynch, Kendall had anything but a sleepy temperament. Soon after they met the two men got into an altercation in the shower room that had to be broken up by crewmates. According to Lynch, a verbal disagreement over Kendall's stated treatment of a woman he had gone out with precipitated the fight. Neither man was put on report for this incident. Their feelings diffused over time; not because of friendship, but rather the need to work together.

Sergeant Charles F. Cumings, the top turret gunner and flight engineer, was the least likely person one might expect to find on a combat aircrew. Small in stature and shy in nature, Cumings was often seen by Addison, Paul and the others clutching the Holy Bible. "He read it when he felt threatened," Paul opined. "I think he was told it would protect him." Paul added: "I never thought the Bible served this purpose." This became a cause of concern for his crewmates as Cumings manned the key defensive position on the B-17. In many situations, it would be up to Cumings to sound the alarm, that is, to alert the crew via the intercom, "Five O'clock high!" Paul and the others wondered: when the time came would he shout this or would he freeze up? And when attacked, would he reach for his Bible or the trigger?

Being fearful was not something one could control, and no one, including the plane's commander, Dave Bishop, could really know how Cumings might react until an actual situation happened. Cumings was a decent person, not yet 20, and he was given the benefit of the doubt in crew training at Gulfport. He came from Neenah, Wisconsin, and had worked for a short period at the Gilbert Paper Company following graduation from high school.

Ball and waist gunner Sergeant William "Billy" Robertson had a sweetheart waiting for him in Philmont, New York, and he became a good friend of both Addison and Paul. Paul regarded him as one of the two enlisted men on the crew that he had most confidence in. Addison and Billy took a few days leave at war's end and visited Scotland together. They also kept in touch after the war.

The other ball and waist gunner was Sergeant Earl Sheen. "He wasn't easy to get to know," Paul said about him. "He did his job and stuck to himself." Later in the war, flying combat with a different crew, Sheen saved a man's life. He was a native of Idaho. A thin man like Robertson, Sheen was small enough to curl into a Sperry ball turret.

Then there was Owen Monkman, 20, the lanky sergeant from Choteau, Montana, population 2,000, who everyone on the Bishop Crew, without exception, trusted to do his job properly and really liked. "Owen never complained about being assigned the most dangerous position of tail gunner," Paul Lynch noted. "He just crawled back like he belonged there."

Monkman grew up on a cattle ranch near the town that had a view of the magnificent Teton mountain range to the east. The land was arid, however, and the winters severe. Temperatures sometimes dipped to 40 below zero. The younger of two sons, Owen worked long hours on the ranch. A friend, Andrew Jensen, working a nearby spread, wrote: ". . . after school we had chores to do such as milking cows, feeding the animals, haying, harvesting, fencing and lots of other jobs; when we were old enough, of course, we drove tractors and other heavy equipment." Owen played the trumpet and enjoyed jitterbugging.

In 1942 Monkman graduated from Teton County High School and the next year enrolled in Montana State University in Bozeman. A year later he volunteered for the U.S. Army Air Forces hoping to become a pilot. His selection as pilot did not happen, however, and Owen ended-up at the same gunnery school in Las Vegas as Paul Lynch. It was there that the USAAF made him a bugler and tail-gunner. Invariably positive about life, Owen wrote to his parents who were trying their hand at sheep farming: "I'd sure like to be home for shearing . . ."

Last but not least, there was first pilot Flight Officer David Bishop, who had also grown up on a farm. "He was reserved," Paul Lynch said about him. "He was friendly, yes, but not like Addison. Addison was more like one of the boys, and Bishop a senior member." Paul added: "Addison liked to joke. Dave, no." The fact that Bishop chose to remain aloof in Paul's mind was an attribute. "Dave seemed to fit the job of what a plane commander should be," he noted.

Addison Bartush, who grew to respect Bishop over the two months they spent together at the University of Pittsburgh, and who later enthusiastically asked Bishop to assume the first pilot job, obviously agreed. "One wouldn't swear in front of him," Addison related about his boss, a twinkle in his eye. "I doubt he knew what the inside of an Officers Club looked like," he added, mischievously. "He read the Bible daily." In saying this, Addison did not need to clarify that Bishop read the Bible for a different reason than Cumings.

Addison explained why he focused in on Bishop: "I sensed he would make sound decisions as a pilot," he said. "I felt I could work with him on the flight deck." The fact that Bishop would not become a drinking buddy and was in daily communication with God did not trouble Addison Bartush one iota.

As mature and reserved as he was, Dave Bishop was not beyond having some good fun, however, even if it meant violating a USAAF flight plan. The South Carolina farm that he grew up on was within the flight range of a B-17 departing out of Gulfport, and Bishop would make a once-in-a-lifetime memory for himself, his parents and crewmates.

The Bishop Crew soon got into a routine at Gulfport. "There was PT in the morning followed by classes in such things as the newest changes to radar, survival training, and other topics," Paul detailed. "We also took a lot of training flights together, practice bombing Dallas and other assigned locations." Paul added that the crews flew in whatever B-17s that might be made available by the Army Air Forces; that a specific bomber was not reserved for the exclusive use of any individual crew. This practice also applied in the European Theatre.

Owen Monkman wrote home: "This is the wettest, swampiest country I have ever seen." He also told of how enthusiastic he was to fly, even if it meant flying every day. Not everyone on the Bishop Crew felt the same, however. As time progressed it became apparent to crewmembers that Charles Cumings did not like to fly. For Addison's part, he wondered why Cumings even joined the U.S. Army Air Forces. Being pasty-faced while taking off or landing, however, was not the same thing as complaining, which Cumings never did; nor did he ever ask to be relieved from flying duty. Cumings was a hard worker. "He did extra things for Dave Bishop," Paul Lynch recollected.

Shortly after arriving in Gulfport Addison read of a new USAAF policy that permitted flight officers to apply for a commissioned status with the rank of second lieutenant. "I did it and got Dave Bishop to do the same," Addison related. Up the chain-of-command their applications went. "I never understood coming out of flight school why some men got flight officer and others, second lieutenant," Addison said. "Dave was selected for first pilot but not given the higher rank."

On August 19, 1944, a concerned father wrote a letter to his son:

Dear Addison:

Do you like to fly the B-17? Will you be able to fly home or near here . . . Selfridge [?] Why don't you try and make it before you go across. Will you fly them [the B-17's] over or will you go on a ferry? If you cannot come home let me know and I will try to come there . . . Do you want anything— if you do let me know. I hope this war will be over before you get there . . . Addison, let me know all about your next move if you can—how and where you are going.

Love, Dad

As hard as the Bishop Crew worked, there were a few days off now and then for rest and relaxation. Addison told of one such occasion when he ran into Paul Lynch in New Orleans and the two of them spent time together sightseeing and drinking beer. Addison had been surprised to encounter Paul in the city. Always resourceful, Paul Lynch explained how: "New Orleans was off limits to enlisted personnel because of the high VD rate," he chuckled. "But I found a way around that. I knew that Army MPs routinely checked second-class passenger rail cars bound for this city and removed the enlisted men. So I traveled first class."

It was mid-September on a routine training flight over Georgia that Dave Bishop made his decision to pay an unscheduled visit to his family. "I want to go to Spartanburg, South Carolina," he announced over the inter-com, "and fly over my parents' farm."

As the crow flies, Spartanburg is only 50 miles or so from the Georgia border, but Addison recollected: "It was a long, long ways away from where we were supposed to be!" The distance from Gulfport to Spartanburg is 572 miles.

Of course the crew, including its second-in-command, immediately thought this was a grand idea, and endorsed the diversion wholeheartedly. Not only would the prescribed flight route be abandoned, the Bishop Crew would fly in at low altitude! And at full throttle! What could be more fun? This was to be barnstorming at its best, and in a 36,000-lb., four-engine "heavy" bomber no less!

To avoid alerting the USAAF, the trick would be to return to Gulfport within a reasonable period of time. This required increased speed and it was discerned the fuel supply was adequate. Bishop ordered Flight Engineer Cumings to juice up the carburation and do other things to make the bomber go faster. Nervous as always, but happy enough to be part of this joy ride, Cumings complied. As the South Carolina border approached Bishop did not need the services of navigator RJ Miller; he knew what country roads to follow.

The first pass over the farm terrified the animals. Owen Monkman wrote home about chicken feathers flying and cows "running all over the place."

Addison Bartush remarked, coyly, "We were too low." Paul Lynch, standing at a waist port, enjoyed a wondrous view, as did the other crewmembers standing at similar positions or, even better, crouching in the confined plexiglas nose. Circling, Bishop was confident that on his second pass he would see his loved ones on the lawn waving up. Surely his mom and dad realized that this had to be him! It had not occurred to Dave, however, that the buzz produced by propellers driven at 4,800 horsepower from a low-flying warplane might cause someone in a house below to reasonably flee to their cellar.

On the second pass, Bishop took it even lower, "nearly shaking the roof off," Monkman wrote.

Addison lamented: "I held onto the wheel for dear life." Disappointed at not seeing anyone, Bishop was not to be deterred. Peeling off, he "radioed the Spartanburg airport control tower," Addison explained, "and asked them to telephone his folks and tell them to step into their backyard."

On the third and final pass Monkman reported seeing Mrs. Bishop, "waving up at us like crazy." He even described her as, "wearing a flowered dress and apron." Addison recalled seeing both parents.

After returning to Gulfport Army Airfield it was discovered that one of the co-conspirators had screwed-up. Flight Engineer Charles Cumings had been trained to keep a log of his in-flight activities. On this occasion as with all earlier occasions he dutifully entered into his log what he had done to increase airspeed, and also the time or times that he implemented changes. "The poor guy," Addison chortled, referring to Cumings, "he caught hell for something he'd been ordered to do!" Addison explained that, "Bishop went in with him" to see the training command officer-in-charge and fessed-up that the blame was his, not Cumings. "Both were disciplined," Addison stated, richly smiling at the memory.

"Bishop and Cumings never shared with the crew the punishment meted out," Addison said. He also recounted that no one verbally branded Cumings a Mr. Dumbsquat, but more than one crewmember thought of him that way on account of his log entries. "They rode the beam!" Addison rejoiced, thinking of Bishop and Cumings nervously bracing to face the music. From this episode Addison learned something—sometimes being a second pilot could be a positive thing.

"Buzzing" friends and loved ones was a phenomenon that often happened in the United States during World War II. Would the person manning the control tower at the Spartanburg Airport report this incident? Would neighboring farmers? No, they would not, for they knew that a hometown hero was up in the sky. And that these young men were honing their flight skills to defend the nation; they were to be cheered, not jeered. "300 feet," Addison said, then modified his recollection slightly. "Maybe lower."

Addison's only real regret over this incident was the fact that the distance between Gulfport and Detroit and back was farther than a B-17 could fly. He was both proud and jealous of Dave Bishop.

Around this time Addison had a surprise visitor. His father, Stephen Bartush, had arranged for a business meeting in New Orleans through Mr. Schaefer, and he made a side trip to Gulfport. "It was wonderful to see him," Addison recounted. This was a difficult period for the Bartush family. Middle son Jack was already in the Coast Guard and destined to perform convoy duty in the North Atlantic. It was only a matter of time before the youngest son, Chuck, would be drafted or would volunteer to take the oath. Recounting this visit decades later, Addison wept. "My parents were so good to me," he said. "They were so good to all of us." Addison then related a story about his father's brother, Frank, who had a falling out with his father and later fell on hard times. Addison's father reconciled with Frank and took him into the family business.

On October 1, 1944, Captain Sam A. Tomaino, adjutant, administered the oath of office commissioning Addison as a second lieutenant in the U.S. Army Air Forces. A base newspaper article reported this was the first ceremony of its kind at the Gulfport Army Airfield. The ceremony was witnessed by the commanding officer of the field, Lt. Col. George L. Holcomb.

"For a short period Addison outranked his plane commander," Paul Lynch recounted. "We [the enlisted crew] started calling him 'Big Wheel.'"

Addison and Dave would fly to the war zone wearing new gold bars and be paid a higher salary. More important, perhaps, the two would now wear the exact same crush hat worn by such notables, as say, General Jimmy Doolittle. They were now fully accepted members of the club. They could slouch on the tarmac, as General Carl Spaatz often did with his shoulders conspicuously slumped, and in front of cameras no less, and, if discretion permitted, with hands comfortably placed in pockets. They wore the Great Seal of the United States of America. They were full-fledged U.S. Army Air Forces officers.

As October approached, when the Bishop Crew expected that orders to deploy would soon be issued, bombardier Ray Peacock informed crewmembers that his request to remain in the United States for a short period had been approved. Peacock offered to train one of the enlisted men on the use of the Norden bombsight, and Dave Bishop, with the concurrence of Addison and RJ, agreed that Paul Lynch should be the one to receive the training. At this juncture in the war, many heavy bomb squadrons (typically a squadron would consist of 12 or more aircraft) operated with only two or maybe three bombardiers. The lead plane bombardier would do the targeting using his Norden and the other bombers would drop their bombs at the sight of the lead dropping its bombs. If the lead were to be shot down before "bombs away," the bombardier on the deputy lead would take over using his Norden. The loss of Peacock, although a setback for the Bishop Crew, was not critical. Unless flying lead or deputy lead, all the Bishop Crew would need would be someone to toggle the bomb rack and RJ or one of the gunners could do that.

All bombers were equipped with the Norden bombsight, however, and Paul explained why he received this training: "If our plane got separated," he said, "with the bombsight we could still press an attack on a target of opportunity." He added: "That is, if we had someone on board who knew how to work the thing."

Training was done in a hanger with the bombsight mounted on a tall, electrically driven rolling gurney-like platform simulating an airplane in flight. The operator tried to guide this platform with the bombsight to hit a target painted on the floor. "It seemed easy inside," Paul laughed, then added humbly: "There was little unexpected movement and no flak to deal with."

In a real situation a Norden bombsight would act as an autopilot of the lead plane during the bomb run. "It took over the airplane," Paul explained. "Bombing accurately from four to five miles high in the sky while traveling at hundreds of miles per hour is a difficult assignment," he amplified. Indeed, an analysis of the results of a major raid conducted in late 1943 with the Norden revealed that only one of every ten bombs dropped "landed within 500 feet of the target."[1]

Still, the Norden was a great improvement over visual dead reckoning. The mechanical computer took into account altitude, air speed and winds. Paul finished his training in only three or four two-hour sessions with Peacock, and felt he could handle the job.

On October 3, 1944, the aircrew received "shipping orders" that they would be moving out. "Everyone thinks our final destination will be Europe," one crewmember wrote. The enlisted men would be going over as sergeants, or if not, promoted to that rank before flying combat missions. This was an important distinction, as the Geneva Convention, which the Nazis had ratified, provided that prisoners of war holding that rank could not be made to do manual labor. At war's end the Nazis held some 30,000 U.S. airmen as POWs and approximately half of them were sergeants and the rest officers; none went to labor camps.

The Bishop Crew was given a few days off before departure and Paul and a few other airmen took a train to Tampa, Florida, in the hope of going on to see Miami and possibly even the Keys. Money was tight, however, and the travelers took a temporary dock job unloading a banana boat. It was here that Paul learned firsthand about racial attitudes in the South. Upon entering the boat's hold, the airmen saw that their co-workers were African-

American. "They looked at us strangely," Paul recounted. Not knowing quite what to make of this situation, the airmen started working alongside these men while on the dock a group of white "Southern boys" (Paul's description) assembled. "They had a fit," he related.

One Southerner confronted Paul as he carried out a stack of bananas. "You went down in the ship's hold with those [expletive deleted]?" he barked.

The tense situation diffused when Paul explained that this was a one or two day opportunity to raise a little travel cash. When he said this, however, Paul could not resist pushing back a little. One of the African-Americans had been kind and warned Paul and his companions to look out for tarantulas. Paul told the Southern boy of this and also blurted: "The white boss who hired us didn't mention those poisonous things."

Paul and his friends returned to Gulfport having never made it to Miami or the Keys, but the trip did make an impression on Paul. "Tampa was a dirty port city," he recalled.

An *Officer's Pay Data Card* for Addison was completed on the date that he departed Gulfport, on October 9, 1944. At the time he received a monthly base pay of $150, additional pay for flying of $75, and subsistence of $21, for a total of $246 a month, or $2,952 a year.

Addison and Paul had trained in Miami, Pittsburgh, Nashville, Montgomery, Clarksdale, Greenville, Lawrenceville, Fort Myers, Biloxi, Denver, Las Vegas and Gulfport, for a total of 29 months training between the two of them. They thought they were as ready as they could possibly be.

The Bishop Crew, sans Peacock, took a 20-hour, stop-and-go train ride to Savannah, Georgia, had physicals and a records check there, and picked up a shiny, spanking new B-17 for delivery to the Eighth Air Force. They flew it first to Bangor, Maine and en route came within 20 miles of Paul's hometown of Leominster, Massachusetts. Looking down, Paul spotted a church spire he recognized. "We were so close I could have bailed out and walked home," he recalled.

The flight over the Atlantic Ocean, given the technology at the time, was not without risk. A number of U.S. aircrews perished on the long journey over, though most died on a route different from the one the Bishop Crew would take. Still, any overseas airplane route could be dangerous.

They left the United States from Bangor, Maine, on Sunday, October

15, 1944.[2] Most aircrews flew what was known as the "North Ferry Route" that started at Gander, Newfoundland, and after stops at Greenland or Iceland, ended in Prestwick, Scotland. For their flight however, the Bishop Crew had been directed to fly to Goose Bay, Labrador, and then on to Iceland and finally to Valley, Wales, a city on the northwest corner of the Welsh coast, in latitude across from Dublin, Ireland. Only crewmembers flew; no passengers were taken.

The only mechanical glitch on the crossing occurred on the approach to Goose Bay. "We had a several day layover there due to low oil pressure in one of the engines, and by the time that got fixed the weather turned bad," said Addison. Paul Lynch recalled how remote and lonely Labrador seemed. At 53 degrees N latitude and being mid-October, snow was present.

The flight to Iceland proved to be an adventure of sorts. The distance, practically 100% over water, was approximately 1,500 miles—almost as far as a B-17 could fly. Without a bomb load to carry, this was doable. Still, the flight would be mostly in darkness attributable to the lateness of the season and the need to start at a time so they could land in daylight. The weather over the North Atlantic could be fickle, to say the least, and a magnetic compass that far north was useless.

It was on this ferry crossing that Addison received a true appreciation of the concept *Ride the Beam*. "It was cold," he related, referring to what it had been like sitting in an unpressurized cabin and staring into nothing outside for seemingly an eternity. "The flight deck had a heater and this helped some."

"We flew at less than 10,000 feet and this eliminated the need for us to use our oxygen masks. We were told to maintain radio silence and not to turn on our running lights as there might be German subs on the surface with their deck guns manned. We flew alone; that is, not as part of a formation."

The flight had been an eerie, no doubt out-of-world experience for Addison and Dave, who at least had a lighted instrument panel to focus on. The other crewmembers could do nothing more than sit in total darkness and absorb the monotonous drone of four powerful engines and the vibration of large propellers.

"The only hope to get to Iceland was to ride the radio beam. It made an audible 'beep, bop or beep, beep, bop, bop' sound or something like that. After a while the noise drives one crazy." Addison added: "You're following the beam when it makes a straight, solid continuous beep."

"Dave and I took turns flying," Addison continued, and he explained why: for the sake of sanity, the earphones needed to be removed now and then. An impish grin came over Addison's face. "One time while I was flying to Iceland, trying to follow the radio beam, I got a little mixed up. I got off course." The grin widened at the memory. "I poked Bishop and said to him, 'I think we're in trouble and he said, 'Yes, we're off course, what the heck did you do?' " Addison laughed. "Dave got us back on course."

Dave Bishop did not get upset with Addison but rather simply did what needed to be done to correct the situation. The term "Ride the beam, Cadet!" or, "Ride the beam, Lieutenant!" was a phrase of art in the USAAF in World War II, denoting the need to stay sharply focused, that is, to think about what one needs to do in order to get to where one has to go.

The landing in Iceland was not without stress. "It was cloudy and hazy on the approach," Addison related and he remembered it being gloomy-darkish.

Paul Lynch also remembered it: "We kept looking for a hole in the clouds and were still in them when the descent began. The clouds seemed to hang on forever and all I could think about was running out of gas. Finally a hole appeared . . . up ahead was land." Crouched in the nosecone alongside the nervous navigator RJ Miller, upon first sighting the tarmac Paul broke the tension: "Look," he said to Miller pointing at parked aircraft, "aren't those Japanese?"

"I was extremely uncomfortable during our stopover in Iceland," Addison indicated. "It was so cold there. It was penetrating cold even with the heavy jackets we had been issued. I couldn't wait to get back on the plane as it had some heat."

The final leg of the ferry trip proved to be an easy, even enjoyable flight. This was because it was made in daylight and with 100% visibility. The flight could have encountered peril, however, due to the notoriously unpredictable British weather. The aforementioned more dangerous "North Ferry Route" with its terminus at Prestwick witnessed 17 bombers crash during the war on a mountainous island off the Scottish coast named Arran.[3] The cause of each crash was abrupt weather deterioration. Addison and cohorts would stay as far away as possible from Scotland, but nevertheless, the weather could have turned on them, too. Blessedly, it did not.

The Bishop Crew came in by way of the North Channel and passed over the Irish Sea. "At that time Ireland was independent," Addison said, meaning neutral in the war. "We could not fly over Ireland so Northern Ireland had huge arrows on the ground showing us where their boundary was. It was OK to fly over Northern Ireland."

"We left our ship at Valley, Wales. And it was a brand new B-17," he added, speaking softly and looking pitiful at the memory. Every rookie crew that ferried a newly made bomber overseas invariably desired to possess it, paint individualized nose art on it and protect it from all others who might bring it harm. The problem for these crews was the aircraft distribution system did not work that way. Once assigned to a bomb group, rookies would start at the bottom and suffer their fair share of "hanger queens." In the USAAF, a patched-up bomber with plenty of flight hours on it went by that derogatory name.

Addison and his crewmates were sent by rail to Stone, an old market town in Straffordshire, England. There, they awaited orders to join a bomb group.

At this stage of World War II, that is, late October 1944, the U.S. and British Armies were stalemated before the Nazi Gothic Line in Northern Italy, not far south from the city of Bologna. In Western Europe however, the situation was looking more favorable. On October 21 Aachen fell to the U.S. First Army—the first major German city to do so. In the east and south all of Romania had been liberated a few days later by the Soviets, and in the north the Red Army was deep into Poland and only some 300 plus miles from Berlin. Troubling to the U.S. and British leadership, however, was the pattern and manner of the Soviet advance. Rather than thrust directly at the heart of Nazi Germany, the Soviets were advancing steadily along a front extending all the way from the Adriatic Sea to the Baltic Sea. What was the Soviet intention? Equally troubling was way that the Soviets recently captured Warsaw. On August 1, 1944 the Red Army advanced to the outskirts of the city and the Polish resistance started an uprising against their Nazi occupiers in anticipation of Soviet assistance. The dictator Joseph Stalin then halted the advance of his army for 63 days—giving the Nazis enough time to regroup and destroy the Polish resistance. What Machiavellian perfidy was this?

On October 26, 1944, shortly after the Bishop Crew was assigned to a bomb group, the U.S. Eighth Air Force operating from Great Britain attacked military targets in western Germany with 1,225 heavy bombers accompanied by 674 fighters, with the loss of only one fighter. The U.S. 15th Air Force operating out of Italy would have launched a large mission against the southern part of Germany that day but for inclement weather.[4]

The Nazis were being viciously assaulted on the ground and pummeled from the air. Some thought the war might be over by Christmas.

91st Bomb Group—Bassingbourn

By pure happenchance the Bishop Crew ended up being assigned to one of the most, if not *the* most storied USAAF bomb groups in World War II, and within that group to a very famous squadron; famous because it had been honored by the King and Queen of England and because it had been singled out and publicized by Hollywood. In the latter stages of the war this squadron achieved additional fame in the person of its commander, who would become an Army Air Forces legend.

In addition to the accolades, the 91st Bomb Group also had the dubious distinction of having experienced the largest number of losses of any heavy bombardment group in World War II.[1] With this distinction, however, came a special form of recognition—". . . more Distinguished Service Crosses and Silver Stars, a measure of high valor of its combat crews."[2]

Two years before the Bishop Crew arrived, the 91st Bomb Group landed in Great Britain on October 3, 1942, becoming the first American bomb group into the fray. On their initial ferry trip over the Atlantic, one of the original 91st bombers was lost, crashing in the fog.

The 91st started offensive operations on November 7, 1942 by sending 14 bombers to attack a German submarine base in France. Missions continued regularly after that date, and by mid-1943 the USAAF felt confident enough to attempt something really bold. The U.S. was determined to prove the efficacy of deep-penetration daylight bombing of military targets. The British had eschewed daylight bombing in favor of nighttime carpet attacks, claiming the latter achieved satisfactory results at much less risk to bomber crews.

The seminal test came on August 17, 1943 and the 91st Bomb Group was in the thick of it. The Eighth Air Force sent 230 U.S. bombers on a

1,000-mile round-trip mission—a force that included 24 B-17s from the 91st, with the 91st commander in the lead.

They headed for Schweinfurt, in central Germany, to destroy three ball bearing plants critical to the Nazi war effort.

The Americans made mistakes during the raid.

Strike timing was not coordinated with a separate U.S. attack that day on a Me-109 fighter plant at Regensburg. As a consequence the Luftwaffe was given time to attack the Regensburg raiders, land, refuel, rearm and rise again to attack the incoming Schweinfurt raiders.

Going in, the U.S. commander for the Schweinfurt raid chose to fly below a cloud cover ranging between 17,000 and 21,000 feet, "which showed the Fortresses up beautifully and made them easily visible for fifty miles."[3] The Luftwaffe, however, effectively used this same cloud cover to mask its attacks.

At day's end, the Schweinfurt mission cost 36 B-17s. The 91st, flying the always-dangerous lead position, lost 10 bombers, a loss rate of 42%. Thirty-six airmen from the bomb group were killed. The ball bearing plants were damaged but soon repaired; German war production was not seriously interrupted. News releases touted the raid a success; the reality was otherwise.

After the war, Gregory Peck starred in the popular film *Twelve O'Clock High*. A work of historical fiction, it was loosely based on the early days of a U.S. bomb group stationed in Great Britain and focused on the introduction of strategic daylight bombing. The film's major raid was based on the real Schweinfurt mission and the B-17 bombers in the film had a large and distinctive "Triangle A" painted on their tails exactly as the planes flown by the 91st.

After the devastating results of the Schweinfurt raid, it took the 91st over a month to recuperate in terms of men, material and morale. When it did recover it came back with what one might characterize as an *attitude*. On October 9, the 91st participated in what would become known as the Battle of Anklam. The name "battle" derived from the fact that so many bullets were fired. Again trying to prove American daylight air superiority, six U.S. bomb groups, comprising 115 B-17s (including 17 from the 91st) faced-off against approximately 300 German fighters. Anklam, a good-sized city approximately 90 miles north of Berlin near the Baltic Sea, was a deep penetration mission for the attackers and beyond the range of U.S. fighter support. This time the 91st flew tail-end Charlie, another dangerous position in a bomber formation.

What made this raid tactically different was the fact that it was a diversion. Ostensibly sent to destroy an aircraft components plant in the city, the real intent of the mission was to serve as a ruse to draw off German fighters from a much larger U.S. attack planned for eastern Germany via the Baltic Sea coastline. A commentator wrote: "As an additional temptation to the Luftwaffe they [the Anklam attackers] would fly at only 12,500 feet."[4]

Bomb-laden heavy bombers usually operated at high altitude, often at 24,000 feet, for two reasons: one, planes flying at high altitude were more difficult to shoot down from the ground; and two, enemy fighters were less maneuverable and effective at higher altitudes. In going into Anklam the way it did, the Eighth Air Force issued a special challenge to the Luftwaffe: "We are willing slug it out in the airspace favorable to you."

The Germans pilots took the easy offering and allowed the larger more destructive main U.S. force to proceed unopposed.

Aerial combat in the Anklam battle was fierce.

The Luftwaffe came on aggressively with repeated head-on attacks followed by hits from all directions. German fighters attacked singly and in groups of two or four. The B-17s held to a tight formation that optimized the many gun stations on each ship. Several U.S. gunners were severely wounded but stood to their posts and continued firing. The Luftwaffe flew through its own rocket fire and flak to get at the U.S. bombers. Planes on both sides ran out of ammo. Eighteen of the 115 B-17s that started out that day were lost, including 5 from the 91st. Thirty men from the 91st were killed."[5] The contest had been waged in perfect visibility.

As for Anklam itself, the city was seriously damaged. A German woman would later write about her experience on the ground. This had been the first bombing of her city. She reported that the attack lasted only four minutes and that most of the city center was destroyed. "The sky darkened into night and 350 civilians died."[6]

The raids at Schweinfurt and Anklam set into play what would become a tradition for the 91st—an aggressive eagerness to engage and a willingness to sacrifice to obtain victory. The bomb group would both lead from the front and defend from the rear. Casualties or not, this bomb group was unstoppable. The press said as much and a reputation came into being.

The 91st had completed some 250 missions when the Bishop Crew arrived at Bassingbourn in late October 1944. When the crew started flying combat approximately a month later, there remained another 82 missions for the 91st to fly before the Nazis would capitulate. Addison Bartush would fly 31 of these 82 missions—representing a normal combat rotation for a pilot at the time.[7] Paul Lynch would fly but once.

Being the first U.S. heavy bomb group to arrive in Great Britain in 1942, the 91st had dibs on available airfields—well sort of dibs, anyway. The commander of the 91st, Col. Stanley Wray, whose bomb group had been billeted at Kimbolton (a less-than-desirable metal shack kind of a facility), had been ordered to inspect and report on an air station at Bassingbourn, near Cambridge and not far from London, for a possible move of the 91st there. Seeing the pristine, fully completed permanent structures at Bassingbourn, Wray ordered his men to immediately truck in everything they could in order to take squatter's possession! The reputation for aggressiveness of this bomb group started right then and there. After "occupying" Bassingbourn, Wray pleaded for, and begrudgingly obtained, forgiveness from a frosted USAAF brigadier general.

Wray chose Bassingbourn, a base built by the RAF before the war, because it had a large number of hangers, well-built permanent brick buildings (no cold-water-only Nissen huts or out-houses that would become the bane of later arriving USAAF operational groups) and perhaps, most wonderfully, per Addison, concrete sidewalks. "There was no mud!" Addison exclaimed. "We were the country club of air stations! The dance floor at the Officer's Club was made of real wood," he effused. Officers lived in one area of the base and enlisted men in another; both had it as good or better than their USAAF counterparts elsewhere in the ETO. Bassingbourn's close proximity to London did not hurt 91st morale, either.

Paul and Addison's squadron, the 324th, was one of four squadrons comprising the 91st Bomb Group—the others being the 322nd, the 323rd and the 401st. The 324th was the unit made famous by the bomber *Memphis Belle*, whose crew, on a 1943 cross-country promotional tour, had visited the University of Pittsburgh when Addison and Dave Bishop were student cadets there. "I remember meeting them," Addison said. This had been a big deal for Addison, Dave and all the cadet-students.

Under Eighth Air Force rules in effect in 1942, when the U.S. air war started, a bomber crew had to complete 25 combat missions, referred to as a "tour," to be eligible to return to the United States. At that time, many knowledgeable of German air defenses thought that surviving 25 missions was not statistically possible. On May 17, 1943, the crew of the *Memphis Belle* proved them wrong; they were the first crew to accomplish this feat. An elaborate ceremony was held at Bassingbourn to mark their success— one that included a visit from the King and Queen of England.

Memphis Belle proved to be a big morale boost for the Eighth Air Force and the event was made famous in a documentary by Hollywood director William Wyler. The movie proved to be a huge hit stateside and in the United Kingdom. "I knew about the *Memphis Belle*, of course," Addison said. "But I didn't know it belonged to the 91st."

By the time the Bishop Crew arrived at Bassingbourn a year-and-a half later, the war was going much better for the Allies. The odds for bomber crew survival were better in large part because U.S. fighter planes, flying from forward bases in liberated France and carrying external fuel tanks that extended their range, could, for the first time, escort heavy bombers all the way to their targets and back. When Addison and Paul and the others arrived on the scene, a "tour" had been upped to 35 missions. Although the survival odds had considerably improved by late 1944, flying combat missions was still extremely dangerous work. "Flak," or anti-aircraft artillery fired from ground stations, accounted for the majority of bombers downed—even early in the air war—and flak could not be stopped.

Upon arrival, the Bishop Crew was put to work almost immediately, but not at flying combat. Things were going so well for the USAAF at this juncture that it had the luxury of training newly arrived crews for approximately a month before exposing them to harm's way. "We had to fly around the area to get used to the local topography," Addison explained. "We flew a lot."

The Bishop Crew had barely settled in when major tragedy struck on November 2, 1944. The 324th Squadron was idle that day, but the other three squadrons of the 91st put up 37 bombers and flew to Merseburg. Only 24 returned. Eighth Air Force-wide, a total of 38 B-17s were lost on the mission.[8] Several B-17s belonging to the 91st went down because of flak damage taken during their bomb runs. After "bombs away" things became far more deadly. The Luftwaffe, that had not been active for some time in order to conserve fuel, came out with 500 fighters and sandbagged the returning American raiding force. The 91st happened to be in the always vulnerable tail-end Charlie position and consequently absorbed the worst of the attack. In its largest single-day loss of the war, the 91st suffered 49 members killed and 5 wounded; another 68 were taken prisoner of war.[9]

Addison had been away from the base when this happened, but Paul Lynch was at the field when the shattered bomb group limped home. "I recall watching those planes return with all their structural damage and wounded," Paul remembered. "This was my first real exposure to the fact that war is hell and I soon would be right in the middle of the whole mess."

Thinking back on this event, Addison recounted a similar event that later affected him: "I once saw a plane pull-up and a body removed from a ball turret. The sight made me grow old quick."

The November 2 Merseburg raid dispelled any thoughts that Bishop crewmembers may have harbored about the air war winding down, or that it was becoming relatively safe to fly combat. True, at this stage of the war the casualty percentage rates for bomber crews were not nearly as high as it had been previously, but there still remained a present and real danger. "When I flew combat, enemy fighters were few and far between," Addison remarked, "but they could always surprise you." In the lore of the 91st Bomb Group, November 2, 1944 would become forever known as the *Massacre at Merseburg*.[10] That the 324th Squadron did not fly that day was purely a matter of chance. Unless the Eighth Air Force had a "maximum effort" on, it was customary for bomb groups to send out three squadrons on any given mission day, allowing the fourth squadron, on a rotational basis, to stand down for a day of rest. It simply happened that the 322nd, the 323rd and the 401st Squadrons were assigned to fly on November 2, 1944, and not the 324th.

Paul had a thought-provoking reaction to what happened on November 2. As bad as the Merseburg raid had been for his bomb group, he felt America's conduct of the war was the proper approach. He said: "U.S. airmen had a certain pride that we bombed only military-specific targets and in broad daylight. The British bombed whole cities at night. There was an undercurrent among U.S. airmen that the British raids were revenge for the German blitz over London that killed thousands of civilians, and that this was wrong. The 49 U.S. airmen from the 91st who died over Merseburg that day were trying to knock out a Nazi fuel-making plant. This was a right thing to do." The Blitz lasted from September 1940 through mid-May 1941 and witnessed the Nazis attacking many UK cities, including 71 assaults on London. Approximately 60,000 British civilians were killed during the Blitz, and a majority of those perished in London.[11]

During late November Paul recounted a training mission to Paris where communications were lost on the way back resulting in an emergency landing. Addison described it this way: "We couldn't get back because the weather had gotten so bad. We passed over a small RAF fighter base and circled several times while Dave initiated radio contact for permission to make an emergency landing. They granted us permission and the landing wasn't easy because of the short runway. We spent the night there and the British were very, very helpful. When the weather finally cleared, we flew back to our base."

"We were fortunate for that one-day emergency layover," Paul recounted. Had we made it back to Bassingbourn, at least some of us would have flown combat the next day on a B-17 that ended up being shot down."

The commanding officer of the 324th Squadron who was responsible for training the Bishop Crew, Lt. Col. Immanuel J. Klette, had a real persona. He was the son of a Lutheran pastor who detested the Nazis, and "Manny" Klette vowed to continue flying combat until the Third Reich was smashed.[12] To him the war was personal—he abhorred "a totalitarian government headed by a megalomaniac racist."[13] Klette took command of the 324th Squadron on July 30, 1944. By the end of the war he would hold the Eighth Air Force record for most heavy bomber combat missions flown—coincidently the same number as his bomb group—91.

"He was a disciplinarian," Addison said without hesitation. "You had to obey the rules and always be a good pilot." The manner of Addison's delivery left no doubt about what he meant to say: Klette was a CO who commanded respect.

Like Addison, Klette started flying combat as a co-pilot. Blond, handsome and 27 years old, Klette was the first known B-17 pilot to pull out of a spin with a full bomb load.[14] When he was climbing at near stall speed through clouds he had to maneuver sharply to avoid a collision. The sudden veer caused him to lose air and put him out of control. Somehow, miraculously, he was able to re-stabilize his airship. Another first was a crash landing under instrument conditions in the woods near an RAF base with only one engine and a flat tire.[15] Although there were miraculously no crew fatalities, this flak-caused downing put Klette in the hospital for five months with a fractured pelvis and leg injuries. After he was released he was selected to command the 324th. Addison told of a social event involving his commanding officer where Klette's human side came out. "We really got to know him when he married," Addison offered. "He married an American nurse, I believe, in a church at Cambridge and we all attended." He added, "She died young and he remarried."

Asked if Klette had a sense of humor, Addison replied, "I think he did," then smiled wide at the memory and qualified his response. "Later in life," he chuckled, meaning *only after* the war. As a combat commander, Klette had been all business but also not a vainglorious, strutting peacock militarist. "We all wore crush hats and walked around with our hands in our pockets," Addison confessed, looking positively refreshed at the recollection. "Klette did not swagger or project hot pilot."

"He was shorter than me," Addison observed. "But not a whole lot." Addison stood at about 5' 9" and readily agreed that in the air combat profession it was an advantage to be of modest stature. "It helps when exiting an airplane with a parachute," he observed smiling wryly. It was telling, when reminiscing so many decades after the association, that Addison could not bring himself—not once—to refer to his former commander as "Manny."

Klette could be very aggressive. On one occasion while in the lead he dove the bomb group from a perch of 27,000 feet with no visibility to a position at 17,000 feet with clear skies and did so through a major flak barrage. Some of his airmen felt this dive was foolhardy, exposing the group to flak at the much lower altitude, but the 91st hit the target and Gen. Doolittle gave Klette a letter of commendation for the result. Only one B-17 was lost.[16]

"Klette was a tough guy," Addison remembered. "Aggressive is right."

At the time the Bishop Crew arrived on the scene, Klette had completed 32 missions as squadron commander of the 324th—this, in addition to 28 earlier missions. With such a combat record any crew, rookie or not, would have looked upon him with veneration.

By the time Klette finished flying combat with the 91st he had led "either group, combat wing, division, task force or Eighth Air Force" on 30 missions.[17] This was a remarkable accomplishment. More astonishing however, was the fact that during these missions, the 91st Bomb Group lost only two aircraft.[18]

Safe as it may have been to fly with Klette in the lead, one had to be on his guard. "He had a real temper," Addison said. "All of us were aware of this." Addison would later relate an incident that occurred on the last mission of the war that sparked this temper.

"There is always someone giving you the, 'go, go, go, go out and fight' pep talk," Addison observed. Klette's passion for the righteousness of the Allied cause was well known, Addison admitted, but he also indicated his commander led more by example than rhetoric.

Addison told of another leader at Bassingbourn who made a huge difference: an American chaplain named Father Michael Ragan. "He gave comfort and support to Catholics and non-Catholics alike," Addison related. "He really cared."

"He was a character," Addison continued. "Everyone loved him."

What Father Ragan did that so endeared him to the 91st was to *always* be at the airfield in the early morning to give the combat aircrews a group blessing and to offer communion for Catholics like Addison who wanted it. When the mile-long procession of bombers rolled around the airbase perimeter road, queuing up for an operation, Father Ragan would stand on the grass next to the runway at the spot where they would start the take off. He held up a horseshoe as a symbol of luck. As each bomber accelerated, he blessed it. For a number of these airmen who saw him do this, either though a plane window or out of a waist port, it would be their last sight of a man standing on the earth.

While the bombers were gone Father Ragan made the rounds of the ground crews and chatted amicably about anything they wanted to talk about. He thanked them for the invaluable service they performed and the long hours that they put in doing it; he also invited them to come and see him at any time and for any reason. It did not matter what religion someone observed or even if the person had a religion: Father Ragan viewed his job as listening, spiritually consoling and advising—not converting.

When the bombers returned in the afternoon, he would always be there with hot chocolate at the ready, enthusiastically waving them in. Father Ragan appreciated the stress these warriors endured, and their need to be assured that God flew with them; that faith would save their soul even if the worst should happen; that the war they fought was just and needed to be prosecuted; that Nazism, with its penchant for military aggression, was an abrogation of God's law and the teachings of Jesus Christ.

He even blessed B-17s on the tarmac and sprinkled holy water on them; he was known to talk to birds. He was not, however, lacking something those of Irish descent cherish most: a solid sense of humor. He was in the habit of concluding Sunday worship service by removing his habit, one sacred vestment at a time, and trying to explain its meaning and history within the Church. When an airman invariably yelled, "Take it off!" (as happened every week) he did so—right down to his army uniform. No one laughed harder at this pretend strip tease than did Father Ragan.[19]

"He really cared," Addison elucidated, tearing up. "He was from Youngstown, Ohio, and got killed in an automobile accident in the summer of '49." One of the regrets in Addison's life was not learning of Father Ragan's death in time to attend his funeral.

Paul Lynch was not at Bassingbourn long enough for Father Ragan to make an impression. In Addison's case the priest's contribution was cumulative, starting in earnest when he commenced flying combat. When the going got really tough, and it did, it was Father Ragan who more than anyone else held Addison together. "He was always there," Addison exclaimed, emphasizing his lifelong appreciation. In a bitter comparison he blurted: "One rarely saw the Protestant chaplain."

"I had a couple of Jewish friends," he said, wearing his trademark grin, the one that foretold a punch line coming. "One arrived, I think in January, and I had lunch with him. He was from Detroit and that's how we got acquainted. Anyway, at our first lunch together we were having pork and it was the first time he had ever eaten pork, so I said to him, 'Well, this is the first time I ever ate meat on Friday.'"

Addison's friend was pilot Lt. Marvin Goldberg, and they maintained their friendship after the war. "He was very religious," Addison held, "Although not a rabbi, he conducted Jewish services at Bassingbourn for his fellow Jews." Addison later related how poorly some members of his squadron treated him simply because he was Jewish.

At the end of November, Bishop crewmembers started flying combat missions, but not as a team. "They broke our crew up at the start so that we could gain experience working alongside seasoned airmen," Addison explained. "Dave Bishop flew his first two missions as a co-pilot before I flew my first mission, and of course my first mission was with someone other than Dave." After flying five or so missions with other crews, the 91st plan called for the full Bishop Crew to reunite and fly combat together.

At the time their combat duty began, Addison, Dave and RJ lived in a bunkroom with several other officers. Conditions were spartan, but the building was made of brick, not corrugated metal, and was well insulated and heated. It had sashed windows that opened and closed. The men slept on army cots with a footlocker nearby for uniform items, toiletries, stationary, photographs and personal effects.

By this time in the war, U.S. mail arrived regularly. At mail call Addison received more letters than the others; in addition to the usual letters from family and friends, he received correspondence from his father's business associates and letters from some of the 4 M's.

Addison and Paul wrote home frequently, as surely did the others.

On the night of November 24, Addison turned in early. "Good luck, tomorrow," Dave said to him, and RJ echoed the same sentiment.

"Thanks, guys" Addison replied. "I'll try not to make too much noise when I get up."

CHAPTER FOUR

The "Oil Campaign"

I n the late summer of 1944, as Addison and his crew trained in Gulfport, Mississippi, for deployment, the Red Army captured the heavily damaged oil fields of Ploesti, Romania, denying the Germans access to natural crude oil. To counter this, the Nazis, under the ever-resourceful Reich Minister for Armaments, Albert Speer, accelerated the production of synthetic fuel from coal at two-dozen plants situated inside Germany itself.[1] The Allied air campaign against these fuel plants commenced in the spring of 1944 and continued throughout the summer and fall of that year. Addison's first mission would be to the largest fuel plant in Germany and it would prove to be a dangerous one. The target city was Merseburg, a name that was all too familiar to members of the 91st. Addison would experience combat for the first time in the company of eight veteran crewmembers; men that he had never flown with.

"I didn't expect a tough one like that for my first mission," Addison bemoaned, describing what it was like in the briefing room that morning when the target was identified. The large curtain was drawn back to reveal a map. "A string showed the route we were going to take," Addison said. "A groan went up in the room."

The Eighth Air Force mission #723, on November 25, 1944, Addison's first, involved 1,043 bombers and 955 fighters dispatched to make radar-guided attacks on oil targets and a marshalling yard in Germany.[2] Addison's bomber was among the 766 that were directed to make a deep penetration attack on the enormous I.G. Farben chemical factory named Leuna Werke.

Located in central Germany in the city of Merseburg, not far from Leipzig, Leuna Werke was one of the best-defended targets in the Third

Reich. Nazi Germany possessed approximately 25,000 total anti-aircraft guns,[3] mostly of the 88 mm caliber variety, and a hefty 7% of these guns, or 1,700, were placed in defense of Leuna Werke.[4] Such was the importance of this fuel plant to the German war effort.

A German 88 could shoot as high as a B-17 could fly, and a typical gun crew could put out between 15 and 20 exploding rounds per minute.[5] The Germans never developed a radio proximity fuse that would cause a shell to explode near an aircraft (this was a top-secret American innovation) but using radar and visual sighting techniques they could manually set their fuses so the shells would detonate at or near intended targets. With all of these guns firing, the Germans could put up nearly 30,000 rounds of exploding flak per minute. This was as concentrated as flak could become.

The first of 20 Eighth Air Force missions to be flown over Leuna Werke took place on May 12, 1944. A commentator referred to this series of attacks as *Twenty Missions in Hell*.[6] Addison participated in two of these missions: on November 25 and again on December 12, 1944. Collectively, the 20 USAAF missions to Leuna Werke and the additional missions to other synthetic fuel plants became known in military aviation history as "the oil campaign." With each succeeding mission to such targets, enemy flak and fighter attacks intensified. Yet, only 11% of total Eighth Air Force resources had been allocated to the oil campaign,[7] and when Addison attended his first combat briefing he had reason to hope for another, less dangerous assignment.

"We all knew where the heavily defended targets were," Addison said, "and Merseburg was the least popular place for a mission." Addison further explained that it was common knowledge at the time that Merseburg produced the highest USAAF casualty rates. "I'd have rather gone to Berlin on my first mission," he indicated. After he did go to Berlin months later he still felt the same way.

This round-trip for Addison would be approximately 1,200 miles, with a good portion of it over enemy territory. Addison's first mission would be a long one, taking approximately eight hours.[8]

The 91st BG's operations officer spoke at the early morning briefing and he covered the route and the planned rendezvous with other Eighth Air Force groups. The weatherman followed. Addison indicated that the weather forecast for the return trip was critical; that the squadron might take off in lousy weather and even bomb through clouds, but that good weather was essential for finding one's way home and getting safely down. U.S. Navy ships stationed in the Atlantic were tasked with reporting approaching weather conditions.

"Pilots with prior experience with the target would speak," Addison said, "to share what they knew." The commanding officer of the 91st, Col. Henry W. Terry, would be present at the briefing and offer words; that is, if he felt anything needed to be added. Terry was well regarded and had a reputation for listening. "We were 'Terry's Tigers'," Addison proudly noted. "He called us that." Indeed, the bomb group had a B-17 that went by that name. Terry commanded the 91st from May 1944 through May 1945, the end of the war in Europe.[9] The Colonel led from D-Day on.

The fuel plant at Merseburg bore the nickname "Flak Hell Leuna" or "flak alley" or even "flak den," as it was at all times truly a dangerous place for Americans to fly over. The worst of the November 2 *Massacre at Merseburg* however, had been caused by German fighters and not flak, as there had been no in-flight diversions to fool the Luftwaffe as to the intended target.[10] Addison confirmed that this was not the case for his first mission on November 25. "That string on that big map on the wall had a number of bends in it," he recalled.

Addison could not remember what position in the squadron formation the bomber that he flew in occupied that day, but he did remember vividly other things about the mission. The experience terrified him. "It was at the target area that I *thought* I saw enemy fighters. Our fighters were diving all over the place and it was wild. I believe they were engaging enemy aircraft, I'm not sure, but for sure all hell broke loose." Addison explained: "I cannot tell you how many fighters I actually saw. It was a fighter campaign, though, no doubt. I couldn't tell you if I saw 20 or 50 or even 100, but they were all maneuvering."

Addison had flown into the middle of a dogfight and he confirmed what scores of other U.S. bomber pilots reported: in aerial battle it is extremely difficult to distinguish friend from foe. "It was pandemonium and we were following a lead bomber to make an attack," Addison said. Addison and his pilot focused on staying in formation as the "initial point" approached for the bomb run. On the run itself Nazi and American fighters alike pulled out to avoid being hit by flak.

"We bombed from twenty-four thousand feet," Addison explained. "And as soon as we dropped our bombs we would turn either to the left or right and drop down a couple thousand feet. We wanted to get out of there as fast as possible." This maneuver, that is turning and dropping altitude, was called a rally and it was very important for the bombers to hold a tight formation. "The [flak] shells had been programmed for 24,000 feet and we wanted to get under the explosions," Addison related. "They would re-program them, yes, but that takes a little while." Diving would enable the bombers to immediately boost needed airspeed and without a heavy bomb load they could fly faster and be more maneuverable.

Addison pointed out that the tight formation was needed for defense against the expected re-emergence of enemy fighters. Multiple machine guns from different bombers could be concentrated on the same targets and dangerous passing lanes denied to the enemy. Loose formations were preferable in flak barrage situations to allow room for individual evasive action, that is, to anticipate where the gun batteries might shoot next and dodge and dart accordingly. Klette, however, had a bias for "holding extremely close formations."[11]

"Klette did order close formations," Addison agreed, and then that wry smile came over his face, and he chuckled. "But there were always some who did what they wanted," he said, implying that an individual bomber or even several bombers might maneuver in an unauthorized fashion in order to dodge incoming trouble, such as being charged directly by a Fw-190.

What Addison described had to have been a gut-wrenching experience: four or five hours of nerve-wracking flying in the sure knowledge that when one reached the target area an incredible violence would occur and that people would die both in the air and on the ground. The mental build-up for this had to have been an almost out-of-world experience, particularly for those new to the fight. "We zigged and zagged all the time," Addison indicated. "We did not fly a straight course coming in." He added: "The enemy knew what our target was going to be; that is, they knew what we were going after. The Germans were prepared."

"We generally flew the bomb run straight and level," Addison said but then qualified his statement indicating that Klette might make a route deviation if he spotted a flak field ahead that could be avoided. "Everyone was supposed to follow." Addison again laughed. "I don't know what went on behind me."

The *USAAF Chronology* for the November 25 raid on Leuna Werke indicated that a radar attack was made. "I never saw the plant," Addison recollected. "Never. The sky was full of smoke and clouds that day, it was also dark in November." Visibility from the air may have been diminished in part by the Germans who were known to spray acidic fumes into the air to produce a dense smoke screen and hide their factory.[12] Addison had no knowledge of this, however.

As regards to flak bursts he said: "They were orange and angry. Some left white smoke and others, black. I guess it depended on what kind of shell they shot at us. The explosion sound was drowned out by our engine noise and the fact that we wore earphones. We could feel the explosions, though. They moved the plane around like it was passing through a storm. It was very rough." Addison could not remember whether his airplane suffered flak damage that day. "We would have inspected the plane after we got back," he explained, "but I don't recall if we had any holes."

For Addison, Leuna Werke had lived up to its USAAF reputation. "I was terrified," he admitted. "The flak was so thick one could almost roll on it." As co-pilot his duty had been to be prepared to take over. He also was an extra set of eyes. "You might see an enemy fighter coming at you," he said, indicating that was what the intercom was for, to sound the alarm.

"A smoke bomb from the lead plane would signal the drop and then it was simply a matter of someone throwing a switch. There was a back-up toggle on the flight deck but I never saw it used. As the bombs released, the plane rose like an elevator."

In World War II bombers did not delay turning in order to track the downward descent of their bombs. "We turned immediately," Addison re-emphasized, "and dropped down to get under the flak." He added: "We flew these missions at 150 miles an hour airspeed. We needed to get out." What Addison said made sense. Photos might be taken from a waist port or another station on a ship but the pilots were only concerned with skedaddling. A photoreconnaissance airplane such as the fast P-51 Mustang or a British Mosquito could gather evidence of bombing effectiveness after the fact.

The Nazis used slave labor at Leuna Werke and other fuel plants in a frantic effort to ring the factories with thick walls of concrete in order to minimize blast damage.[13] This effort failed completely.

Asked if he encountered any German fighters on the way back, Addison replied, "I don't recall any." Fortunately for Addison, he did not witness any B-17s blown out of the sky this first day, although it happened.

As an aside, Addison recollected that on all of his missions, only on one occasion did he see a fighter that he could clearly identify as German. This fighter flew through his formation from the rear and he spotted the swastika. There was talk it might have been a ME-262 jet as it traveled so fast. Addison did not know this, however.

Thinking back on that day Addison pondered whether the training he had received had prepared him well for aerial combat. "I came out of it alive, that is all I know," he declared, meaning that the end result for him justified the means and validated his training.

On the way back the bombers stayed at 24,000 feet and zigzagged until they were safely into friendly territory. Addison hardly noticed the ferocious cold in the unpressurized airplane. The small cockpit heater helped some, he supposed, but then he offered this: "One would perspire occasionally," referring to his reaction to combat. "One tended to generate internal heat," he laughed.

Relieved and exhausted, Addison participated in his first mission debriefing. "They sat the entire crew down at a table and they gave us each a half-full coffee cup of bourbon. They asked us to tell them what we saw and took notes. It was over in 15 minutes or maybe a half hour." Addison described what it was like to have that bourbon—"the best elixir in the world." After the briefing he went to chapel. He knew that it would be a long time before he would enjoy the concept of seri*ass* again. For now everything had turned serious. Whether he drank any of Father Ragan's hot chocolate he did not mention.

One mission down and 34 to go!

That evening in the bunkroom he told Dave and RJ about his mission. Dave and RJ were assigned to fly the next day along with four members of the Bishop Crew. Things had progressed well so far for the young men who had trained together at Gulfport, and it was expected that after a few more missions the nine Bishop crewmembers would fly and fight as a team.

Wake-up for those on the duty list was between 2:00 and 3:00 a.m. A duty officer with a flashlight would be assigned to make the rounds of the dorms to make sure no one scheduled to fly overslept. The next day,

November 26, Addison would not have that flashlight shined into his face; Addison would not have to ride the early morning beam.

The Eighth Air Force Strategic Mission #723, Addison's first, witnessed moderate losses. A total of 671 Fortresses attacked the Leuna Werke synthetic fuel plant. An additional 95 B-17s failed to make it to the target area due to one reason or another—weather, mechanical failures, navigational errors and the like. The *USAAF Chronology* report states, as regards B-17 bombers: "lost 8," "damaged beyond repair 4" and "damaged 197." Additionally, six fighter escorts were lost. All bombers belonging to the 91st returned safely to Bassingbourn. The numbers that were most important, however, for the mission as a whole, were reported as "KIA," "WIA" and "MIA." For Addison's day of indoctrination, November 25, 1944, these numbers for B-17 crews were 7–5–64. Fortunately for Addison and his bomb group, no casualty report needed to be filed.

The sacrifice of the Allied airmen who participated in the oil campaign was not in vain. By war's end, 220,000 tons of high explosives had been dropped on the production plants and this reduced the Reich's synthetic fuel output to a mere 5% of what it was before the campaign began.[14] When Hitler launched his final offensive in Belgium on December 16, 1944, his panzers had less than a week of fuel supply available. The Nazi fuel shortage proved to be a critical factor in the U.S. success in the Battle of the Bulge and it equally served as an advantage to the advancing Soviets. Near the end of the war the Luftwaffe was grounded days at a time for lack of aviation gasoline.[15] The Germans had no shortage of airplanes; only fuel and experienced pilots to fly them. As a strategy, the oil campaign was a total success.

The bombing of the Leuna Werke synthetic fuel plant, Addison's first mission, epitomized the execution of USAAF strategic bombing doctrine at the time: high altitude, precision, and daylight bombing of military targets only.

CHAPTER FIVE

Tragedy for the Bishop Crew

The briefing Paul Lynch attended the next day was better received than the one Addison experienced. No groans went up when the intelligence officer promised, "The area is not heavily fortified and the Luftwaffe has been quiet recently."

Looking at the map with two of his fellow gunners sitting next to him, Paul could see that this would not be a deep penetration raid. The red-circled target was a railroad viaduct, or land bridge, near Osnabruck, Germany, about 40 miles east of the Netherlands and 90 miles south of Bremen. "The town where the viaduct is located is named Altenbeken," the briefing officer said, pointing to it on the map.

Paul glanced at Owen Monkman and sensed Owen was thinking the same as him; he smiled, and Owen acknowledged the exchange with a return smile and nod. Without saying a word, both men had agreed that a short mission to a quiet sector was a good way to break the ice. Paul tried the same reassuring smile on Charles Cumings, but Charles did not make eye contact.

Paul, Owen and Charles were the chosen gunner contingent from the Bishop Crew for this mission. Bishop Crew radio operator John Kendall would also fly it, but at this moment he was being briefed at a different location with the officers; Dave Bishop would fly as co-pilot and RJ Miller would navigate. Almost the full Bishop Crew, Paul thought; only three veteran airmen filling in as replacements. Soon all of the men that he trained with at Gulfport would operate together.

For Dave, RJ and John this would be their third combat mission; for the three Bishop gunners this would be their hair of the dog—a cure for the hangover of never having flown combat. "I had great anticipation," Paul made clear, recollecting his emotional build-up for this event. This was what he and his friends had trained for. Paul was just 19 and this was the start of the adventure; his flight into the unknown. Paul had been pumped up since the day before when he saw the duty sheet posting.

"This should be a milk run," the briefing officer said. Paul cringed when he heard this. Was it not briefed (or so Paul had been told) that the Luftwaffe was "inactive" before the tragedy of November 2? "I didn't know whether I had confidence in the assessment of this intelligence officer or not," Paul asserted. There was nothing to be done about it, however. It was the Sunday after Thanksgiving and Paul would fly regardless of the mission.

This mission day called for 1,137 bombers and 732 fighters from the Eighth Air Force to attack targets all over Germany with 118 B-17s specifically tasked to take out the viaduct. Each heavy bomber carried approximately 5,000 lbs. of ordnance, or two and a half tons. Paul did the calculation in his mind: the viaduct would have approximately 300 tons of high explosive bombs dropped on it today. It would be blown to smithereens.

"The pilot was a Lieutenant Flint," Paul said. "Kendall, Cumings, Monkman and I were given our normal positions. Two veteran gunners filled out the rest of our crew. Dan Hiner took the nose gun and Sergeant Bart Zanotto the ball turret on the floor. Both were staff sergeants."

Following the briefing the crew was trucked to their assigned bomber which awaited them on a concrete hardstand, serviced, fueled and armed. "We were shocked when we saw *The Wild Hare* on the flight line," Paul shuddered at the recollection. "The old lady had patches on patches and lines of bombs painted on her nose." Indeed, *The Wild Hare* had arrived overseas at the end of 1943 and had seen continuous hard use. Paul whined: "We figured this hanger queen was saved especially for the new kids on the block: us."

Doing all of the pre-flight checks required of gunners, Paul and his cohorts had the opportunity to talk to the two veteran gunners. The men readily volunteered the specific personal information that the Bishop crewmen wanted to know. For Dan Hiner, who would also act as bombardier, this would be mission number 26. For Bart Zanotto it would be 35.

He'll be home for the holidays, Paul thought of Zanotto.

Paul noted how far down the runway it took to get airborne with a full bomb load and also how the flight in the early daylight hours had been pleasant and even a secure-feeling experience. "The flight was beautiful high above the clouds in the early morning sun, and with the comforting sound of the four engines I took a nap," Paul recollected. *The Wild Hare* climbed and climbed and after a bit it got colder.

As Paul slumbered, Addison Bartush rose. This would be a good day to visit London, he decided. He needed a winter uniform coat, something less than a greatcoat, and he knew just where to go in the city to purchase one. There would also be sightseeing to do and perhaps a spot of lunch? Yesterday had been awful, yes, but yesterday was over. Maybe he had seen the worst?

Before leaving the base, Addison purchased two London editions of the *Stars and Stripes* newspaper. Yes, his mission was prominently reported on the front page. On each paper he placed a tiny black ink dot over the word "Merseburg." He mailed one copy to his parents and kept the other in his footlocker.

Paul awoke. It was 10,000 feet and time for the oxygen now. This raid was to be a quick in-and-out, bombing from a high 26,000 feet. Paul witnessed the better part of a 1,000 or so U.S. warplanes queuing up in the morning sky, forming up for their assigned strikes—his reaction was one of awe; he had never seen anything like this. With 118 of these monsters to protect him at Altenbeken, what could go wrong? This number meant that well over a thousand .50 caliber machine guns in his attacking force could be brought to bear on one or more targets. Moreover, the B-17 machine guns were not "fixed" rifle barrels—each could be swung to the right or left, raised or lowered—that is, each could be specifically *aimed*. Paul sensed that it was the Luftwaffe that needed to be careful.

Over the English Channel the bomber crews test-fired the .50s. It grew even colder and the gunners huddled in front of the waist ports to avoid a lashing wind, thankful for their electrically heated flight suits and boots and the oxygen hook-up. The Altenbeken bound B-17s droned on and on in the blinding sunshine in what seemed like a long time but in reality wasn't that long. Presently the word was passed. Aboard *The Wild Hare*, Lt. Flint gave the order over the intercom: "Don flak jackets, assume stations."

"Our squadron was almost at the end of the formation," Paul noted. "I helped Owen into his jacket and watched him as he took his position in the tail. It wasn't long before we were picking-up puffs of smoke."

"I manned my waist gun and it was announced that we were approaching the IP for the bomb run." Maybe another 15, minutes, Paul thought, maybe a little longer. When they did the bomb run, Paul knew the Norden bombsight on the lead bomber would be used. When Sgt. Hiner, who was in nose of the *The Wild Hare*, observed the lead bomber drop its bomb load all he would need to do was to throw a switch. Thereafter, *The Wild Hare* would turn and head for home, a lighter and faster airplane.

It all seemed so simple, so clean.

Everything was going as planned, Paul felt. The flak was there, but not too close or thick. The enemy was shooting at him, but missing! Soon they would be flying straight and level, Paul knew, no more zigzags. Paul stared out of the left waist window, alert for anything that he might spot. He was the only waist gunner for this mission; it was his job to man both sides of the plane. The intercom remained silent.

Paul could see glimpses of the ground. We will hit the target today, he believed. It was merely a matter of the lead bombardier spotting that railroad track and following it to the viaduct. This would happen.

What Paul could not see was the large flock of German fighters tens of thousands of feet below traveling in the opposite direction. These fighters knew where Paul's bomber force was, and moreover, likely what it was going after. A perfect time for them to press an attack would be on the bomb run or the preparation for it, these Luftwaffe pilots knew.

The intercom aboard *The Wild Hare* remained silent; the bandits had not been spotted. Kendall at his station in the radio shack received no warning transmissions from other U.S. aircraft in the vicinity.

The German pilots could scarce believe their good fortune. They had passed under the bombers without encountering a single American interceptor, then quickly turned 180 degrees and climbed as fast as their engines would pull.

In the meantime, the formation of 118 B-17s droned onward toward the target area, oblivious to the approaching danger. Soon the order would be given to open bomb bay doors, Paul reckoned. Paul's heart was in his throat. He had practiced this many times, both stateside and on training runs over parts of non-hostile Europe, but what he was about to participate in would be "for real" warfare. This was the stuff stories are made of Paul thought; his almost 14-month anticipation was about to be realized. The bombs he would see falling would destroy or kill anything or anyone in their path.

Instead of seeing bombs falling, however, Paul spotted something else.

"I noticed we had drifted out of formation," Paul said, "away from the protection of the other gunners."

Paul added: "This concerned me."

"I called the pilot and told him if we didn't catch-up we would be out of range of the guns in our formation. He told me he was pushing her as hard as he could. It was then that I looked out the other waist port and saw number three engine ablaze. I assumed we had been hit by flak."

The Wild Hare had sustained serious damage and Paul had not heard or felt a thing, not even a faint shudder. The engine drone of the airplane had not changed. And as related, none of the men at the many gun stations had sounded an alarm. There was no reason for him or any crewmember to believe that this was anything other than flak damage.

"The pilot yelled: 'Fw-190s ten o'clock!'" Paul recalled.

Paul immediately manned the left waist port gun but not before the attackers fired. "Cannon shells ripped into our plane making a hissing and popping sound," Paul related. "I witnessed Kendall, our radio operator fly out of his chair, killed. I managed to squeeze out a few shots at this attacker and I believe Zanotto in the ball turret did the same."

In that instant, Paul's life had forever changed. What began as a very cold but beautiful and sunny day had turned into hell. Paul later elucidated: "I had no idea that the ten o'clock sighting was a second fighter attack," he exclaimed, "and that we had already been attacked from the rear by German flyers."

As it turned out, nobody in his B-17 wing had a clue that an aerial attack was in progress. It would be after the war that Paul learned that up to 75 Me-109s and Fw-190s had attacked. An analyst described it: "The enemy came in line abreast with guns blazing and knocked three 91st aircraft out of formation and finished them off almost before anyone knew what was happening. The escort had apparently been decoyed away and the enemy struck when they were elsewhere. *The Wild Hare*, flown by Lt. Robert J. Flint of the 324th Bomb Squadron, was hit before the IP was reached and had No. 3 engine set on fire in the first pass. The Fortress dropped out of formation and began a gentle dive and then exploded."[1]

With no U.S. fighter cover there had been no advance radio warning that the attack was coming. The German pilots dove from a higher altitude behind the B-17 formation.[2] *The Wild Hare* was flying the tail-end Charlie position. Gaining speed, the fighters got slightly underneath the bombers, came up, leveled and fired. U.S. fighter pilots referred to this technique as "the perfect bounce." From the 6 o'clock position (directly behind) the Germans circled to attack again from 10 o'clock (left frontal quarter). The first aerial assault happened so fast that none of the rear gun stations had time to react, and for *The Wild Hare* and other B-17s, even to report sightings.

After the second attack Flint ordered the crew to prepare to abandon ship. Listening to the responses over the intercom, Paul's blood curdled: "There was no acknowledgement from Owen in the tail," he said. Looking towards Owen's battle station, Paul hoped to see his friend crawling out of

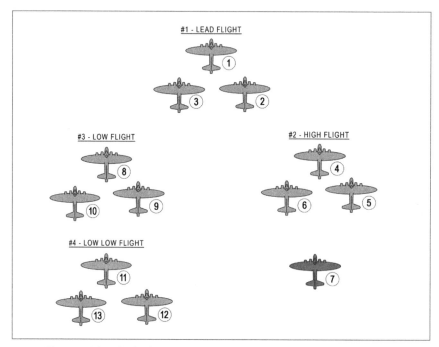

Flying "Tail-end Charlie" position. Paul noted, "We were in position #7 for the Altenbeken Mission. Lucky us."—Formation drawing by Mark Allison from a base drawing provided courtesy of 303rdbg.com, the website honoring the 303rd Bomb Group (H)

his turret, as he should have been after such an order had been issued. Paul saw no movement.

"I opened my duffle bag and snapped on my chute," Paul recounted.

"Then I spotted another Fw-190 slowly sliding in for another shot from ten o'clock. I grabbed my gun and called the top and ball turret men. The ball responded but the top did not. I fired at this fighter until it disappeared under us. The ball followed him under and continued firing at him as he flew away. I don't know that either of us got a piece of him. I checked the windows and saw three engines out. We were really shot-up. This was the end of the fight for us. Our pilot made the only decision, the correct one: abandon ship."

"Zanotto pulled the door release and I gave the door a hard boot and it went flying into space." Standing in the waist, Paul had no view of what was taking place in the forward section of the airship. He knew that those in the front, however—Flint, Bishop, Miller, Hiner and Cumings—had their own exit door, and moreover, there was absolutely nothing he could do to help them in any event. Zanotto had his chute on and was ready to go. Paul did as ordered—he jumped. The decision-making for Paul was not over, however.

"As for me," Paul recounted, "I decided I was going to get more oxygen and as soon as possible. I didn't want to be caught in the middle of an air battle floating to earth under a chute." He added: "Also, this way there was less chance of detection by ground observers," meaning less opportunity for the Germans to find him right away or worse, shoot at him as he floated down. This was to become Paul's first and only practical application of the principles he had learned in Colorado. It was his first and only jump, and most of it was free-fall.

At a minimum Paul Lynch hurtled four miles through the atmosphere. The "gentle dive before exploding" of *The Wild Hare* gave precious time for some to get out and survive.

"We had been instructed to watch for tree limbs," Paul explained, referring to his survival school training. "If one could see tree branches, then it was time to pull the rip-chord."

The free-fall terminal velocity of a human body is between 100 and 200 mph depending on body position and weight.[3] Using an average for the two speeds and doing the math, Paul's free-fall lasted approximately two minutes with little air to breathe at the onset.

"I learned after the war that five men jumped and four survived," Paul said. "Charles Cumings apparently was the first out, exiting in the front, and he was the one who did not survive the fall. After the war Dave Bishop told me that he had quite a time in the forward section trying to convince

Cumings to bail out. He was terrified and almost completely unresponsive. Dave finally put a chute on him and forced him out of the plane."

On January 17, 1945 the U.S. War Department reported Cumings KIA.[4] He died November 26, 1944 and it took almost two months for the Germans to find and identify his body, using his dog tags no doubt, and notify the International Red Cross. Perhaps Cumings had been so traumatized that he simply failed to pull the rip-chord, but there was no way of knowing this. Perhaps his parachute malfunctioned? Or maybe . . . some Nazi in the air or on the ground? That happened in World War II.

Charles Cumings had volunteered for the USAAF, yet during training developed a fear of actual flying. Despite his trepidation, he flew because his country expected him to do so. For this determination he would be remembered as a special person. He was decent and hard working. His loss, as with the loss of the others on November 26, 1944, would be mourned. And as for his screw-up on that training mission detour to overfly Bishop's folks in Spartanburg? "He was good-natured about it," Addison reported. What a wonderful memory Cumings created for the Bishop Crew—the best they would ever have.

Navigator RJ Miller almost bought it on the way down. He had been wounded in the leg and Staff Sergeant Hiner spent valuable time that he did not have helping him put on his parachute and exit through the forward door. RJ chose to pull his rip-chord early and soon regretted it. He later told Paul that a German pilot tried to kill him as he floated down by spilling air out of his parachute. The pilot passed him as close as he could without getting entangled in the shrouds. RJ also told Paul that Sgt. Hiner was a hero for helping him; he could have put on his chute and jumped and lived, instead he stayed to help a wounded man and presumably died while putting on his own chute.

Flint and Bishop made it out of the B-17 and both lived. Hiner and Zanotto did not make it out in time, and Paul had no answer for why Zanotto did not jump. Paul would catch a brief glimpse of Bishop on the ground; he would learn about the others after the war. He did not witness *The Wild Hare* explode. With 5,000 lbs. of bombs and a considerable amount of fuel aboard, the fireball had to have been huge. Sgt. Zanotto, flying his 35th mission, had completed his tour this day but he would not return home for Christmas.

"My chute caught in one of the top branches of a tree," Paul continued, "and I swung into a large lower branch hitting my shin. It hurt badly and at first I thought I had broken my leg. Fortunately, I was only ten or so feet above the ground. I made it down by jumping and landing on my good leg. It was with a great deal of pain, but I survived my parachute landing fall!"

"I saw Bishop on the ground a short distance away. A German spotter plane, an Me-109, flew over and I believe the pilot saw us. Bishop ducked into the woods as I stuffed my parachute under a log and also thought of evasion. My leg hurt terrifically, however, and running was not an option."

Even if Paul had not been injured his chance for evasion would not have been high. For one thing he wore a USAAF flying suit and useless boots wired for electricity; for another, he was in Nazi Germany proper—there would be no partisan support. Paul did not have a sidearm.

Paul continued: "I spotted some wormy apples and pocketed them. I also fashioned a walking stick out of a tree limb. Otherwise, I just sat and waited, and in a great deal of discomfort."

"Two German farmers armed with antiquated rifles had no difficulty locating me and taking me prisoner. I rose up lamely on my walking stick and they could see I was injured. The first word I understood was 'Vor-wartsgehen.' I started hobbling using the stick and mercifully they let me proceed at my own slow speed."

Addison returned to Bassingbourn that afternoon from London, carrying his prized purchase; he intended to start wearing it the next day. The U.S. Army officer short coat cost him 5 pounds, 15 schillings and 11 pence at the QM London Sales Store.

Entering his dormitory room, Addison glanced around and asked, "Where's Dave and RJ?" His heart sank when he saw the expression on the faces of the men in the room.

"Haven't you heard?" one asked.

———

When Addison learned of a tragedy that would haunt him for the rest of his life, he was dumbstruck. Six of his crewmates, six of the young men who had trained with him stateside, six of the airmen who only weeks earlier had flown with him on that long and adventurous trip over the Atlantic, six of his friends had gone down at a place he had never heard of. And two other B-17s from his bomb group were lost on the same mission.

Addison had been told that several parachutes had been spotted but there was no certainty as to a number—three, maybe four. Nothing else. All he knew for certain was that some of his crewmates had died and some had possibly survived. Nobody knew anything more.

Not being able to ascertain the status of any individual airman, the 91st Bomb Group listed all nine crewmembers from the *The Wild Hare* as "missing in action." One of the circumstances that made the air war in World War II so uniquely horrible was its incredibly high number of "MIAs." Tens of thousands of parents, loved ones and friends were forced to wait, worry, pray and hope. Airmen jumped in World War II without radios—no one but the enemy would know whether a parachutist made it safely to the ground. Still, there was good reason for hope. Substantially more American airmen survived this ordeal than were killed. At war's end approximately 1,150 airmen from the 91st Bomb Group were taken prisoners of war compared to 600 killed.[5]

Concerned that the loss of B-17s might get reported in the United States, or that families of missing Bishop crewmembers might in a panic somehow contact his parents and put them in fear for himself, Addison had the presence of mind to telegraph home. "I sent them a cable the day that I found out my crew was lost," he said. Addison wired his parents: "I'm OK."

Addison would soon enough learn firsthand how families stateside networked for information in World War II. This prospect had already become a source of stress for him. As second-in-command, he pondered if he should write the parents of his missing crewmen. He had never met any of them, since the only parent to visit in Gulfport had been his father. What news could he tell them? He didn't know anything.

In the aftermath of the tragedy, members of his squadron maintained a respectful silence in Addison's presence. There was nothing anyone could do or say that would change what happened and no one, including Manny Klette himself, or even his boss, Col. Terry, could promise that what had happened would not happen again. Inside, Addison Bartush was beside himself. This, the loss of six his crewmates, had followed the day after his trauma in the sky at Merseburg. He could not bring himself to talk about his innermost reaction, that being the primal need for personal security; he reacted as a condemned man might—Addison clammed up.

Addison was not resentful of his commanders. "Manny Klette had been through it himself," he asserted about his boss. "He had been hospitalized."

He also volunteered that Col. Terry took turns flying combat. Addison respected these two leaders, and wanted to be like them.

The night of the 26th and subsequent nights in the bunkroom were extremely difficult for Addison. "Dave and RJ's personal things were gone a couple of days later," Addison said. "They sent someone in to do it and I don't know who." Bishop had displayed family pictures on his footlocker that no occupant of the room dared to touch. Addison had tears in his eyes when he recounted, "Miller's cot was nearby too." The word he used to describe his sleep was "restless."

Grief counseling from a medical standpoint was unheard of in 1944, and Addison did not seek, nor was he directed, to see the squadron flight surgeon. And having flown only one combat mission himself, he was certainly not a candidate for battle fatigue counseling—a recognized and treated psychological condition at the time. It never occurred to Addison to ask for sleeping pills or other medications that might alleviate the stress he experienced.

The day after the tragedy Addison met outside with crewmates Earl Sheen and Billy Robertson. He recalled that someone took a photograph of them standing together and that he always knew what date this photograph had been taken because in it he wore his new coat. "None of us looked happy," Addison remarked. Addison later lost or misplaced this photograph, and the fact of this did not trouble him at all.

At this meeting it dawned on the three airmen that they were no longer a team. They would continue to remain in the same squadron and have the same obligation to complete 35 missions, but they would not necessarily fly together. Each would go into a pool of available names, to be drawn upon and used as needed to fill a vacancy caused for whatever reason. Addison was to be a substitute, or supply co-pilot, Sheen and Robertson extra gunners. To be equitable to all of its combat flyers, the 324th would endeavor to ensure that these alternate airmen flew combat neither more nor less than those permanently assigned to crews.

Recollecting this meeting Addison said: "We shared what little information we had and talked about what we might do." The three somberly concluded that "not a thing" could be done, however.

Depressed, discouraged and for the first time in his life really frightened, Addison knew who he could turn to for support. Catholicism had been an integral part of his life. Indeed, he had gone to a parochial school and a church-sponsored university; the "four M's" were all good Catholic girls; he wrote letters to and received letters from his priest in Detroit, and he received periodicals from his church even while overseas.

Addison sought out and found Father Ragan. "I probably saw him somewhere other than the chapel for he was always around everywhere," Addison related. When he found the priest Addison did not mince words with him: "I just told him," he said. Father Ragan knew what to do.

World War II was fought with such a magnitude and events happened so fast that there may have been, from a practical standpoint, little opportunity to properly commemorate casualties as they might be honored in the U.S. military today. By the end of the war, 40,061 USAAF airmen had died in all overseas theaters.[6] For the 1,347 days that the U.S. fought the Axis, the average daily loss of U.S. airmen was 30 a day. It may have been that all each bomb group could realistically accomplish was to plan for the next day's mission. Also it may have been that the command back then might have been skeptical about memorial services being tied to specific adverse events; such services might prove demoralizing to the surviving aircrews. In any event, Addison had no recollection of there being a ceremony of any kind held at Bassingbourn related to the loss of November 26, 1944. Father Ragan gave the spiritual guidance Addison sought out on a one-on-one basis.

Three days before the downing, Flight Officer Ray Peacock, the bombardier who did not make the Atlantic crossing with the Bishop Crew, wrote Addison a letter from Gulfport which Addison would have received several days after the event. His salutation read, "Dear Gang," so obviously he intended Addison to share his letter with his crewmates, almost certainly the officers, Bishop and Miller. In his letter Peacock thanked everyone for "the swell letters" and also wrote this: "We have our minimum so we'll soon be on our way. Tell RJ to stay out of the crap games." He signed his letter in an unusual manner for a guy-to-guy communication: "Love, Ray." None of the letters Addison wrote during World War II survive, but Addison believes he wrote Peacock back and told him what had happened. One can only imagine how Peacock reacted when he received that letter.

As an aside, USAAF records reveal that Peacock deployed overseas and was assigned to the 490th Bomb Group near Eye, Suffolk. This Bomb Group experienced 47 non-combat related accidents over a 14-month period[7] and Peacock survived one of them. On April 22, 1945, while turning off the runway after a routine landing, the B-17's left landing gear collapsed, resulting in considerable damage to the airplane. No one was injured and a faulty jackscrew was determined to be the cause. By this time Peacock and Addison no longer corresponded.

Addison remained on the combat rotation schedule for the 324th, and on November 30 he flew his second mission to Zeitz as a substitute co-pilot. "Headquarters of the famous optical company," Addison observed, "but I recollect we were after a fuel factory there." Addison's recollection was accurate and this mission was no milk run. A total of 451 B-17s, mostly from the 1st Air Division (to which the 91st belonged) flew to hit targets in southeastern Germany. Eleven B-17s did not return. Addison and another 131 B-17s broke off from the larger pack to attack a synthetic oil plant in the city.[8] While Addison's memory of the target was correct, he did not re-member something significant that happened on the mission: the fact that one of the B-17s lost—blown up that day with all but one airmen lost—was from the 324th.

Thinking back to the Zeitz raid, Addison admitted to being terrified about flying combat again, and offered this as his reason for doing so: "I knew that I had to get back into it, otherwise I'd become a complete wreck."

In World War II, the USAAF did not compel airmen to fly combat. One could voluntarily ground oneself and not end up punished for cowardice under the Articles of War. The psychological price to be paid for grounding oneself however, could be devastating, and in the mind of a 22-year-old, even catastrophic. A pilot who refused to fly might end up working on the same base in a different capacity where he would come into contact with those who knew what he had done; he would also be denied continued mess privileges with those officers who flew combat. Flight surgeons would do everything within their power to insure that those having second thoughts about continuing to fly combat resolved their reservations in favor of a full mission roster (the author Joseph Heller addressed this issue using slashing and often angry humor in his brilliant literary novel *Catch-22*).

In the last month of 1944 and the days leading up to it, Addison Bartush lost something that had always served him well. The world to him could no longer be seri*ass*; there would be no more Mr. Dowilly's to laugh at, and it did not matter if a person was a Spoony or not, or even a Dawn Patroller.

The person who Paul Lynch described as "more like one of the boys," the second-in-command who "liked to joke" had lost his sense of humor—at least for a period. The real war was not at all as depicted by Hollywood, Addison explained. An adventure? "Hardly," he said.

On December 3, Addison wrote a letter to his brother Jack who was in Boston at the time waiting for his Coast Guard ship the USCGC *Tahoma* to be assigned to another convoy. Only 165 feet long, the *Tahoma* had been built to serve as a Great Lakes icebreaker, but now had escort duty transiting coastal routes near the northeastern United States, Canadian Maritime Provinces and Greenland. In his letter, Addison apparently told Jack about what happened to his crewmembers and also likely the B-17 loss to his squadron at Zeitz. Addison and Jack evidently shared things about the war that, for reasons entirely understandable, were not shared with other members of the Bartush family. "I served as my own censor," Addison observed, referring to the loosely enforced security procedures at Bassingbourn that enabled him to share militarily sensitive information with a brother.

Four days after Zeitz, Addison had another combat assignment. This time it was to a marshalling yard at Kassel where the bombing was done through winter cloud cover using pathfinder force ("PFF") techniques involving H2X, a form of airborne radar used on a lead bomber. Addison explained: "That's the one where a guy sat in front of a screen in the radio room with a hood around him so it would cover any external light and he could read what was below him, that is, pick out cities and rivers." By attacking a marshalling yard, the Eighth Air Force took the battle directly to enemy combatants on the ground. One B-17 from the 91st was damaged by flak and made a forced landing on the Continent.[9] By 1944 the era of "blind bombing" was well at hand.[10] The British developed PFF for night-time bombings; the pathfinders would go in first, find the target using radar and other means and mark it with flares. The main force would follow going directly for the flares, with little or no time lost by a lead bomber searching for an aiming point.

On December 11 and 12 Addison participated in back-to-back missions to Frankfurt and Merseburg, both done by PFF. In a maximum effort on the 11th, the Eighth Air Force put up a record 1,586 heavy bombers, escorted by 841 fighters. The 91st bombed a marshalling yard at Frankfurt and the next day, the Leuna Werke fuel plant at Merseburg. The Luftwaffe did not challenge either attack[11] in the air, but "Flak Hell Leuna" lived up to its reputation. No planes belonging to the 91st went down. "It was exhausting," Addison commented on the circumstance of flying combat two days in a row. "Really tiring."

It was during this period that Addison stopped writing regularly and mailing newspapers to his family at home. In mid-December one of the four M's wrote him a letter undoubtedly intended to cheer him up but it may have had the opposite effect of reminding him of what he might never see again. She wrote: "Remember how I always loved your house because your mother had flowers around all the time."[12]

That Addison was having a tough time of it both mentally and physically there can be no doubt. A friend serving with the 15th Air Force in Foggia, Italy, John Antes, replied to one of Addison's letters with this: "You said you were lonely being the only one on a crew. Care to comment?"[13]

And brother Jack's reply dated December 13 did not offer Addison encouragement. After mentioning that a sister ship to *Tahoma* had recently been sunk near Greenland, Jack wrote:

> *You aren't the only one that should be worried. You are right when you say things aren't as easy as the general public thinks even in the North Atlantic. Since I've been up there, there has been three to five ships sunk and I've been saying my prayers like mad and also including you and Charlie in them. By the way, Charlie will be sent to Burma when he finishes his course as a radar technician—at least he and the other fellows he is with think so.*

Jack signed his letter "God bless you," and added a postscript: "Does what you said about your [crew] being shot down mean that the fellows whose pictures are with you are missing?"

Asked if he had feelings of guilt over not being with his crewmembers when they were shot down, Addison responded, "I don't remember if I did or not," then admitted, "but I could. We were friends," he explained.

Asked if he had feelings of guilt over not writing the families of his downed crewmembers, Addison snapped: "I didn't have the courage, is that what you would say? That I didn't have the . . . guts?" Yes, Addison felt guilty about that too. Just about everything that could go wrong in Addison's life short of himself being shot down had gone wrong.

The trail of letters and Addison's own recollections strongly suggest Addison very likely suffered from what today is known as post-traumatic stress syndrome—an anxiety disorder caused by exposure to a terrifying event or events resulting in serious physical harm or the threat of harm.[14] By mid December Addison had stopped writing long and descriptive letters. His family received only three letters from him in the month of December. "They were short with no news and [stated] he was always tired and that war was hell," his mother wrote to Paul's mother at year-end.

Events in the ground war did not help Addison's state of mind either. When he flew his first mission on November 25, the Western Front was, relatively speaking, quiet. Many assumed it would remain so until spring-time, or that the Nazis in the interim might come to their senses and sur-render since they were losing so badly. On December 16, 1944, however, the German army launched a surprise offensive in Belgium and Luxem-bourg that came to be known as The Battle of the Bulge, and this signaled an abrupt and stressful mission change for USAAF airmen. The initial Ger-man attack met with success, and for a period U.S. commanders did not know whether it could be stopped. The Battle of the Ardennes, as it was officially named by the U.S. Army, lasted until late January 1945, when all of the ground lost to the Nazis had been retaken. The Allied victory was secured at the cost of 80,000 U.S. Army casualties.[15]

Addison described the problem the 91st had in helping U.S. ground troops: "It was fog, fog, fog," he said. On December 18 Addison flew a high altitude "screening force" mission to the Luxembourg area. "No bombs were dropped, only chaff," Addison related, and it had been dropped to jam German radar. "We got it up to 31,000 feet or higher," he reported, "and could barely control the airplane. There was a little chute on the airplane for the chaff. The crew would dump it out." Addison also noted that the chaff floated down like strips of tinsel from a Christmas tree. Klette as group leader recorded "none, none, none" for claims, casualties and battle damage for this trip, which counted as a combat mission since it was over enemy-held territory.[16]

During this period Addison received a letter from his father's chief salesman asking Addison to take over sales in the Midwest and East after the war so that he, the salesman, could focus on sales in the West and most particularly, California. "Sales are not doing so well in California," this man wrote. As an inducement for Addison to consider this offer, the salesman reported December projections for Shedd-Bartush Foods, Inc., in the market area he proposed for Addison: "Chicago should do 100,000# [sell 100,000 lbs. of margarine] and New England 250,000#."

What import this letter may have had on Addison's morale at the time he did not indicate, but chances are his mind was on other matters. Addison noted, however, astutely, that this salesman hailed from California and his true intent was to return to his home state and with a job.

POW Paul Lynch, by this time in northern Poland, learned the news of the initial success of the Nazi army in the Battle of the Bulge. Paul now appreciated why the Luftwaffe came out to defend that railroad viaduct he was going after at Altenbeken—it would be useful to them in the upcoming battle.

During the critical period from December 19 through December 23 the Eighth Air Force continued to be unable to fly because of horrible weather. As one writer put it: "mist, fog, snow, frost, and drizzle."[17] Aircrews stood on the ready only to have planned ops scrubbed after anxious long hours of cigarette smoking, pacing and waiting. Addison was honest in his reaction to these cancellations: "Yeah, I was relieved," he admitted, "but at the same time I felt sorry for the poor guys out there in the trenches, in the snow."

Addison recalled that there were no special briefings on the situation on the ground at the front. "The only thing we knew was what we read in the *Stars and Stripes* and also heard on the radio. We listened to the B-band [BBC] and also our own, U.S. radio station." He added that being Christmas time, the American network played, "Bing Crosby, that sort of thing."

Christmas Eve 1944 was a low point for Addison. He did not fly that day but the 91st did, and it was another record-breaking mission for the Eighth Air Force: a total of 2,046 heavy bombers protected by 853 fighters attacked airfields and communications centers throughout western Germany.[18]

"None of our planes returned to Bassingbourn that Christmas Eve," Addison said. "A deep fog set in and the pilots had to find other bases. Our bomb group landed wherever it could at bases all over England, and this resulted in a huge mess. In some cases there was literally no place for our aircrews to sleep."

Addison attended a midnight Catholic Mass at Bassingbourn. "There were just a handful of persons there because our planes had not returned," he explained. Addison recounted that this had been an especially tense time because everyone was still upset over the whole bomb group having to divert; that all present were painfully aware that emergency landings brought on by bad weather were scary events. It turned out that all of the 91st bombers made it down safely on this special day, but this did not serve to lessen the shock over what had happened. While they sang *Silent Night* Addison and others wondered if the 91st would be required to take such a risk again. "Things were not going well," Addison admitted, talking about his emotional state. "Everything seemed . . . well, tight."

On Christmas Day Addison received a telegram from his father: "WHILE WE HAVE NOT HEARD FROM YOU SEVERAL WEEKS WE ARE CABLING OUR BEST ALL ARE WELL—STEPHEN BARTUSH." This was followed five days later by a letter from his kid brother Charlie, who now went by the nickname Chuck. Chuck was stationed at Boca Raton at the time and expected to soon receive orders overseas. He joked about his upcoming promotion to corporal and being able to pull rank on Addison with his two stripes. Chuck wrote:

> *Add, just how does it feel being there [?] I know you don't like to talk about it because you are busy going on many missions. And now with the Jerries putting on a little pressure I'll bet it's awfully nerve-racking. If you ever get a chance to write, let it all out, and don't mind the language. It makes a fellow feel a lot better. I received a letter from mother and she said you were too nervous to think or write. So do what I say and just write and write about nothing.*

Addison wrote a single word on the reverse side of Chuck's letter: "Ashamed." When confronted about this well over a half-century later, Addison balked: "That's not my writing," he first protested. Then the sheepish grin appeared. "Maybe I wrote that down to see how to spell it." Finally, the confession popped out: Addison laughed and admitted he had been ashamed for not writing home.

Chuck's letter was not the end of it for Addison from his family, however. The next day his 12-year-old sister, Mary Cay sent him this V-Mail:

December 31, 1944
Dear Addison,
This is not going to be a friendly letter. Yesterday Mom got a "special delivery letter" from Mrs. Lynch [who] said that her son was reported "missing" over Germany. She would like to get all the information she can. I told Mother that he was the boy that was taken off your plane in Gulfport. If this is true you don't need to answer but if it isn't true and you know some information that you can tell us let us know. Mother is writing her now and telling about being taken off.

Mary Cay had mistaken Paul Lynch for Raymond Peacock.

In early 1945 Addison's spirits picked up somewhat. He had survived enough missions—five were required to wear the Air Medal, which signified he was a veteran combat flyer. There would be close calls ahead, he knew, but he resolved not to let the prospect consume him. Addison *had* become a combat veteran.

Years later, with a friendly gleam in his eye, Addison offered insight on the subject of physical courage and did so without giving credit to himself: "I was young!" he exclaimed, as in too inexperienced to know any better. He agreed readily that 30-something-year-olds could not easily be made to do the line of work known in World War II as combat air.

CHAPTER SIX

Paul's POW Odyssey Begins

After being captured by the armed farmers, Paul Lynch was escorted to an uncertain destination and fate. "Presently we were on a road and came into contact with a person that I presumed to be, from his appearance and demeanor, anyway, displaced," Paul said. "He was Polish and spoke fluent English. The farmers allowed me to speak to him."

Paul continued: "The Pole wanted to know where I was from and what I was bombing. I figured that I had better tell him about the viaduct because a stray bomb might have fallen close to a civilian area and I wanted to let him know we were after a military target."

Under the Geneva Convention the only information Paul was obligated to give out was his name, rank and serial number, but Paul had done what tens of thousands of other American parachutists had done, that is, he immediately disclosed to those who captured him that he had not participated in a terror bombing. In the USAAF during World War II there was an adage that it was "not a good idea" to parachute into a population center not far from a site one had just bombed.

"I asked this man," Paul said, "if there was any way out of here and he just smiled. That was the end of my hope of escaping."

Paul spent the night at the local jail and was fortunate to do so. Following the war, a fact-finding commission at Nuremberg exposed the very real hazard Paul faced as a parachutist:

When Allied airmen were forced to land in Germany, they were sometimes killed at once by the civilian population. The police were instructed not to interfere with these killings, and the Ministry of Justice was informed that no one should be prosecuted for taking part in them.[1]

While in jail, leg pain notwithstanding, Paul had time to reflect upon John Kendall's death. He had never seen a man killed before. Paul and John had had their differences, but somehow any personal animosity that might have lingered between the two of them had been expunged. Paul felt terrible over John's loss.

And as for his friend Owen Monkman? Paul could only hope that Owen met his fate as painlessly as he knew John had met his.

"The following morning an old truck pulled up and they put me on with several other prisoners," Paul said. "Most were with planes from other outfits and I didn't know any of them. I asked the driver if there were any more survivors from my plane and he told me that they recovered six bodies from the wreckage." When he heard this Paul did not know whether to believe it or not. He knew Kendall and Monkman were dead and he saw Dave Bishop on the ground, but beyond that he knew nothing.

While waiting for the truck to move, an oddity of war took place. Several young, giggly German girls came over to Paul and the other Americans wanting to practice their English. This was unusual, Paul thought, "in that they would be so friendly towards us in spite of the bombings."

Paul experienced additional German friendliness. Taken to a Catholic-run hospital for his leg injury, the nuns there treated him with the same kindness and care they extended to a wounded German pilot. While there he also ate the same food as the nuns—primarily potato soup with a little meat in it, "but only now and then." Paul suspected it was horsemeat.

"The hospital was spotless and I was permitted to walk around." Thinking back, Paul added something of a wistful note: "I wished I could have stayed there for the duration of the war, but alas, it was not to be." Paul sensed what might be coming and kept his wormy apples.

"When I was released from the hospital after a short stay, I was taken to a railroad station under guard along with several other Americans. No one seemed to notice or care as we stood on the platform wearing our flying suits. In fact, some of the time we couldn't even see our guards. It would have been senseless to try to escape however, dressed the way we were.

There were armed German soldiers everywhere. I did something foolish on the platform. I flirted with a very attractive blonde."

Paul remembered what she wore: a navy blue beret, a silver fur jacket, blue skirt and black knee boots. "She noticed me looking and smiled," Paul recollected. "I smiled back and she smiled again. I thought she might come over to talk to me."

"One of the older Americans elbowed me to knock it off. 'You could get shot for that,' he warned me. I broke off eye contact immediately and later realized that I had taken a risk. She could have been SS or Gestapo." Paul had been wise to heed the advice of the older American; both Nazi organizations employed female operatives, and some were known to bait with good looks.

"On the train I sat next to a German soldier," Paul continued. "He looked interested so I took a chance. 'My name *ist* Paul,' I said to him and he responded. Neither of us could communicate in the other's language but I recognized the word 'haus.' I mentioned 'Massachusetts' and his face went blank. I then tried 'Boston' and he recognized the name. Eventually I found a piece of paper and drew a rough picture of a bridge and a train carrying a tank being bombed. He laughed."

Paul attempted to find out where the soldier was going and after a period heard the word "Russia" spoken.

"Then he fell silent and didn't want to talk," Paul related. "I wondered if he wanted to trade places with me."

The train trip was uneventful and of relatively short duration. Paul and the other Americans ended-up at a Luftwaffe POW processing facility near Frankfurt known as Dulag Luft, which was a collection and interrogation center for newly captured Allied aircrews.[2] There were other Dulag Lufts established by the Nazis during the war in different locales, but the one near centrally located Frankfurt was the oldest and by far the largest. The rooftops of buildings and other sections of this approximately 500-acre compound were marked with the huge white letters "POW," to warn Allied bombardiers not to attack. Officer and enlisted POWs, American and British, would be processed through a Dulag Luft before being sent on to one of the "Stalag Lufts"—the name given to the chain of POW holding camps for Allied airmen set up throughout Germany and occupied Europe. The Stalag Luft camps for officers, and most particularly pilots, were among the most heavily guarded of all POW camps run by the Third Reich.

The Nazis did not want POW flyers to break out or be liberated by a raiding party, and took extra precautions accordingly.

At Dulag Luft, electrified flight suits and boots were exchanged for POW uniforms and trench boots supplied by the International Red Cross; interrogations generally followed periods of solitary confinement. Dulag Lufts had a reputation for not being nice places to stay.

Paul's period of solitary confinement lasted four days.

"I was put in a small cell with just a cot," Paul said, "and now I felt like a real prisoner. That night I heard a slight knock on the wall and an American voice. He was a fighter pilot and he had been there awhile. He told me not to talk during the day but talking was overlooked at night because the guards wanted to hear the progress of the war from the new prisoners. They would listen at the doors. He also told me to watch out for a huge German Army Sergeant as he had severely injured several prisoners during interrogation."

It never occurred to Paul that the person speaking behind the wall may have been working for the Luftwaffe and that he intended to plant fear in Paul's mind about being physically abused in his upcoming interrogation. In 1960 a commentator had this to say about the modus operandi of the camp:

At Dulag Luft each prisoner was studied by psychologists in order to learn his likes, dislikes, habits and powers of resistance. The method of procedure was then determined, and the machinery was set into operation to destroy his mental resistance in the shortest possible time. If the prisoner showed signs of fright or was nervous, he was threatened with all kinds of torture . . .[3]

"I don't think the fighter pilot was a Nazi," Paul opined, "but in any event, I didn't give him information." Paul explained the basis for his opinion about the fighter pilot by stating that before he went into solitary confinement he had heard from several POWs about a large sergeant at interrogation who mistreated POWs; that the fighter pilot had not told him anything that he did not already know.

From his cell, Paul heard explosions in the distance. When Paul learned that Dulag Luft was approximately 13 miles from the center of Frankfurt, he said, "There were many targets in the industrial area of Frankfurt, and in my opinion bombers could have been closer than 13 miles." Paul added: "My barred window was high so all I could do was listen."

"My turn for interrogation came up and I really dreaded it. I was taken to a large room with a number of booths. My name was called and I stood up. The interrogator came over, grabbed me by the collar and told me in a very loud voice to stand at attention when a German officer spoke. I did. 'You Americans have no military discipline'," Paul reported the man saying.

Although Paul was understandably anxious about the treatment he might receive, he also knew that America was winning the war and this fact stiffened his spine as a U.S. soldier. He resolved to tell his interrogator nothing more than the Geneva Convention required. It turned out the German officer already knew Paul was from the 324th Squadron of the 91st Bomb Group.

"I was led into a booth and the atmosphere changed completely. Things got relaxed and informal. I think the scene in the main room was to put on a show. Questions were routine and even some about family. I stuck to name, rank and serial number. He asked me if the apples I carried were from Washington State."

Paul was in for a surprise, however. "I saw a huge bear of a man thump across the main room with some papers in his hand." This of course startled Paul as it was undoubtedly intended to do. Paul did not visibly react, however, but rather continued chatting amicably, and when questioned directly again only politely offered his name, rank and serial number. After a period of this, Paul made a bold move: he complimented his interrogator on the quality of his English and asked him where had he been educated.

The friendly exchanges abruptly stopped. Paul reported that his interrogator snorted: "I ask the questions." Almost immediately thereafter Paul was dismissed; his interrogation at Dulag Luft was over.

By refusing to show fear in the presence of the gorilla-sergeant, Paul Lynch extricated himself from a situation that could have become more serious. As stated, Dulag Luft was not a nice place to stay, yet Paul never suffered the "dog tag" or "heat" treatments, but other airmen did. Dog tags were sometimes taken away from a confined prisoner to make him feel vulnerable, like a citizen stripped of a passport. "I always had my dog tags, even at the end," Paul remarked. The "heat" treatment was done during the summer months by placing a space heater that could not be turned off into a solitary confinement cell. At the interrogation session the next day, the interrogator would apologize profusely and explain that this was a simple mix-up easily rectified. The fake apology delivered the Nazi message:

cooperate by giving information or suffer the consequences.[4]

Paul confirmed that his German captors never mistreated him. With respect to his stay at Dulag Luft, however, he observed: "I was pleased to get out of there. The place was no playground."

The heavy-duty winter clothes and footgear issued to Paul by the International Red Cross were important items for him to have; the footgear, especially. A pair of proper fitting rugged military-style boots was almost as important as a parachute. The boots Paul received fit him properly. Paul probably could not have appreciated the importance of this good fit at the time, but he would later on. Not every POW was as lucky as Paul; the consequences of ill-fitting boots often proved deadly.

On December 7, 1944, while at Dulag Luft, Paul completed a pre-printed "Postkarte" that he addressed to his parents. No individualized message was permitted on the card but it did convey that Paul was in good health and that he would be transported to another POW camp. This postcard was a requirement of the Geneva Convention. One can only imagine the joy that came to the Lynch family household when this card arrived in the mail, made all the better because the limited handwriting on the card was Paul's own.

The rail trip from Middle Germany to northern Poland where Paul would be incarcerated at Stalag Luft IV encompassed approximately 400 miles, five times as long as his rail trip to Frankfurt, and it was not made on a comfortable passenger train. And in December 1944, increased distance meant increased danger.

"One day a large number of us were marched to the rail yards and divided into groups," Paul related. "Then we were loaded onto cattle cars." The "cattle cars" Paul mentioned were standard 40 and 8 boxcars—the same type as used by the SS to ship Jews to the death camps. And not unlike with the Jews: "There were no amenities, not even benches, only straw on the floor. We improvised a toilet by prying up some loose floorboards." The comparison to how the Jews were transported ends there, however.

"The only humor on the entire trip was someone's observation that our makeshift john allowed us to spread our stuff all over Germany."

Paul indicated that none of the rail cars bore large letters denoting "POW" or the telltale red cross on a white background. "This was a cause for concern," Paul noted. "We were locked in with no way out."

On the first day out an incident happened that captured Paul's attention:

"Later that day the train came to a screeching halt and we could see the engineer and guards running for the ditches—an air raid. Our doors remained locked and a few of the fellows were getting excited. Some of the older fellows calmed them down by telling them that our fighter pilots liked shooting the engine to watch the boiler blow. Things finally settled down and in about 20 minutes the train was moving again."

Paul was correct to be concerned. The famous "Ace of Aces," P-47 Thunderbolt pilot Francis "Gabby" Gabreski, wrote about his 400-mile train trip to Stalag Luft I on the Baltic Sea coast north of Berlin. Gabreski was captured in late July 1944, and saw his situation the same as Paul:

All of us knew there was no way a P-47 pilot up there could tell our train was carrying a bunch of "Kriegies," as we POWs called ourselves. And we all knew how much damage a P-47 could do to the train—and us. Luckily for us, the train wasn't attacked.[5]

As it happened, the Germans were not required by international accord to mark rail cars to denote that they carried prisoners of war. The 1929 Geneva Convention, specifically Eight, "Transfers of Prisoners of War," however, obligated them to pay the expense of Paul's transfer and to forward correspondence and packages addressed to him.

Paul could not recollect the number of days the trip took but estimated "four or five." Paul said: "Conditions in the car started out well but each day they worsened. A few got sick with diarrhea and the smell was rank. Progress was slow as we made many stops. One day we just sat on a siding and I think that was the worst day of all. It seemed to last forever." Paul added a reason for all the stops: "Our Army Air Forces was doing its job."

Paul continued: "As we got farther into Germany the guards became more relaxed. There was another air raid and this time they opened the doors and permitted us to dive into ditches near the tracks. We heard it from a distance."

Paul described an act of kindness on the part of his captors, who were not SS: "Several evenings, the guards would have fires outside the cars and drink schnapps, then they would open the doors and we exchanged family pictures and found some areas of understanding to talk about. We were not allowed outside but at least we got aired out."

When Paul and his POW traveling companions finally arrived at their destination in northern Poland, they discovered they were in the boonies. "There was a little depot and a peasant woman sweeping the snow off the walks with one of those stick brooms. We were ordered out of the car and lined up beside the train. The place reminded me of Labrador with the stillness of cold, snow and fir trees. No other buildings in sight. When the train was unloaded, we were walked to the prison camp. It seemed good to get out and be able to move again." The walk to the camp was approximately two miles.

At the time Addison was sweating out the prospect of flying dangerous and desperate missions during the Battle of the Bulge, Paul adjusted to daily prison life at German Stalag Luft IV. Opened in May 1944 in Tychowo, Poland, which the German's called Gross Tychow, the camp was not far from the German border, and about 25 miles from the Baltic Sea. In January 1945, according to a report of the International Red Cross, Stalag Luft IV held 8,033 Americans, 820 British (likely including Canadians) and a smattering of other POW nationalities.[6] Most POWs were gunners like Paul; practically all were non-commissioned officers. These numbers would grow to approximately 9,500 in a month's time. As stated, the Geneva Convention provided that non-commissioned officer POWs could not be made to do manual labor. Stalag Luft IV was not a work camp.

The POW camps designated as "Stalag," as opposed to "Stalag Luft," held significant numbers of privates and corporals, and these men of lower ranks were required to work and often under slave labor conditions. For point of example, the working POW rank and file of the large, defeated French Army was *decimated* by five years of Nazi forced production activity.[7] To a very limited extent Paul, as an airman NCO-POW, had privilege.

Upon arrival at the train depot outside of camp, Paul and the other POWs were not harassed by the German guards who were there waiting for them. That was not the case with a large group of POWs who arrived at the camp the previous summer, as they had been received in a very rough manner.[8] "I recall that we lined up for a roll call and marched to the barracks," Paul said.

The POW camp that Paul stayed in for approximately two months was rectangular in shape and surrounded by countryside. It was composed of four equal-sized sections or "lagers" named for simplicity "A," "B," "C" and "D."

The lagers were also rectangular shaped and separated by razor wire and guarded by towers containing searchlights and machine guns. The fencing into separate sections prevented the camp prison population from massing together, or as one inmate at another stalag luft put it, ". . . the divide-and-conquer theory at work."[9] The lagers filled up one at a time, starting with "A." By the time Paul arrived at Stalag Luft IV in mid December 1944, Lager "D" was in use and that is where he was quartered.

Paul could see the camp main gate from where he was and also a structure outside the wire known as the "Russian barracks." Each lager was surrounded by two rows of barbed wire, with the outer row being electrified. A "warning rail" inside the lagers ran parallel to the barbed wire. If a POW ventured beyond this rail, the guards in the watchtowers were under orders to shoot to kill.

"One of our limits," Paul volunteered, "was that we were not allowed to visit another barrack." There were no prisoner shootings when Paul was at Stalag Luft IV, but in June 1944 a G.I. POW had been shot and killed while jumping out of a window; the camp had a rule against inmates exiting through windows to prevent contraband from being removed during surprise inspections.[10]

Paul reflected on day-to-day life at Stalag Luft IV: Daily POW formations—the standing in ranks outside to check attendance—were conducted in the mornings and afternoons. "It was a head count," Paul said, meaning not a roll call where names were yelled out.

Paul confirmed there was a POW chain-of-command established at Stalag Luft IV. "Sort of," he chuckled, remembering. "It was primarily the POWs who had been in camp the longest and had the most advice to give. They informed us what our limits were."

In this regard, the 9,500 enlisted POWs at the camp were organized quite differently than officer POWs at other stalag lufts. Gabby Gabreski in his autobiography wrote that the commissioned officer POWs of Stalag Luft I, some 200 miles west on the coast (where Dave Bishop and RJ Miller were confined) had the senior U.S. colonel act as "wing commander" for the camp. Field grade POW-officers were designated "group" commanders for the individual lagers. Finally, going down the chain, each barrack was designated as a squadron ". . . with sections for intelligence, supply, and all the rest," Gabreski observed.[11] Stalag Luft IV had none of this. Paul's memory about the military organization at his POW camp was accurate. The American camp leader was Sgt. Richard M. Chapman who ". . . came to camp in May [1944] with the first arrivals."[12] Sergeant Chapman performed an important function in dealing with the Luftwaffe chain-of-command but no one saluted him!

Two months before Paul arrived at Stalag Luft IV, the International Red Cross sent representatives to inspect the camp and issue a report on conditions there. The section of the report entitled "Accommodation" contained this:

> *Today [5–6 October 1944] Stalag Luft IV has twice too many inmates. The men are housed in 40 wooden huts, each hut containing 200 men. The huts are only partially finished; new arrivals are expected and more huts are being erected. The dormitories have been prepared for 16 men in two tiered beds. But there are not sufficient beds for some rooms [that] contain up to 24 men each. At camps A and B, a third tier of beds has been installed, whereas beds have been removed from camp D. There is not a single bed in camp C and 1900 men sleep on the floor. 600 of them have no mattresses, only a few shavings to lie on. Some have to lie right on the floor. Each prisoner has two German blankets. None of the huts can be properly heated. The [IRC] delegate only saw five small iron stoves in the whole camp. Some of the huts in camp D have no chimneys. Each camp has two open air latrines and the huts have a night latrine with two seats. The latrines are not sufficient as they are not emptied often, the only lorry for this work being used elsewhere. The prisoners have no means of washing; there are no shower baths as there is only one coal heated geyser in the camp of 100 liters for 1000 men. Fleas and lice are in abundance; no cleansing has been done.*[13]

"I don't recollect ever sleeping on a floor," Paul said in reference to this report. "As I recall, each POW had a bunk on a double-decker bed along with the two blankets described. Also the cold weather did not seem to be a problem in the barracks."

"I think I recall a small stove in the middle of the room," Paul added. "Fleas and lice were not a problem as it was late in the season. There were no showers or clean clothes."

In the section entitled "Food" the IRC report gave faint praise: "The German food is no worse than at other camps."[14]

Paul had this to say by way of example about the food supplied by his captors: "German 'black bread' consisted of 50% bruised rye grain, 20% sliced sugar beets, 20% tree flower and 10% minced leaves and straw." He then explained that "tree flower" was sawdust. The other German staple was a thin, potato-based soup that was not very nourishing. "We lived off Red Cross food parcels," Paul explained. "They were quite good but the supply got less as the war progressed." He added: "I suspect the Germans enjoyed them as well."

After reflecting, Paul observed that the living situation at Stalag Luft IV, primitive as the IRC reported, was bearable. "Most of the POWs in my immediate area were late arrivals. They did not know what to expect. Conditions were just accepted." The seminal truth was that these POWs were glad to be alive, under a roof and out of harm's way.

Although isolated in a camp in the wilds of an occupied country, Paul was able to be in touch with the outside world and what's more, his family. "I was able to write several letters home," he said, "and found later that they had been delivered." After Paul's family obtained his new mailing address, they of course wrote him immediately back, but again there were the postal delays. "I only received a few," Paul indicated. As regards to his first letter from home he related: "I was thrilled of course. Mostly to learn my family was OK. I can't remember details of what it said. It was receiving it that mattered most." About his personal outgoing correspondence, he observed: "My letters were certainly censored but I was careful not to be pessimistic about conditions. What good would it do to cause more worry at home?"

While Paul's family was undoubtedly also circumspect about what they wrote to Paul, particularly as it might concern the subject of Allied progress against Axis forces, Paul had a surefire way of keeping abreast of the action. "A short wave radio was hidden in one of the barracks," Paul explained. "We would get periodic news updates from Britain so we could follow the course of the war. I understand that the radio had been put together by one of the radiomen from a downed B-17." This hidden radio gave all the POWs at Stalag Luft IV daily hope for the future. "I think the general spirit in camp among American POWs was, 'Let's sweat it out 'til we win this war,' " Paul explained.

An intriguing aspect about this "hidden" radio was that Paul suspected the German guards were complicit in its existence. Paul questioned: "How did he [the USAAF radioman] get the materials into prison? Why hadn't the Germans discovered the place where it was hidden? We would have periodic inspections of the barracks by the guards but they were rather perfunctory. They never seemed as if they were really searching. I wondered if the messages were monitored and the Germans wanted to keep this as a source of news."

Paul's suspicion made perfect sense. If a guard were caught listening to the BBC it undoubtedly would be a regulations violation that would spell trouble for him. But if a POW happened to tell that very same guard what news was coming in over the airwaves how could this be a regulations violation for the guard? *Nein verboten BBC!* The historical fact is, several or even most of the Stalag Lufts had hidden radios.

Paul made no mention of it but a German guard had a clever way to trade for cigarettes or soap or whatever else might be found in the Red Cross parcels. The POWs wanted photographs to show their loved ones upon their return home. Of course cameras in a POW camp were *absolutely verboten*— but this did not deter one entrepreneurial German sergeant. Because of his illegal trading, an important historical photographic record survived.[15]

"The celebration of Christmas was subdued," Paul recollected. "And I don't recall ever seeing a chaplain in camp." Per the IRC report there were three POW chaplains serving Stalag Luft IV, but with 9,500 inmates it is not surprising that Paul did not encounter one.

Paul was not in a position to appreciate the rich irony of his Christmas being far less stressful than the one celebrated by his friend, Addison Bartush. Paul's time for personal stress would soon be at hand, however. In the near future he would look back at his stay at Stalag Luft IV as a good place to have been shelved during a time of war.

Paul witnessed no abuses of POWs during the short time that he was at Stalag Luft IV. He was cognizant how the Japanese treated POWs, and particularly so after the Bataan Death March which happened early in the war. Japan, unlike Germany, never ratified the 1929 Geneva Convention. Moreover, the Japanese, unlike the Germans, tended to view POWs as contemptible cowards, even if they became POWs by parachuting from a crippled airplane! Japanese guards routinely inflicted indiscriminate beatings with fists and sticks, nonsensical harassments (like requiring POWs to salute when passing by an unoccupied window) and also verbal abuses. POWs held by the Japanese had little hope. They had no way of learning how the war progressed. Arbitrary rules like no smoking, card playing, singing,[16] or holding worship services were enforced haphazardly by the Japanese, and differed from camp to camp.

Paul Lynch was subjected to none of this. "I don't think there is much comparison between Japan and Germany in regard to POW treatment," Paul opined. "I also believe that the Germans generally tried to live up to the Geneva Convention."

Paul buttressed his statement about non-abuse on the part of his captors by offering this about his camp commandant, a Luftwaffe lieutenant colonel named Aribert Bombach: "I don't think he was a strict military man," Paul observed. "The story I heard is the Germans caught a couple of guys trying to tunnel out. He [the commandant] told them if they tried it again they'd be shot." Paul explained that his barracks had little contact with the German commander. "The only time we saw him was at formation in the morning, and sometimes we didn't see him then as it was done by subordinates." Paul described the commandant as "a moderate fellow." "He was not out to make life miserable for the prisoners."

The historical record indicates that quite a number of Stalag Luft IV inmates did not agree with Paul's assessment of the commandant, and in particular, the approximately 2,500 POWs who arrived in July 1944 shortly after the camp opened. Based upon testimony of many of these men and a U.S. flight surgeon who arrived at the camp at a later date, Bombach and others were arrested by the Allies following the war on suspicion of having committed or having ordered war crimes while at the camp. Bombach, who was commandant of Stalag Luft IV during the entirety of the camp's existence, would also be investigated for acts of criminal negligence in connection with a forced POW march that commenced February 6, 1945 that came to be known as *The Black March*. Ultimately Bombach and the others were not prosecuted, though some of the evidence on the record against him and the others was strong.

Stalag Luft IV opened in the spring of 1944 with a handful of POWs. In mid-July about 2,500 Allied noncom POWs were shipped in from long distance by a sea-going vessel followed by a short trip by rail. These prisoners came from another POW camp in Lithuania that was then threatened by the Red Army. The boat trip was a five-day ordeal in cramped holds, but what awaited them when they arrived at the train depot, the same one that Paul described as tranquil, was terrifying. The Nazis turned this short march from the train depot to the camp into a really vicious gauntlet run. An authoritative commentator described this horrific event as follows:

> *The POWs' shoes were taken from them; they were chained in pairs—many of them ill and wounded—then double-timed three kilometers through a cordon of guards who used bayonets, rifle butts, and dogs to keep them moving. Some were seriously injured. (German doctors later testified the injured suffered only from sunburn.) They had had neither food nor water for five days . . . [and] . . . they were strip-searched and had most of their clothing and possessions taken from them.*[17]

Fifty years after the fact the U.S. Congress commemorated this shocking event for the veterans who endured it by reading into the Congressional Record: *"Many were forced to run two miles to the camp at the point of bayonets. Those who dropped behind were either bayoneted or bitten on the legs by police dogs . . ."*[18]

The accusation was made, but not sufficiently sustained, that Bombach ordered this wrongful and inhumane treatment as a special "welcoming" gesture for POW internees at the newly opened camp. Supposedly he initiated this in order to traumatize this large body of initial POWs to show them he was boss, and to make them fearful and compliant. There were some black-shirted SS men spotted in the vicinity at the time, however, and the incident happened outside of the camp. This circumstance, and the fact that no one died as a result of the gauntlet run, probably accounted for Bombach's release after the war. Reportedly the SS had hidden machine guns ready to use on POWs who might attempt to break away from the harassment being foisted on them in the column. While the SS may have orchestrated part or all of this, it was the Stalag Luft IV guards and a Luftwaffe officer under Bombach's command who carried out the acts of violence.[19]

In 1947, sworn testimony on this horror was given by U.S. Army Flight Surgeon, Major Leslie Caplan, M.D., who, as a POW himself had served as Allied Medical Officer at the Stalag Luft IV Camp Hospital from November 1944 forward and had treated one of the victims a half-year or so after-the-fact. Caplan made this statement to the U.S. War Crimes Office:

"Yes, I personally saw the healed wounds on the legs of a fellow . . . who had been severely bitten. There were approximately 50 bites on each leg. It looked as though his legs had been hit with small buckshot. This man remained an invalid confined to his bed all the time I was at Luft #4."[20]

Paul Lynch was aware of this gauntlet incident from stories he had heard while at the camp, but was quick to point out: "I did not experience anything like it." He added: "In my opinion the camp commander never seemed oppressive. He was just there as commander."

Paul related only what he witnessed. It is possible that Bombach could have started out cruel and oppressive and as the war went on he saw the writing on the wall and moderated his behavior.

Paul stated he had had heard stories about a brute of a Luftwaffe sergeant who supposedly abused POWs at Stalag Luft IV by cuffing their ears. "I never had dealings with him," Paul pointed out.[21]

Bombach was also accused of stealing POW food. One author described it this way:

In September [1944] a Red Cross shipment came into camp, but even then conditions did not improve. At the end of the month, prisoners stood near the warning fence and watched as a truck left with their shipment of clothes. They suspected that food had also left the camp. The commandant would not let the American and British camp leaders verify shipments with the invoice, so they never were sure if they got the entire shipment or a portion of one.[22]

Upon considering this observation, Paul chuckled, reiterating: "I always thought the Germans enjoyed the Red Cross packages."

One of the early photographs of the camp showed a concrete building outside the gate near Lager "A" with the notation "solitary confinement prison." The Geneva Convention authorized arrest not to exceed 30 days for disciplinary infractions but Paul never witnessed or heard of a POW removed to this facility. Likewise, Paul could add little about the nearby Russian barracks. The Soviets never ratified the Geneva Convention and all Soviet POWs could be made to do manual labor. A report indicated that the Germans used the Russians to drain and dispose of human waste from the outdoor camp latrines.[23] Paul said: "I was aware of the Russians but never saw them perform this responsibility."

Paul met no one that he knew during his stay at Stalag Luft IV. "I was a short-timer with the 91st," he observed, pointing to his brief stay at Bassingbourn. He indicated he did make several friends at the POW camp, but added: "We got separated during the march."

At the time Paul started his forced march, that is, early February 1945, the American bombing campaign over Europe greatly escalated. The United States Army Air Forces changed its heavy bomber policy and started hitting German population centers. The huge numbers of German civilian deaths caused by this decision, one that Roosevelt approved, served to put Paul and his fellow POWs at real risk. Gabreski noted: 'The German population at that time was very hostile and in disarray, so the likelihood of our getting away alive [escaping] was very, very slim.'[24] Another writer described a deep concern of Allied airmen POWs in general at this juncture in history:

> *The principal fear stemmed from . . . [a] rumor that Hitler had ordered the execution of all of the captured bomber crews that had wreaked so much death and havoc on the Fatherland. There was no reason to doubt that this order could still be carried out.*[25]

Paul observed: "There was a constant concern about Hitler's orders to kill POWs. We heard it often. Also, I would add that during our captivity we had no idea that [German] population centers were being targeted. During my stay with the 91st, military targets were attacked. I think that I can say that most of our crews would not have supported this change."

CHAPTER SEVEN

USAAF Heavy Bomber Policy— *Operation Thunderclap*

I n early 1945 Addison's father mailed Addison a news article about his acquisition of the Pearsall Butter Company in Elgin, Illinois, along with a short note saying, "Just getting ready for after the war so you boys will have more to do." The article read:

> *Mr. Bartush, who becomes president of the new company under the new ownership, is a figure of national prominence in the food industry. The story of his success is typically American—the story of a small town boy, raised in modest circumstances, who has risen to the top of his chosen field. Mr. Bartush is noted in the industry for two attributes: his rigid practice of maintaining highest quality in the foods his company produced, and the firm's exceptionally considerate policy in regards to the employee family. Coming up through the food industry from a modest beginning in a corner grocery store, Bartush knows every job because he worked at it. The Detroit industrialist has been the guiding genius back of Shedd-Bartush for three decades.*

Addison was justifiably proud of what his father had accomplished. "It was a large acquisition at the time," he observed, "but there were even larger ones to follow. Pearsall Butter Company originated the butter package, that is, four wrapped sticks in a box. It is still used today." Addison continued: "The company was mismanaged," he explained. "They could not get enough vegetable oil to make oleo-margarine during the war and lost out to competitors." Addison father's prediction proved true—following the war Addison did run this company for a period.

105

Addison's loneliness about being the only one he knew on a crew was cured by early to mid-January 1945. For one thing, flying with pilots that he had never trained with and who might be more or less unknown to him proved to be not that big of a deal. "We were all taught the same way," he observed. "We all knew our respective jobs." For another thing, Addison began to see personal benefit to himself in his role as a supply co-pilot: "It certainly gave me a lot of experience," he observed, extolling the virtues of variety. "That is, in dealing with different people." Finally, Addison found that there were some pilots and crews that he simply enjoyed flying with. "I did fly a number of missions with two other crews. I cannot recollect the pilot's names after all these years, but I believe one was from Baltimore and the other from somewhere in California."

In mid-January Addison flew a mission with a pilot he both liked and remembered, and aboard a bomber with a name that he could never forget: "*Skunkface III*." The January 15 mission was to a marshalling yard at Ingolstadt.

"I remember Balaban," Addison said about his pilot. "Chicago." Addison related how Balaban was a famous name in that city. "They owned theaters," he explained. "The previous week," Addison recalled, "Balaban made an emergency landing in France. His plane had been all shot up. Balaban's mission with me had to have been near his last. I enjoyed flying with him. I considered him lucky. As for this mission," Addison continued, "I recollect it was a milk run."

Addison's recollection about it being an easy mission was correct. The Ingolstadt 324th post-mission squadron report stated "no flak," "excellent fighter support" and "bombing results unobserved."[1] *Skunkface III* and 110 other B-17s made the attack using H2X radar. While the 324th passed over the target area without encountering flak, five other B-17s were damaged but with no casualties.[2] The mission had a new aspect to it, however: a V-2 rocket was spotted on its way to England.[3]

"I saw one once but on a different mission I believe," Addison said. "It was probably 15 or 20 miles away and we clearly saw it come up and arch towards England." Addison told of flame and smoke. "It was their big rocket, no doubt."

The Nazi terror-rocket campaign against England lasted approximately nine months and ended March 27, 1945, when the last rocket, a V-2, killed a 34-year-old housewife in her home. The V-1 rocket, the smaller "buzz bomb," is attributed to have killed 6,184 persons and injured three times that number. The much larger V-2, that Addison witnessed in flight, was launched an estimated 3,000 times. With a ballistic trajectory of 50 miles high and an operational range of 200 miles, the V-2 delivered a large (2,200 lb.) warhead. The V-2 reportedly killed 7,250 and wounded many more.[4] A macabre fact about this weapon is that more human beings died producing it than were killed from its use. An estimated 20,000 slave laborers from the Mittelbau-Dora concentration camp assigned to the project perished from exhaustion, execution, disease and starvation.[5]

Allied airpower was unable to destroy a single "Meillerwagen"— the mobile launching pad that deployed the rocket to forested launch sites over country roads.[6]

While the V-1 and V-2s had little chance to change the outcome of the war, these "vengeance weapons" had a hand in causing a significant policy shift in USAAF bombing. The horror associated with these indiscriminate rocket weapons (the V-2 was supersonic and could not be heard on its approach) coupled with the horrible casualties and Nazi criminal behavior at the Battle of the Bulge, where the SS murdered approximately 100 American POWs, caused Roosevelt, after consultation with Churchill, to re-think the U.S. doctrine of precision bombing only military targets. Although Addison could not have known it at the time, he was to become an eyewitness participant, in 1945, to what later would be referred to as "the most destructive year in human history."[7] Much of this destruction was wrought from the air upon German civilian population centers by the USAAF.

Addison told of German rocket attacks at Bassingbourn. "Occasionally I would hear them," he said, referring to the V-1 buzz bomb. "They made a chug, chug, chug sound. On one occasion, I heard one blow up in the distance. I also saw one once, that is, the flame coming out as it traveled past. We had a couple air raid shelters, but I never used them." Addison explained that to the best of his knowledge Bassingbourn had been hit only once, and that was by a V-1 that exploded on the drill field prior to his arrival.

On at least one occasion Addison dined at the Cumberland Hotel in London. A note in his World War II document file indicates that a few weeks after this dinner, a rocket dropped in the park in front of the hotel on a Sunday morning and that three people were killed.[8] Records show that this rocket had been a V-2, the date was March 18 and the time was 9:31 a.m. The rocket landed near Speaker's Corner and blew out windows in the hotel. A large march by the National Fire Service had been scheduled to go through that area that afternoon. If the rocket had been fired a few hours later, thousands could have died.[9] Londoners deemed the death of only three as "fortunate."

Addison flew four combat missions in January—two against marshalling yards, one attacking an airfield and one assaulting a rail center, all clearly defined military targets. His mission on January 29, the attack on the rail center at Niederlahnstein-Koblenz had been again aboard *Skunkface III* and without casualties for the 91st. Things were looking up for Addison—January had been far easier than December.

As an aside, *"Skunkface"* proved to be an unlucky name. The original *Skunkface* was lost in February 1944 with two KIA. *Skunkface II* was transferred to a different bomb group in early 1944[10] and *Skunkface III*, the one that Addison flew on twice, was lost April 17, 1945 over Dresden with eight of its nine crewmen killed.

The 91st Bomb Group had a myriad of fanciful and sometimes ribald names for its airplanes, as did all of the bomb groups of that era. The name perhaps most clever was, *"The Fuhrer the Better,"* which belonged to the 322nd Squadron. The planes assigned to the 324th Squadron tended to be named on the tame side. *"Extra Special," "Shure Shot," "Ah's Available," "Terry's Tiger," "Lorraine," "Klette's Wild Hares"* and (uniquely) *"Chippewa The Milwaukee Road"* are but a few examples. Paul Lynch noted that the less-than-raunchy appellations attributed to his squadron did not result from Klette being a preacher's son. "The 324th was just a group of decent fellows," he remarked proudly.

Nose art turned into a competition of sorts between aircrews. Addison brought back with him a photograph of a B-17 named *"Rhapsody in Red,"* that had on it a well-done painting of a pretty lady dressed just enough to be respectable. This was not the situation with all aircraft nose art, however.

It turned out that *"Rhapsody in Red"* would be the bomber on which former Bishop crewmember Earl Sheen would perform a life-saving act. Also this aircraft would finish out the war in a very memorable fashion, only to be retired and ingloriously junked in Kingman, Arizona, following almost two years of continuous combat.[11]

As January 1945 came to a close, Addison received two letters from Dave

Bishop's sister, Pearl, posted in the middle of the month, days apart. The first letter conveyed bad news and the second good news. These letters typify what ordinary folk went through on a very imposing scale in World War II.

January 17, 1945
Dear Lt. Bartush,
We received word today that the engineer, Sgt Cumings, was killed. We were so sorry to hear it, and it makes us that much more anxious to hear something from David. We got another letter from the War Department today. They just said that they haven't found him yet. They said his name was not on the prisoners list. We were so glad you were not on that mission. We have an uncle, who lives in Detroit, so I asked him to find your Dad and he did. He gave us the information about you . . .

David really did think lots of you. He often spoke of you in his letters. In fact he was well pleased with the whole crew . . . I know you can't write us some things due to Army regulations but do write us anyway. Then you can tell us anything that you're allowed. We would like to hear from you so much.

January 20, 1945
Dear Lt. Bartush,
We just received a telegram from the War Department saying that David is a German prisoner . . . We are just thrilled.

Addison related what it was like to fly a B-17, indicating that the controls were light and not sluggish. "Pretty good," he said, describing how the Boeing-built aircraft handled. "The plane responded." Addison pointed out that the bomber was considerably easier to fly after the bomb load had been dropped, however. "Much of the fuel was consumed at that point," Addison added, "which also made it easier. The long climb to altitude burned a lot of fuel." Regarding the bomb drop itself, he noted: "Up we went, like an elevator."

Long mission flights in or back while not near enemy airspace, or training flights provided the opportunity to listen to the Armed Forces Radio Service or the BBC. "Our radio system was unusual," Addison observed. "We could put it on in our airplane, and when we had the direction finder going it would switch back and forth and we never knew where the signal was coming from, that is, where it was being transmitted from. This kept the Germans from homing in." He added that when it wasn't news it was entertainment. Comedy was popular during this era, with American stars like Jack Benny, Groucho Marx and the duo of Burns and Allen being in demand by the USAAF.

On a number of occasions co-pilot Addison was called upon to take over from the pilot. "Not usually during the combat [bomb drop] but often on the way in or out."

The relief tube near to the flight deck could be problematic: "We had a hose with a funnel on it but I didn't use it because it froze at altitude." Addison then smiled mischievously: "And if one did use it and forgot to tell the ball turret gunner to turn around he might get it in the face!" He laughed and added: "It was used only at low altitude and generally speaking we were able to hold it." Addison then posed an out-of-the-ordinary question: had the practice of retention for long mission periods been unhealthy for him in later life?

As an aside, the Army Separation Qualification Record issued to Addison following the war stated, "Flew 31 combat missions and 238 combat hours." Doing the math, that averaged to a mission length of 7.7 hours. The actual average time per mission may have been somewhat less however, because some of his combat hours were for missions that were aborted. This document supports the contention that Addison did experience many time-consuming flights. Whether this may have impacted his health in later life is unknown.

Addison did not question another malady known to afflict bomber crewmen years later, probably because it never afflicted him: deafness.

Addison had been fortunate in that he never experienced a really close call during a combat mission landing. "One time we had to go around again because we weren't sure all the wheels were properly locked," he related. He allowed, however, how this had not been a crisis situation. He never had to return aboard a plane made hazardous to fly by battle damage.

Landing in extremely cold winter conditions could be a challenge for any airplane in that era. Slush picked up on takeoff could freeze into a solid block of ice, locking wheels in an upright position for the return. This was particularly a problem with the B-24 Liberators produced by Consolidated Aircraft, and later Ford Motor Company; that model of aircraft also struggled with a hydraulic system that became sluggish and unresponsive in extremely cold weather. B-17s used electroserver motors instead of hydraulics and were better suited for winter high-altitude flying. Addison believed his B-17 to be the superior bomber, its slower speed and slightly lower payload capacity notwithstanding.

The winter of 1944–45 in Europe was more severe than usual. "One of the earlier missions I was on, just across the river from Cologne, there was a 60-mile-an-hour winter headwind," Addison said. "Our actual speed over the ground was only 90 miles per hour." With the temperature hovering at near minus 50 degrees Fahrenheit at 24,000 feet, the crew managed to finish the job. "Fortunately, it wasn't a long mission," he explained. "We were able to hit the target and get back." He confirmed that the waist gunners probably had it worst because of winter winds. Exposure to the elements at the large open gun ports was unavoidable.

Addison told of an occasion when a flak shell passed through a wing and failed to explode, leaving a large hole that looked like an Easter lily made of aluminum petals. Addison did not feel the impact. "We were passing through a flak field," Addison explained, "and I looked out to the right and saw the damage after it had been done. I shouted [into the intercom] 'My God! There's a hole in our wing!' " He added: "I smelled gasoline."

"No smoking on the way home," he chuckled, shaking his head at the incredible memory. "It was a self-sealing tank," he explained. "Rubberized." The German 88 shell had a diameter of 3.5 inches. This would tear a large hole in a wing, indeed.

"I saw small holes caused by flak fragments and also cracks in the Plexiglas. I saw that, yes," Addison said, but he also had the good fortune never to see a crewmember wounded by one of these flying shards or get hit himself. "I remember one of the guys who I bunked with, kind of a character, who wanted a Purple Heart because a piece of Plexiglas nicked him on the chin and he bled a little." Addison chortled at the remembrance. "He was from Maine." Asked if this man received the decoration, Addison replied: "I don't think so. You need a little more than that."

A glimmer crossed Addison's face as he remembered a close call. "There was one time," he recounted, "when I grabbed the controls without asking and put us in an emergency dive." After a pause, he explained: "We were approaching the target, and there was this airplane, my God, I could have almost touched it! I shoved the wheel down. I don't know if the pilot knew what I had done or what was going to happen."

Addison's decisive action in taking control of the airplane in an emergency situation is what the author Tom Wolfe described in his book *The Right Stuff*. "Oh, yes!" Addison blurted for emphasis. "We'd have not been here." The intensive psychological testing that the Army Air Forces had put Addison through in Nashville, Tennessee, to see how he might react in an unexpected crisis situation had in this instance paid off. That and the training, training and more training that he received. By his spontaneous action Addison had avoided disaster.

Addison reported that his gunners engaged often, "particularly in some of my early missions," and most particularly in his first mission to Merseburg. The vibration from firing guns would reach the cockpit, but not always from the far away tail gun. Regarding the tail gun position, Addison noted that there was a tail gunner door, an escape portal, on the G model, but that the earlier F version had none. "For structural reasons there could not be one," he explained about the earlier model. The tail section bore considerable stress even in normal, non-combat, flying, he pointed out, and a door there was not at first possible. And getting into and out of the tail gun position was itself a challenge. First, a large rear wheel strut stood in the middle of the airplane partly blocking the passageway to the tail section, and second and even more cumbersome to traverse, the tapered fuselage became progressively narrow towards the end of the bomber. One had to crawl through a contracting tunnel to enter a very confined space and wiggle out the same way. When Addison talked about this the expression he wore was serious. Undoubtedly he was thinking about his lost friend, Owen Monkman, and the model that he flew on. Addison identified what he thought was the second most dangerous position on the ship: "The ball turret was tiny and the gunner had to get up and out quickly," he said.

A manual reported a 267 mph maximum airspeed for a B-17 but upon hearing this Addison disagreed: "I don't buy it," he asserted. "More like 150 mph or maybe a little faster." Technology was primitive in World War II compared to today. The slow-moving aerial leviathans from World War II had no ability to quickly extricate themselves from harm's way. And B-17s and B-24s did not operate together in formation. The B-17 could fly higher, and the B-24, faster; to combine the two operationally would weaken the overall capability of both.

Addison never saw the 88mm ground flak batteries that shot at him. "I recall seeing flak towers," he said, "but at quite a distance." The Germans erected numerous enormous reinforced concrete towers in population centers to serve the dual purpose of supporting heavy (128mm) anti-aircraft guns on top and providing civilians with bomb shelters within. Bombs that exploded on the ground near these towers might not take out or damage the artillery on top of them because of the angle, and the thick walls at the tower bases were built to sustain powerful nearby explosions. All of the towers survived the war, and afterward proved so hard to demolish, even with tons of carefully placed explosives, that several still exist to this day.

Addison mentioned once jettisoning a bomb load into the English Channel. "I flew as the pilot one time and we got recalled," he added, smiling proudly. "And I got credit for a combat mission."

Addison also told how after hostilities ceased he went into the bomb group map room and helped himself to one of everything that he could find. "I boxed them up and mailed them home," Addison recalled, obviously pleased that he had done this. "I knew they would never be used again." The maps were all standardized at 25 by 30 inches in size to fit the navigator's table, and were brightly colored—dark blue for lakes and rivers, bright red for highways, and light green for forested or rural areas. The maps were works of art.

One of these maps was used for Berlin, where Addison would fly to on Saturday, February 3, 1945. On that day he and many thousands of other U.S. airmen struck the heart of the Third Reich as part of a new mission-strategy codenamed *Operation Thunderclap*—the largest raid ever to hit Berlin. It happened that the 91st Bomb Group was designated group leader for this attack and would be the first over the target. This raid ushered in a change in heavy bomber policy in Europe for the U.S. Army Air Forces; it foreshadowed the U.S. participation in the raid on Dresden and other central city-bombings.

Addison would not have known it at the time but a far-reaching decision had been made in Washington, D.C. The Germans, who had fought aggressively and ferociously in two world wars, were about to be punished in a special manner that would, or so it was thought, make them forever renounce war as a means for advancing their national interest. At least that was the hope of the U.S. President and the Prime Minister of Great Britain.

THE RHYTHM OF THE EUROPEAN AIR WAR 1944–1945
91st Bomb Group Missions at War's End
November 25, 1944–April 25, 1945

Mission attacks flown by Lieutenant Addison Bartush appear **bolded** below; three additional recalls over enemy territory are not shown. The mission resulting in Sergeant Paul Lynch being shot down appears in *italics* below.

11/25/44	**Merseburg**		01/10/45	**Ostheim**
11/26/44	*Altenbeken* (six Bishop crew members shot down including Paul Lynch)		01/14/45	Cologne
			01/15/45	**Ingolstadt**
11/27/44	Offenburg		01/17/45	Paderborn
11/29/44	Merseburg		01/20/45	Ludwigshafen
11/30/44	**Zeitz**		01/21/45	Aschaffenburg
12/04/44	**Kassel**		01/22/45	Sterkrade
12/05/44	Berlin		01/28/45	Cologne
12/09/44	Stuttgart		01/29/45	**Niederlahnstein– Koblenz**
12/11/44	**Frankfurt**		02/01/45	Mannheim
12/12/44	**Merseburg**		02/03/45	**Berlin**
12/15/44	Kassel		02/06/45	Gotha
12/18/44	**Luxembourg Area** (screening force— chaff dropped)		02/07/45	Osterfeld (recalled)
			02/08/45	Wesel (recalled)
12/24/44	Merzhausen— Kirch-Göns		02/09/45	Altenbeken
			02/14/45	**Prague**—a secondary target following flight over Dresden
12/28/44	Ludendorf			
12/29/44	Wittlich			
12/31/44	**Bitburg**		02/15/45	Dresden
01/01/45	Kassel		02/16/45	Gelsenkirchen
01/02/45	**Prüm**		02/17/45	Böhlen (recalled)
01/03/45	Cologne		02/19/45	**Dortmund**
01/05/45	**Koblenz**		02/20/45	Nürnberg
01/06/45	Cologne		02/21/45	**Nürnberg**

02/22/45	**Stendal**	03/24/45	Twente/Enschede
02/23/45	Meiningen–Hildburghausen	03/25/45	Zeitz (recalled)
		03/28/45	**Spandau**–Stendal
02/24/45	Hamburg	03/30/45	Bremen
02/26/45	Berlin	03/31/45	Halle–Aschersleben
02/27/45	**Leipzig**	04/02/45	Snrydstrutden (recalled)
02/28/45	**Schwerte**		
03/01/45	Heilbronn	04/04/45	Fassberg
03/02/45	**Chemnitz**–Jocketa	04/05/45	**Grafenwöhr**
03/03/45	Chemnitz	04/07/45	**Kohlenbissen–Fassberg**
03/04/45	Reutlingen–**Ulm**		
03/07/45	Dortmund–Giessen	04/08/45	Stendal
03/08/45	Hüls	04/09/45	Oberpfaffenhofen
03/09/45	Kassel	04/10/45	Oranienburg–Rechlin/Lärz
03/10/45	Sinsen		
03/12/45	Dillenburg	04/11/45	Freiham
03/14/45	**Vlotho**–Osnabrück	04/13/45	Neumünster
03/15/45	**Oranienburg**	04/15/45	**Rochefort Area, France**—Addison flew as first pilot
03/17/45	Böhlen		
03/18/45	Berlin		
03/19/45	Plauen	04/16/45	Regensburg
03/21/45	Rheine/Salzbergen	04/17/45	Dresden
03/22/45	Dorsten	04/18/45	Rosenheim
03/23/45	Coesfeld	04/20/45	Brandenburg
03/24/45	Vechta	04/21/45	Munich
		04/25/45	**Pilsen**

Due to planned periods of rest, on average Addison flew a combat mission every five days. The Luftwaffe, by contrast did not have the luxury of advance planning. The only rest available for German pilots was caused by weather or lack of fuel.—Advantage: USAAF.

On January 27, 1945, just a week before the Berlin raid in which Addison participated, the Red Army overran the Auschwitz Concentration Camp, and reports soon began circulating about the Nazi genocide. On that day the BBC reported ". . . gas chambers capable of killing 6,000 people a day." There is no record linking the Auschwitz news reports to the change in U.S. strategic bombing policy, and in fact the planning for *Operation Thunderclap* was done well before Auschwitz was liberated. But the information coming out of Auschwitz surely would have steeled the heart of any commander-in-chief. It would take many years for historical researchers to piece together exactly what happened at Auschwitz, but with the liberation of the camp it became apparent that the Nazis under cover of war had exterminated most of a human race in Eastern Europe, and they had done so by using insect poison. Auschwitz made it psychologically easier for the leadership of the United States to pull the "moral trigger" on the people of Nazi Germany through *Operation Thunderclap*.

What was about to be done would not be publicly revealed for years to come, and only then at the prodding of reporters and research done by objective historians. The argument can be made though, that even if what was about to happen had been publicly revealed at the time, by 1945 the American public was so desensitized to the horrors of war that it would have made little protest. All that was desired at home and in the theatre of war was a swift conclusion to the bloody struggle; if that meant inflicting new and greater horrors on the enemy, then so be it.

There existed another reason for the United States to change its long-standing heavy bomber policy away from hitting only military specific targets. As the European war entered its final stage, the world political and military situation had evolved, and an atmosphere of distrust had settled in. As the leaders of the Allied powers prepared for their February 1945 Yalta Conference, the Soviets knew that they had borne the largest suffering and sacrifice, and believed their Western allies were angling for spoils not earned. On the other side, the Americans and British feared they were dealing with a dictator little different from Adolf Hitler. The Soviets had the largest modern army ever assembled; the Americans and the British had a huge strategic heavy bomber force that continued to grow through breakneck industrial production and the training of new airmen. The Americans and British were concerned that the Red Army might attempt to conquer Europe. As one scholarly commentator drolly understated: "Some Allied officers thought the raids in eastern Germany might serve the additional purpose of impressing the Soviet Union."[12] The real issue was: how would these raids be conducted to impress? Or perhaps more accurately phrased: *to deter?*

The family concern over Addison's state of mind eased somewhat during this time. There is no demonstrative letter to show this, but the tone of the letters Addison received during this period are generally relaxed. Emotions seemed to be settling down somewhat on the home front, and reading these letters one can only surmise that this was caused by Addison writing home more frequently and positively.

On January 21 Addison's teenage sister wrote to him: "Who do you think rang the doorbell? It was Jack Shea" [a college buddy of Addison's]. She reported that Jack wanted to go overseas and added, quaintly: "I thought it might be someone to see me but it was just him." On February 1 Addison's mother mailed him a short unsigned note: "Dear Son: 'Chicken Paprikash' is a good Hungarian dish. The *Hungarian Village* is noted for it." Her hastily scribbled note was done on the reverse side of an invitation to the Detroit Athletic Club "Bowlers Ladies Party" at a cost of $15 per couple. The invitation read: "A novel and unique favor for the ladies."

For Addison's part, by the end of January 1945, he had 12 missions under his belt and was a third of the way through his tour. And had he perhaps added a little "swagger" to his step at this point? After all, "green" replacement crews had to have been then arriving at Bassingbourn at regular, planned, intervals. Surely such "rookie" crews would look upon a veteran of 12 combat missions as someone to be respected! That was generally the way it worked in the USAAF in World War II. An airman wearing the Air Medal ribbon denoting five combat missions completed was someone to be looked up to. And for Addison, he now had more than the ribbon; he wore an oak leaf cluster on it, representing five additional missions (every succeeding five missions completed authorized the wearing of another cluster).

Not only was Father Ragan's support of immense help during his rocky start, but Addison's faith also helped to sustain him during his tenure at Bassingbourn, and he made time for the observance of it in his regular schedule. "They had a small chapel on base," Addison volunteered. "I visited it after every mission and made a prayer of thanks."

The war was again going well for the Americans, which had to have additionally boosted Addison's spirits. The Battle of the Bulge had been won, and U.S. ground forces were again on the move. On January 31, 1945, the XVIII Airborne Corps penetrated the Buchholz forest—progress was again being made against the enemy.[13] One of the headlines of a *Stars and Stripes* newspaper that Addison brought home from this period reported in bolded headline: "German Armor Pulling Back."[14]

The American air war was about to take an ominous new course, however, one that paralleled what the British had been doing all along.[15] RAF Bomber Command under the direction of Air Marshal Arthur "Bomber" Harris had been area-bombing German cities as early as May 1942, when Cologne was attacked in "Operation Millennium," the first 1,000-plane heavy bomber raid of the war. Other similar nighttime British attacks on urban areas followed; the most publicized being the Battle of Hamburg in August 1943, codenamed, chillingly, "Operation Gomorrah." An estimated 42,600 German civilians died as a result of this British bombing assault; another 37,000 were wounded.[16] Until February 3, 1945, the United States refrained from the direct bombing of German population centers.

Heretofore Addison and his bomb group had been ordered to press attacks on military targets only, e.g., synthetic oil plants, marshalling yards, rail targets, manufacturing plants, airfields and the like. To this list they were about to be told to add a new target classification or category: "administrative headquarters." The problem was that "administrative headquarters" were most often located in the center of a city. When used as "aiming points," as they were, the collateral damage could be, and was, significant.

Even with the Pathfinder system and new radar navigation techniques, in 1945 the bombs themselves were still "dumb." Lacking a navigational guidance system, they just fell downwards when released from an airplane, and when dropped from 24,000 feet, even in perfect weather conditions, their impact often resulted in unintended consequences. The first bombers to arrive on scene, however, had an aiming advantage. If the weather was clear they could spot and hit their assigned target. For the bombers that followed in the middle-to-rear sections of a long bomber stream, the sighting conditions were much more difficult. These bombers encountered heavy smoke and dust and debris billowing up from the ground that were pushed in every direction by winds of conflagration. Suffice to say, target identification could be challenging.

An academic commentator, Professor Ronald Schaffer, 40 years after the war wrote about the USAAF rationale for *Operation Thunderclap*. Designed to be a series of missions over cities in eastern Germany (cities about to be occupied by Soviet forces), *Operation Thunderclap* was not the name of any single combat mission but rather a closing series of strikes intended as ". . . a climatic psychological warfare campaign in which massive bombings would panic civilians, who would clog roads and railroads and make it impossible for German troops facing the Soviet army to bring up supplies and reinforcements or retreat in an orderly way."[17]

With regard to the February 3, 1945 raid over Berlin that commenced *Operation Thunderclap*, this professor wrote:

> *As General Spaatz's headquarters made final preparations, General Doolittle, the commander of the Eighth Air Force which would have to fly the mission to Berlin, explained to Spaatz why he did not like this operation at all. American planes would have to pass in range of hundreds of heavy anti-aircraft guns to reach an area where there would be no really important military targets. The raid would not succeed even as a terror attack because German civilians would have ample warning to take shelter. Besides, terror was induced by fear of the unknown, not by intensifying what the people of Berlin had experienced for years. And Thunderclap, which would be one of the last and therefore presumably best remembered operations of the war, would "violate the basic American principle of precision bombing of targets of strictly military significance for which our tactics were developed and our crews trained and indoctrinated."[18]*

Addison remembered seeing Tempelhof Airport on the way in to Berlin on February 3, but that was not his squadron's target. A commentator wrote: "The bomber stream was so long it stretched from Holland all the way to Berlin."[19] The following day, Addison's father, assuming correctly that Addison was in this raid, mailed Addison an article from the *Detroit Free Press* that had this headline: *Sky Train Stretches 300 Miles—Fighter Diversion Stuns Defenses.*

Traveling at approximately 150 mph, by Addison's estimate, the bombing of Berlin took two hours to complete, start to finish, give or take. The mission had been planned that way; that is, to employ an extremely long, slow-moving column.

A diversion was used to fool the Luftwaffe and it worked. The *Detroit Free Press* article explained that 900 U.S. fighters had escorted 400 B-24 Liberator bombers on a raid over Madgeburg, a city some 65 miles southwest of Berlin. The Liberators returned home while the fighters proceeded on to Berlin in a swift protective shuttle, cutting down fighter opposition to the incoming B-17s. The German air defenders took the bait, and assumed incorrectly that Madgeburg was the primary target. 3,000 tons of bombs rained down on center city Berlin from approximately 1,000 Flying Fortresses. An estimated 25,000 Berliners died in this raid due primarily to inaccurate bombing.[20]

The *Detroit Free Press* article continued:

It was the 204th raid of the war on Berlin, and brought the total of bombs dropped there to nearly 50,000 tons—seven times the amount the Germans dumped on London during the aerial battle of Britain.

"It was a clear day. I remember going after certain important buildings," Addison said. "One was a communications center, I do believe. My squadron was the first one in." Reports show that other squadrons had been assigned to hit the Nazi party headquarters building, rail yards and the Tempelhof marshalling yard.

With the passage of time this Berlin raid became controversial. In 1981 the editors of *Time-Life Books* published this about the attack:

The raid was directed at rail yards and other transportation targets, but many of the bombs fell on government buildings at the center of the city. Later, Spaatz admitted that his Fortresses had bombed indiscriminately, "making no effort to confine ourselves to military targets."[21]

Asked if he agreed with the *Time-Life Books* assessment, Addison bristled. "We were going after specific buildings," he affirmed. "And I remember seeing pictures of the buildings at the briefing." He also added: "We were not going after libraries or hospitals."

Being part of the lead squadron over Berlin, Addison had not witnessed the smoke and dust on the ground. He saw something else happen right in front of him, however, something that would stay with him for the rest of his life. A historian for the 91st recorded:

The lead aircraft flown by Lt. Frank L. Adams and with Lt. Col. Marvin D. Lord, group leader for the mission, in the co-pilot's seat was hit about ten seconds after bombs away. A direct hit took place in the waist which resulted in the disintegration of the aircraft. The tail section of the plane floated back through the formation and the nose section dived. There were no survivors.[22]

The loss of this lead aircraft was a particular tragedy for Manny Klette. Due to a forecast of foul weather made the day before, the mission had been cancelled and Klette had been given permission to go to London to see his fiancé. After he left for London the weather forecast changed for the better and the mission was rapidly rescheduled. Lt. Col. Lord volunteered to take Klette's place in leading the mission to downtown Berlin. Manny Klette lived; the rest of his crew perished.[23]

In addition to the loss of the lead aircraft, another B-17 from the 324th Squadron was shot down that day. The second plane's crew parachuted safely and all survived to become prisoners of war.

Operation Thunderclap commenced over Berlin without U.S. aircrews being aware that it represented a change in USAAF strategic bombing policy, and Professor Schaffer had this to say about the effect of the change: "Thunderclap did not push Germany over the brink." Schaffer pointed out that this raid and subsequent attacks on populated areas did not cause the German army to stop fighting. Later in life, Paul Lynch, having been in Nazi Germany when *Operation Thunderclap* continued, would agree: "I think it pulled the German people closer together," he said. Did the February 3 USAAF raid on Berlin "impress" the Soviet Union? That question is difficult to answer.

The 324th Squadron report ("claims, casualties and battle damage remarks") prepared immediately after this mission is a testament to the fog of war. In seeming conflict with each other, pilots reported both "unobserved bombing results" and "good hits on target." Four chutes were noted coming out of the lead B-17 whereas in reality there were none. And as for "the second ship lost"? The report misidentified the name of its pilot.[24] Undoubtedly the pilots who provided input for this report had to have been under incredible stress at the time of their debriefings.

On *Rhapsody in Red* that day, one of the young men Addison had trained with in Gulfport and who had flown with Addison across the Atlantic, the "tall thin guy," the toggelier and waist gunner Earl Sheen, had done something special. Sheen died in 1997, never having told his family about it. They learned about it five years after his death when the following email surfaced among survivors of the 91st Bomb Group:

A question was posted on the Ring last week regarding information about Earl Sheen. Nobody seemed to recall too much about him other than he was from the 324th and he came from Idaho. I feel guilty that I can't contribute anything more, for I believe he saved my life. I suppose we're all tired of war stories now, but I hope I may be forgiven if I tell this one, if only as a tribute to Earl Sheen, wherever he may be. I met him just once, and that was inside the nose of a 17 on the morning of February 3, 1945, on our way to Berlin, my 35th mission. He was the toggelier, and I the navigator. We were in the #2 ship alongside the squadron lead ship which was leading the entire wing that day. Over target at bombs away, a burst of flak demolished the lead ship, breaking it in half at the waist [and] shortly thereafter we lost the #3 ship. We were the only ship left in the lead element. I didn't know that the hose between my mask and the oxygen regulator had been severed by flak. When I failed to respond to a call from the pilot, Sheen turned around and saw me slumped on the floor. He had the presence of mind to realize that I had passed out from lack of oxygen. I'll never know how long I was out, but he revived me by connecting me to one of those walk around oxygen bottles. We didn't talk much about it afterward. It had been a rough mission. After we landed, Sheen disappeared to take care of cleaning his guns, and I didn't feel too much like celebrating the completion of my tour, as the base was quiet as a tomb. We all had been close to the guys who had gone down that day. The next afternoon, I left Bassingbourn. From time to time over the next 50 years, I thought of the guy, but regrettably did nothing about trying to locate him. Last week his name popped up in the Ring, and it rang a bell in my mind. Ding, dong. I checked the loading list for my last mission, Berlin, Feb 3, and there was his name. So a long belated thanks from the bottom of my heart, BOMB TG Sgt. Sheen, Earl J. 39919847, old buddy, wherever you may be. Contact me for free beer tomorrow. Sam Halpert.

Survivors of the 91st delivered Halpert's tribute to Sheen's son, Jay. Paul Lynch said that RJ Miller informed him of Sheen's act after the war.

CHAPTER EIGHT

The *Black March* Begins

As Addison was grieving the loss of his squadron members, Paul Lynch was about to embark on a three-month walking odyssey of almost 500 miles that could have taken his life. Paul could have perished from the winter elements, disease, violence or even starvation. Survivors of this event coined a name for what they experienced: "*The Black March.*"[1] *The Black March* was unique in the history of Allied airmen prisoners of World War II in the European Theater. At 25%, the mortality rate of the marchers nearly equaled on a percentage basis the rate incurred on *The Bataan Death March* in the Philippines.[2]

There were other POW camps where Allied airmen were forced to march, most notably Stalag Luft III near Sagan with its 10,300 British and American occupants.[3] All POW marchers suffered an ordeal of one sort or another, but on a comparison basis, the prisoners of Stalag Luft IV—the Black Marchers—got it the worst. Their distance on foot was tenfold more.

By early February 1945 the Nazis were losing badly. The main Soviet spearhead was nearing Berlin, having bypassed the northern coastal part of Poland near the German border where Paul and his fellow POWs were confined. It was simply a matter of time before Soviet forces arrived at Stalag Luft IV, and there was nothing the Nazis could do to prevent it. The Red Army soldiers who broke the siege of Leningrad in January 1944 were moving along the Baltic coast and these soldiers were highly motivated to play a part in the demise of the Third Reich.

On February 11, 1945, in anticipation of victory, an agreement was struck at the Yalta Conference between the Allied powers. The Americans and the British very much wanted help in the war against Japan, and at Yalta

Stalin agreed that ". . . two or three months after Germany has surrendered and the war in Europe is terminated, the Soviet Union shall enter into war against Japan on the side of the Allies."[4]

A Yalta side agreement between the U.S. and Soviets regarding POWs would prove controversial in its implementation and have personal consequences for Paul. At this juncture, however, Paul could not know what transpired in diplomatic circles. The agreement preamble on the subject of repatriation stated:

> *The Government of the United States of America on the one hand and the Government of the Union of Soviet Socialist Republics on the other hand, wishing to make arrangements for the care and repatriation of United States citizens freed by forces operating under Soviet command and for Soviet citizens freed by forces operating under United States command, have agreed . . .*[5]

The Nazis, although pressed and desperate, were not ready to allow any "repatriation." The POWs at Stalag Luft IV represented "bargaining chips" (Paul's words). To permit these POWs to be swooped up by the Soviets would be to lose control over something the British and Americans might well negotiate for. At this late date in the war the Nazis still hoped for a separate armistice with the West. The *Associated Press* reported the following regarding the beginning of *The Black March* and other POW marches:

NAZIS HERD U.S. CAPTIVES
OUT OF RUSSIAN'S PATH

RED CROSS REPORTS MOST TRANSFERRALS
BEING MADE ON FOOT

WASHINGTON, FEB 15 (AP).—*Great numbers of American and Allied prisoners of war, whom the Germans are transferring out of the path of Russian armies, are making the trip on foot. Reporting this tonight, the American Red Cross said the Geneva Convention permits prisoners to make maximum daily marches of up to twelve and a half miles unless longer ones are necessary to reach food and shelter.*[6]

Paul initially reflected that the first week of the march was not very interesting from the perspective of storytelling. When he learned, however, that the events of that first week determined, in many instances, whether a marcher would live or die, he reconsidered his opinion. The first week was the most critical one.

On May 8, 1995, fifty years after VE Day, Senator John Warner read into the Congressional Record a tribute to the Americans who made the forced march from Stalag Luft IV:

> *The 86-day march was by all accounts savage, men who for months, and in some cases years, had been denied proper nutrition, personal hygiene, medical care, were forced to do something that would be difficult for well nourished, healthy, and appropriately trained infantry soldiers to accomplish.*

The Senate tribute suggested that 9,500 suffered the ordeal "on the march." Another account placed the number at approximately 8,000,[7] and still another, "more than 6,000." Accepting any of these figures as accurate, the number of men involved was considerable. The "more than 6,000" figure came from a 1997 *Air Force Magazine* article that explained that in early 1945, "Some 3,000 of the POWs [at Stalag Luft IV] who were not physically able to walk were sent by train to Stalag Luft I, a camp farther west."[8]

This *Air Force Magazine* article also opined that the forced march was ". . . an event of mass heroism that has been neglected by history." This claim is fairly accurate. There are many Internet sites and some published books that contain individual accounts of the march, but it has not received the notoriety proportional to the ordeal that these men were forced to suffer. The Senate commemoration seems to confirm this fact, stating: "Unfortunately, the story . . . is not well known."

Senator Warner's tribute said that the travail ended on April 26 in Halle, Germany, when the marchers were liberated by the U.S. 104th Infantry Division. Research indicates, however, that the march did not conclude in as orderly a manner as Senator Warner stated. Although the 104th liberated a major column of marchers, there were other columns that it did not liberate.[9] Owing to inadequate roads and varying circumstances, not all POWs had taken the same route through Germany. Moreover, in Paul's specific case, because of a fateful decision he and three others made, liberation would come at the hands of a Soviet patrol on April 24. Paul's "march" would not halt, however, until May 12 in Riesa, Germany, four days after V-E Day.

Asked if little food, much filth and no doctors about summed-up *The Black March*, Paul responded acerbically: "There was also the winter." Paul was asked to comment upon a statement appearing in the Congressional record attributed to Major Leslie Caplan, M.D., the same officer who gave testimony against the commandant of Stalag Luft IV, and himself a survivor of *The Black March*:

> *It was a march of great hardship. We marched long distances in bitter weather and on starvation rations. We lived in filth and slept in open fields or barns. Clothing, medical facilities and sanitary facilities were utterly inadequate. Hundreds of men suffered from malnutrition, dysentery, tuberculosis, and other diseases.*

"I don't think I ever slept in the open," Paul observed. "I was always in a barn somewhere and usually you could take your blankets and combine them with somebody else's to stay warmer. Some of the barns had straw that could be used," he added, pointing out that straw would insulate for additional warmth.

Paul explained that by early February he and the other POWs at Stalag Luft IV sensed that a move of some sort was coming. "There were rumors about the Russians getting closer," he said. "I figured we'd be packed into trains but that didn't happen."

The announcement that there would be a march was made on February 6, 1945 at morning formation. Commandant Bombach spoke from a raised platform and without a microphone. "He just told [us] what was going to happen and that was the end of it," Paul indicated. "He spoke good English, he was clear."

Reflecting back on that morning, Paul continued: "There were about 200 to 300 men on the quadrangle which included 100 or so from my barracks. The ones that couldn't make the walk just sat there." Referring to those who stood, he added: "I don't think anybody looked forward to it [the march]. We took it as a matter of course." He then asked: "What could be done about it? We didn't know what was coming up and we were apprehensive." Paul volunteered: "We would have just as soon seen the Russians come in."

With respect to the approach of the Red Army, Bombach had been truthful to the POWs. He told them that this was the reason for the march, and also that there was a lack of rail transportation. Paul and the other POWs had seen no signs of the Soviets. "We were in the country," he said, referring to the fact that it was still and peaceful. "There were no warplane flyovers or the rumbling of far away explosions."

Paul stated that most of the men from his barracks made the march. The POWs in Paul's group, already dressed in winter gear, moved directly out of the lager without returning to their barracks.

"We moved out and they were left behind," Paul said, referring to the POWs who had sat on the ground. He added: "I never knew what they [the Germans] did with them. The Germans didn't say what was happening." No representatives of the International Red Cross were present.

When Paul learned that approximately one-third of the 9,500 POWs at Stalag Luft IV ended-up being removed by train owing to medical reasons, he chuckled and quipped: "I guess I should have been lame."

"It wasn't nasty," Paul remembered, referring to the weather that first day. "Not severely cold, just a normal winter day. We were fairly close to the main gate, but I could not see what was going on in other sections of the camp."

What Paul could not see was that the German guards had emptied the camp one lager at a time and within a lager, one or two barracks at a time. The German design was to send POWs off in separate groupings of approximately 200 each to avoid critical massing. Paul indicated that during the entirety of the march he never saw 6,000 marchers or anywhere near that number. If there were to be a POW rebellion, it would be a small one, that is, localized and more manageable for the Germans.

The evacuation of the camp was accomplished in a day—30 columns on the move, give or take. One of the things that did help that day and for a few days thereafter was the presence of a medical professional. "The Germans appointed a British pharmacist as the medical officer," Paul noted. He was given free movement among the marchers."

"As we were leaving, we passed by tables holding Red Cross packages and we could take all we could carry," Paul said. "This presented a problem because too much weight would be difficult to carry for a long distance. The Germans solved this by marching us by the boxes at a fast walk. My turn came and I saw those Hershey bars. They are light and easy to carry, lots of energy and they are good. I scooped up 8 or 10 bars and wrapped them in some of my clothing as I thought how good these would be along the march." Paul offered that he and the others would have liked to have had an opportunity to think about what food items to select, but this was not to be. "They didn't scream at us," he recollected, referring to the guards, "but the line was moving." The Germans emphasized that this food might be needed for several days and maybe even up to a week; some POWs grabbed more food than they could carry—including heavy cans.

The area in Poland where the march started was latitude 53.56° N—approximately the same as Goose Bay, Canada where the Bishop Crew had briefly stopped. Paul described Goose Bay the previous October, when he landed there in transit, as a place of cold and "never ending snow." Being early February now, Paul was really in a place of never ending snow. The first day may not have been particularly harsh, but many of the days that followed were. A survivor of the march stated: "Many days the weather did not get above zero."[10] Other accounts confirmed frequent sub-zero weather.[11]

"Gloves were available," Paul said. "But I don't remember anything about what kind of hat I wore," he continued, "but I must have had something." Paul wore a heavy wool uniform and greatcoat, carried a blanket roll (with the aid of a shoulder strap) and had this to say about his boots: "They were G.I. styled high-tops like the ones we got in basic training. Tough."

It was not long after the march started that Paul appreciated the significance of having well-fitting boots. "I suspect," he opined, referring to when the boots had been issued to the POWs at Dulag Luft, "that some of the boots weren't the size that the individual needed because they probably ran out . . . so they [the Germans] just substituted something else."

Tightly fitting or loosely fitting boots, uncomfortable as they might be, would not present a medical problem in the confines of a prison camp. On the march, however, blisters would develop and split open and the skin underneath would continue to rub. Exposed and traumatized flesh would become dirty and without proper medical treatment eventually infected. Medications were lacking on the march.

Paul's feet never blistered. He had been blessed with good luck.

The men were issued two wool blankets that they carried as their bedrolls. "I had a tin cup," Paul said, "and may have had a knife and fork, also, I can't remember." He estimated the total weight that he carried was maybe

20 pounds or a little more. Per a number of accounts of Black Marchers, hauling more weight than that in the form of food wrapped in blankets proved to be an excruciating challenge. With only his Hershey bars Paul was in good shape weight-wise. "Really, it wasn't a problem," he observed. "I just threw it over my shoulders and went." Paul also confirmed that the overcoat he had been issued was heavy, long and warm, and that the blanket roll had no tumpline—that is, a relief strap worn around the forehead to shift the weight off one's shoulder onto the spine.

Other than trying to keep Paul's group of 200 or so reasonably together and away from other groups, the German guards were not concerned about a marching order. There were six guards per group and they did not have dogs with them. "The guards were quite old men," Paul said, "and replaced often." At the onset, simply because it happened that way, Paul marched near the front of his column.

Paul finished the first day exhausted, thirsty and hungry, having completed 15 miles. He decided not to eat a Hershey bar, even though he was ravenous to do so; no, best to keep the bars for the long haul he told himself—to preserve what little food he had for future consumption or trading, as the case might be. Using his tin cup, he drank large quantities of ersatz "coffee" made of boiled well water with dissolved lard or grease that passed for butter.

No one had dropped out. "No, not the first day," Paul made clear. There had been foot problems, yes, but "the medic [the British pharmacist] was right there."

There had been no preparation for this march at Stalag Luft IV and to go from an essentially warehoused existence to one involving hyper physical activity in the cold of winter with limited or even no nutrition was indeed a serious proposition in more than one way. In addition to physical health concerns there were psychological health concerns. By the evening of the first day, all of the marchers to some extent questioned what the future might hold for them. Some were in better shape physically and mentally than others, but no one was at ease about the situation.

That first night the guards made the POWs sleep head-to-head in long lines in a barn, Paul explained. "I didn't awake until the morning call," he said. "We were soon on the move and we kept moving most of the morning. Along about noon I decided I would try the first of my Hershey bars so I reached into my hiding place—they were gone! I was angry and very disappointed. It had to have been the fellow in the line just opposite me as none of the others could reach in without disturbing several sleepers. I was so tired I didn't pay attention to who that was and probably so tired I didn't feel him reach in and remove the bars. I watched for a Hershey bar-eater but never saw one. The first few days there was a great deal of food swapping on the march but not for me, I had lost my bargaining chips."

A number of stories about *The Black March* tell of heroic behavior on the part of POWs towards each other, that is, the stronger helping the weaker. Here was something that was, well . . . different. "It happened," Paul confirmed.

The British pharmacist made a huge contribution to Paul and many of the others during the short period of time that he assisted them. He advised the men to huddle together during the freezing cold nights and share blankets for increased body warmth. He also laid down the law about drinking only boiled well water and insisted that the men needed to drink plenty of it. Paul and the others had no canteens, and when marching the Germans did not supply water.

Soon after the march started—in a matter of a day or days—the British pharmacist was gone. "I figured he ended-up somewhere else in the line," Paul said. "But I do not know this." He added: "The German guards could not tell us, either." For the rest of the march, practically the entire 500-mile distance, Paul and his fellow POWs were without the assistance of a medical professional.

The groups trudged on without flags or other visible signals that identified them as POWs. This did not matter though, Paul thought, "Again we were out in the countryside." Paul saw no combat elements of the German Army or pre-made entrenchments; for all intents and purposes, in this area the war did not exist save for old men carrying long bolt-action rifles. "They did not get too close," Paul noted about the guards, but every now and then one of them might initiate a conversation with the friendly question, "Where ist you from?"

Occasionally Paul would see other similar-sized POW groups walking ahead or behind him. "We could not communicate with these other groups," Paul said. "They were too far away."

It was on the second or third day, Paul could not remember which, that he first saw it happen: one of the fellows marching near him developed problems with his feet, and had to be taken to the back of the line. The pharmacist was not available to dress the wounds and there was nothing that could be done for him. "Several men began having trouble and I saw them drop back," Paul remembered.

These men were never seen again; they were trapped in the deep countryside during winter. They lacked the ability to move and the Germans apparently did not have the means to help them. Blisters "caused a lot of problems," Paul noted with characteristic understatement. There were no ambulances or motorized vehicles of any kind; nor did Paul ever see a horse-drawn cart that might be used to help POWs who could no longer walk (this does not mean that such a cart or carts did not exist). There was no Red Cross presence.

The second critical problem confronting the marchers pertained to drinking water. With no potable water available during the day, the POWs had no choice but to hydrate at day's end and into the night and morning, and in this regard many did not have the good fortune like Paul to possess a life saving piece of equipment—a simple tin cup. The problem started the first night. Without a cup, thirsty men were unable to adequately hydrate themselves. Also, apparently a number of marchers—not necessarily in Paul's group, but in the groups as a whole, either did not receive or didn't heed the advice about drinking only boiled water.

According to the 1947 testimony of Major Caplan, the failure by the Germans to supply every POW marcher with a drinking cup was an oversight amounting to criminal negligence. The marchers who could not drink adequate amounts of boiled water during the nightly encampments consequently resorted, in desperation, to drinking tainted roadside water during the marches. The Germans enforced no rudimentary sanitation plans, such as calling for the marchers to urinate and defecate on say, only the left hand side of the road, and consequently the groundwater on both sides became contaminated. A number of marchers ended up drinking water contaminated by earlier marchers, and Major Caplan testified that many took ill and died of typhoid fever because of this oversight. This became a crisis within days of February 6.

Caplan also believed that potable water should have been provided en route by the Germans. Paul said about this: "We drank when we got to our destination and then we usually drank coffee because we did not know how pure the water was." He added: "I wouldn't have wanted to try this in the summer."

The roads in Poland were dirt, Paul related, "but as we got nearer to Germany they were asphalt." This didn't matter, however, as in both countries the marchers proceeded over packed down, or rutted snow.

Paul confirmed that he never saw the camp commandant after that morning assembly. Bombach, undoubtedly aware of what the Red Army would do to him if he were captured, had gone ahead and caught a ferryboat in order to put more distance between himself and the Russians.[12] Although Paul never saw the commandant again, Bombach remained in command of *The Black March* for a period of 53 days after its start.

As the days of the first week wore on, the hardships increased. Some men started out carrying reading books and even small musical instruments, packed in the false hope that a modicum of enjoyment might be eked out along the way. Those had been tossed aside. Also those heavy tin cans—powdered milk for instance—got thrown away. "Anything not needed got quickly pitched," Paul remembered.

The incessant cold of winter made its impact. There was wind chill to contend with and Paul remembered times when he shivered uncontrollably. Asked about the temperature and whether it was near or below zero degrees, Paul revealed a determination that he and others had quickly developed: "We didn't pay much attention to the temperature," Paul answered. "It was either cold or it wasn't cold. We were more interested in where we were, where we were going and where the food was."

The only break Paul and the others received during this period was, surprisingly, the sub-zero temperature. "We had mostly snow, very little rain," Paul said. The snow could be flicked off, keeping Paul and his bedroll dry.

On the march there were no warming fires at intervals along the way, Paul noted. He also noted: "We didn't have heavy socks." Frostbite was a problem, and Paul both suffered from it and witnessed it seriously afflicting others. He explained that after one march his toes had turned color, but that the next day they were OK. "They did not turn black," he said. Others were not so fortunate. "Lost toes were common," he indicated. Asked if anything could be done for these stricken men, he replied: "No. We were on our own after the medical guy left." If someone could not make the march in the morning, he would stay in the barn. Whether the Germans were able to assist him after the column left, Paul never knew.

In some groups there was a shortage of overcoats. A POW might wear a coat for an hour, then lend it out for an hour, then take it back and so forth. This was cited as an example of heroic behavior—and no doubt was. This sharing did not need to be done in Paul's group, however. "Everyone had a coat," he confirmed.

Paul explained that there was no set pattern for stopping the column for a rest break, but rather a stop was made whenever the guards felt like imbibing schnapps. "It's their national drink," he observed, "but not one shared with us." In the evenings the guards bivouacked a short distance from the POWs. "It's hard to tell what they ate because they were off to one side," Paul recalled. "They had their own fire, and I think they had a lot of real bread," which was something Paul and the other POWs longed for. Many of them were in their seventies," Paul said about his captors, "probably retired military." He reiterated that they were replaced often.

As the first week wore on Paul's hunger pains increased but there was nothing he could do about it; he had not yet learned how to forage for farm food, but that would happen reasonably soon. His immediate hope was for a shipment of Red Cross parcels to find its way to him.

Paul did not remember any severe snowstorms or blizzards that first week but this was not the recollection of other Black Marchers. When asked if the visibility ever got so poor in Poland that that one might experience white out and get lost, Paul laughed. "We were always on a road," he commented, indicating "No." He added: "We hoped the guards knew where we were going. We weren't always sure!"

At this time a number of POW groups started taking different routes west; some were able to take the same ferryboat as the commandant; other groups, including Paul's, marched around the body of water the boat crossed. The experiences of groups were different and their stories were often, and understandably, contradictory. Some POWs viewed the German guards in a harsh light; others, like Paul, had a less harsh assessment.

By the end of the first week a routine had set in. Arriving at a barn, the first order of business would be to start a fire to provide warmth and to boil drinking water. "We had the fires outside," Paul explained. Also, "some of the barns had stoves that we used for warming." Extreme caution was used inside straw-filled barns, however, not to use matches as flashlights.

Next, a detail would find an outside area to be used as a latrine. No trenches would be dug, the ground being frozen solid and the marchers having neither the strength nor the tools to dig in any event. Then would come the hours of sipping "steaming hot, freshly brewed German ersatz coffee," Paul said, referring to the awful tasting butter-grease that kept him alive. Practically every account of *The Black March* mentions this beverage; some referred to it as "tea." There was no ability for a Black Marcher to cleanse his body before bunking down; it was far too cold to remove any garments. At sleep time: "We teamed up when we got into a barn," Paul indicated. "Four blankets are better than two."

As thirsty as he got while on the move, Paul never succumbed to the temptation to eat snow or drink ground water. He did experience bouts of diarrhea or even dysentery, however—and he mentioned that all of the marchers did. Paul could not remember whether he experienced periods of fever and shakes but thought that he probably did. "There were days when there was not much incentive to go on, but one did."

Paul explained that he made several friends during the march, one of whom was a musician from Missouri who played a number of instruments. "Early in the march . . . [he] began to have problems with his feet," Paul said. "Every day he would tell us how they hurt and all of us urged him to keep plugging along. One day after a break he just refused to move. Several fellows helped him get to the back of the line. That was the last time we ever saw him. This happened to several others who had medical problems. In order to be fair to the Germans, these people may have been given some medical care. We will never know."

Telling is the fact that Paul could not remember this man's name or the names of any of his other friends on *The Black March*. Asked if he ever witnessed men crawling because they could not walk, Paul replied: "Almost," and then reflected: "I think they would give up before they started crawling. They would sit there on the side of the road and we had to keep moving. [We'd] . . . help them and make them comfortable, and then there'd be a guard on you and you had to catch back up with your group." The toughest part, per Paul, was never learning what happened to these men—not even to this day. Paul also had to question whether the men's loved ones learned anything.

Paul explained that the guards did not threaten the POWs overtly with bayonets or nudge them with rifle butts. "The only thing is," Paul said, "as long as you were helping the fellow [move along] they [the guards] didn't bother you. But as soon as you got him settled, you were advised to get back in the column."

Of the guards using their weapons to prod marchers along, Paul laughed: "They [the guards] were having trouble carrying the heavy rifles!" he joked. "I'm not sure the guards could have used the rifles on us."

As Paul and the others in the column approached the German border they passed through Polish population centers and encountered refugees. At this late stage in World War II there were millions of desperate, displaced persons all over Europe; Paul would see quite a number of them. "Many of these people were not in better shape than we were," Paul opined, and referred to these unfortunate people as "misplaced persons." He described them as: "poorly clothed and without any means to buy things. They just wandered around." He added: "War is not man's greatest achievement."

"We didn't have any idea when we crossed into Germany," Paul said, explaining that there was no remnant of the pre-war border such as a gatehouse, customs office or other identifying structures. Even the architecture remained unchanged. "There were no signs, border guards or anything," Paul added. "When we finally saw some town signs printed in German we knew we had crossed over." Paul joked: "We didn't have a passport."

He arrived in Swinemünde, a port city where there was a large Nazi naval base, on February 15. As the crow flies, the distance he had travelled from Stalag Luft IV was approximately 110 miles. His group had to travel around a large body of water, however, to get to this spot, and the actual distance he walked over a nine-day period was approximately 160 miles.

Major Caplan had been responsible for the well being of 3,000 marchers but not Paul and his group. Caplan arrived at Swinemünde the day before Paul and, as stated, gave testimony before the Army JAG after the war. The question put to him during the inquiry was: "What sort of shelter was provided?" He answered:

On February 14, 1945 Section C of Stalag Luft #4 had marched approximately 35 kilometers [22 miles]. There were many stragglers and sick men who could barely keep up. That night the entire column slept in a cleared area in the woods near Schweinemunde. It had rained a good bit of the day and the ground was soggy, but it froze before morning. We had no shelter whatever and were not allowed to forage for firewood. The ground we slept on was littered by the feces of dysenteric prisoners who had stayed there previously. There were many barns in the vicinity, but no effort was made to accommodate us there. There were hundreds of sick men in the column that night. I slept with one that was suffering from pneumonia.

Paul was asked to comment on Caplan's testimony, and also an account written after the war by a B-17 top turret gunner named John "Pappy" Paris. Paris, who ate snow because he had had nothing to drink for a period of 24 hours, wrote a compelling narrative relating to the same period of the march.

The first weeks of the march saw all of us suffering from diarrhea and dysentery. Many had colds and some had symptoms of pneumonia. When I felt I could go no further, I would tell myself that each foot I put in front of the other brought me one step closer to home. Had I been marching east instead of west I am not sure I could have endured. In addition to my exhaustion and dysentery was the racking pain in my shoulders. The sixth day of the Black March was the turning point for me. All day long I faced a cold wind, with alternate onslaughts of sleet and icy rain. That night they put me in a cold and drafty barn with no food, just a few nibbles from my dwindling rations. The constant dampness never gave me an opportunity to dry out. There were so many kriegies [slang for the German word "kriegsgefangener," meaning "war prisoner"] packed into a small barn that I was unable to stretch out but was compelled to sleep doubled up like a pretzel . . . On the following morning the sun was out even though it was clear and cold. I marched with the sun on my back and soon felt dry and refreshed. I came to the conclusion that my body was able to endure many times greater punishment than I once thought possible. If my will continues strong I shall be able to suffer unbelievable hardships and survive.[13]

Paul responded to each statement. "As I said, I can't remember that there was any time that we had to sleep in the open. There was always some kind of a shelter, usually a barn. Yeah, it got packed, and actually it might have been better off that way."

As regards Sergeant Paris' plight, Paul observed: "It sounds like he had a lot worse time than I did." When Paul said this, a listener could not but help think that Paul had made no mention that his food had been stolen the first night of the march.

Paul had no recollection of that sunny day at the end of the first week. He remembered finally receiving some food, however, in the form of Red Cross parcels. He also remembered something else: "I prayed to get home, and I got home."

Asked what kept him going that first week, Paul responded, "It was the encouragement I got from my fellow prisoners. We shared each other's feelings and had a common ground together. We were confident that the war would end and that Germany would not win, but we did not know when the end was going to come. We just had to hang in until the day of victory arrived."

Paul came up with another reason why he survived: "As I think back, now," he said, "I think that medic [the British pharmacist] who advised us what to do and what not to do had a big part in getting us through. In addition to the water, he also told us to sleep together and share blankets. This might not have occurred to us."

Asked if he was upset with the Germans because so many POWs had perished from causes that could have arguably been prevented, Paul gave a thought-provoking response: "Looking at it from their side," he expounded, "if you're on the German side, you're looking at an enemy. Why would they give special treatment to an enemy? The German guards as a group were quite friendly, as long as one did not challenge their authority, but the higher officials, well, they had a different attitude."

Paul concluded, pointing out that yes, there had been a lack of supervision on the part of the Germans in the evacuation, but he questioned—was it that critically bad in a relative sense? "The Germans did some bad things," he asserted, "and so did we." Without being prompted, he offered as an example: "Look at the bombing of Dresden."

Paul never smoked but he used the wrappers of Chesterfield Cigarette packs from Red Cross parcels to record the names of towns that he would pass through, writing them down as they appeared on road signs. Swinemünde was the first name he recorded.

CHAPTER NINE

Operation Thunderclap Continues—Dresden

"It was the largest bonfire that I ever saw in my life," Addison Bartush said, shaking his head slowly from side to side at the memory.

Addison had been an eyewitness to a very controversial event in World War II: an occurrence that continues to be examined and argued by scholars and intellectuals today. Not only that, he had special status when he witnessed this event: he had been relieved—for this combat mission of all missions—from flying duty.

The USAAF sent Addison out as an official observer; as such he stood in the waist of the aircraft and looked out of the large gun ports and focused on anything within his view. Addison could look directly down, or towards the front or rear. Addison recollected flying the mission in a newer model B-17 where the rectangular shaped ports were staggered in the plane's fuselage, one forward and one aft on opposite sides so the gunners could operate without bumping into each other. Addison stood between these two men as a third set of eyes.

But unlike the gunners, who only looked for fast moving specs in the sky that might spell trouble, Addison took in more. He assessed the spread of his squadron's formation, the approaching flak patterns and moreover, viewed what might be happening on the ground. He transmitted his observations, as needed, on the intercom to stations on the B-17. He was expected to exercise the judgment of an experienced combat officer and exercise sound discretion in regard to the information he might choose to convey.

For this eventful and controversial mission, Addison took in the "big picture" in a way that he never could from inside a cockpit. Pilots must constantly monitor positions and tend to the unending business of staying aloft, which included instrument reading, and in so doing they missed some of the action. Observers, on the other hand, stood to take in much more. Addison served as an observer on three occasions but his other experiences were unlike this one.

Perhaps the most notorious raid of the Allied air campaign in Europe, the bombing of Dresden was significant in many ways. It showcased the ruthless efficiency that had been developed by near war's end for deep-penetration "carpet bombing"; the technique used was to intersperse high explosive bombs that made kindling out of old buildings, with incendiaries to produce a devastating firestorm result. The bombing foreshadowed the Cold War and witnessed the last propaganda coup for the Nazi misinformation machine. Lastly, Dresden left little doubt that the Americans had fully partnered with the British on a new air war strategy to shorten the conflict—a strategy that is widely acknowledged today as not having been militarily successful.

It was just twelve weeks before the Nazi surrender, and some 3,900 tons of bombs would be dropped in four raids over a two-day period on Dresden, the beautiful baroque capital of the German state of Saxony. The conflagration that ensued would consume the city center and 13 square miles of surrounding area.[1] The number of civilians killed is not accurately known, but was staggering.

Addison recalled being scheduled, briefed and readied for a daylight raid on Dresden on February 13 but the American mission was scrubbed because of weather. He remembered this event particularly because he was, for the first time, to be a first pilot.

Two hundred and fifty British heavy bombers struck in the first wave that night, followed by twice that number two hours later.[2]

A British intelligence officer spoke at a pre-mission briefing:

No. 5 Group will open the attack with 250 aircraft to get the fires going with a time on target of 2215 hours. Their marking point will be the sports stadium. There will be diversionary attacks on Bohlen, Magdeburg, Bonn, and Nuremberg to confuse the German fighter controllers as to the main target. One hour and forty-five minutes later, 1 Group will attack with 500 aircraft. The delay will ensure that all emergency services will probably have been called in from outside Dresden, so our attack will knock those out as well. Pathfinders will provide our master bomber, whose call sign will be "King Cole." The Main Force call sign will be "Strongman." The main threat from the enemy tonight will be flak. His fighter aircraft should be chasing the "window" feint force, which we hope will be indicating to the enemy that Frankfurt, Mainz, Darmstadt or Mannheim are the main targets. By the time we get into the picture they will be running out of fuel and therefore landing. But just in case, our night-striking Mosquitoes will be patrolling the enemy's rendezvous beacons and airfields. Now, any questions?[3]

Three hundred and eleven Flying Fortresses, including Addison's, arrived over the burning city at noon the next day, Wednesday, February 14, 1945. "It was flames shooting through smoke," Addison recalled, remembering what the aftermath of the two British raids looked like. The British pre-briefing foreshadowed what turned out to be a flawless mission—the Germans had been fooled as to the target, an extremely deep penetration raid had been accomplished with minimal air casualties, the weather had cooperated, and an entire city had been destroyed. Returning, the British airmen were ecstatic.

At this late stage in the war, the British and Americans were so competent and dominant in the art of air warfare that they could do practically anything they wanted against the Germans, and they did. In 1945 no target was safe in Nazi Germany.

The 91st Bomb Group flew over the city of Dresden on the 14th and 15th of February. As stated, Addison flew as an observer on the February 14 mission, and it turned out that on this mission the 91st did not drop its bombs on Dresden but rather proceeded to a secondary target. Other U.S. bomb groups did hit Dresden heavily on February 14, however, and again the following day.

On the 14th Addison witnessed firsthand the carnage inflicted on this city. He saved a *Stars and Stripes* newspaper that reported the attack as a joint Anglo-American raid. The accuracy of this newspaper article would be publicly challenged by the Soviet Union. The *Stars and Stripes* headline read: *Eighth Hits Dresden to Help Reds.*

The heart of Germany rocked with tremendous explosions yesterday as more than 1,300 Eighth Air Force heavy bombers dropped tons of high explosives and incendiaries on transportation and industrial targets in three important cities—including Dresden, still blazing from the effects of a double RAF blow the night before, and threatened by the advance, less than 70 miles away, of Red Army troops. Both the Eighth Air Force and RAF attacks on Dresden were in support of one offensive of Marshal Koniev's forces, smashing toward the city in a bid to cut the Reich in two . . .

A mission history of the 91st explained what happened that day:

A very long mission was flown on February 14th when the 91st went all the way to Dresden. However, there was so much smoke rising from the city as a result of the Royal Air Force raid the night before the 91st had to seek out targets of opportunity in Prague, Czechoslovakia. Bombing was done visually with good results. [4]

Following the Dresden raids, Nazi propaganda minister Dr. Joseph Goebbels pounced upon a published report of an American journalist in the Associated Press to the effect the attacks were designed to kill as many German civilians as possible, i.e., that the raids were out and out terror bombings. Goebbels issued his own press release falsely inflating the number of dead to hundreds of thousands. He also stated (without specific knowledge) that a million refuges were in the city at the time of the bombing. The press in neutral Sweden combined the two stories into one and ran with it. In a very short period the news of an atrocity had international legs. [5]

After the word spread about the very high number of civilian deaths, the Soviets backed away from ever requesting the air raid in the first instance, or even needing it to help their advancing army. Their disownment served the Soviet interest of painting their British and American allies in the worst light possible in the eyes of the people that they were about to conquer and whose territories they would occupy. The Soviets portrayed themselves as concerned about civilian casualties. [6]

Addison had no recollection of this Soviet reaction, "but I find it interesting," he said. There was one thing he was certain about, however: at the early morning briefing on February 14, no mention of the Red Army or the Soviet Union was made. "We were not told that," Addison noted emphatically, responding to the question whether he ever heard that the Soviets had requested Dresden be attacked or that the attack would be made to assist the Red Army. Without being prompted, Addison then volunteered this: "It would have been better if we had stuck to bombing oil refineries."

Asked how the Dresden raid differed from the raid over Berlin eleven days earlier, Addison responded: "At Berlin I saw buildings. At Dresden I saw no buildings, only fire and smoke everywhere." This difference is likely explained by being first, as opposed to last, over a target area.

Wearing goggles to protect his eyes and dressed in an electric suit and boots and the fleece-lined gloves and helmet of a waist gunner, and donning an oxygen mask, earphones and speakerphone, Addison described his job: "I stood practically all of the time. And I'd be going from one side to the other side continually," he said, meaning from starboard to port. The wind chill from the open gun ports was ferocious, he noted.

Addison also noted there was no idle talk on the intercom. "Not when you are deep in enemy territory," he related. "You kept your mouth shut unless there was something important to report." As for what he might say when he did speak, Addison indicated: "Enemy fighter sightings of course. Also other squadrons like the 323rd or the 401st being out of position. Or that they might be flying tighter than we were, that sort of thing." On February 14, 1945, however, he remembered saying something unique over the intercom: "I told them this was the largest bonfire that I ever had seen," he said for a second time.

As for enemy fighter activity over Dresden, after reflecting a moment, Addison answered that he did not recollect the ship's gunners engaging. "I do not . . . think so," he replied. Addison's answer is consistent with the *USAAF Chronology* that reported only one Luftwaffe plane being downed that day in the whole of the ETO.

The Luftwaffe absence over Dresden notwithstanding, this extra-long mission was no milk run. Of the 311 B-17s dispatched to Dresden on February 14, five were lost, three damaged beyond repair and fifty-four damaged. Four U.S. airmen were killed, fifteen wounded and forty-nine were missing in action.[7] The overall casualty rate was slightly over 2%. While not as bad as the casualty rates the Eighth Air Force often experienced in 1943 and 1944 (5% to 15%), 2% was still significant. "There was always some flak coming up," Addison observed.

"We were to hit a marshalling yard there," Addison indicated, "one that we never saw because of the smoke." Strangely, or perhaps not, Addison had no recollection whatsoever of his bomb group diverting to Prague and hitting targets there. One thing for sure, however, was the fact that what he saw at Dresden shocked him. "There was a city down there," Addison said, "but there was no city, just a big fire. It was gigantic."

It was mentioned to Addison that historians had reviewed the contemporaneous writings of British and American aircrews who participated in the Dresden raid; that is, letters and journals written immediately after the event, and that these records suggested that those who flew the Dresden missions had not been, in any special sense, emotionally troubled by it. The writings suggest Dresden was initially viewed pretty much as any other combat mission.

Addison was asked: "Did you not have a sense, when you returned that afternoon, that is, February 14, 1945, that what you witnessed was morally wrong?"

"I suppose I didn't realize that," Addison responded. He added: "We were in a war." Addison was not defensive in his response, nor should he have been. He had been a young man doing what his country told him to do and in the middle of a desperate struggle for victory. Asked if the Dresden raid had no military strategy attached to it, Addison appropriately responded: "That is easy to say now. We did not know it at the time, however." He added, stoically: "When it came to bombing cities, they were all bad."

Dresden had been a man-made hell. Many of the people there had died not by burning or concussion, but rather suffocation. The conflagrations sucked the oxygen out of the air even in the bomb-proofs.

The initial news reports of the bombing of Dresden were received by the American and British public as pretty much war business as usual — simply that another German city had been hit. The Associated Press story of a terror bombing created a stir that passed rather quickly.

It took the Nazis a month to compile an official count of the fatalities caused by the raids. Horrific as these numbers were, they were a fraction of what had been released in their propaganda effort, and the official numbers were not made public until after the war. They estimated that 18,350 residents of Dresden died in the attack; their bodies had been identified, tagged and later cremated on pyres set up throughout the city by SS veterans of the

Cadet Addison Bartush while attending twin-engine school at George Field, Lawrenceville, IL, during the winter of 1943–44. Deploying to Europe as a B-17 co-pilot in the fall of 1944, Addison's first mission was a difficult one and it was followed the next day by a tragedy for the Bishop Crew. Overcoming fear and adversity, Addison matriculated to become a combat-seasoned first pilot. After the war Addison joined the family business and continued flying. "I would rent small airplanes just for the fun of taking them up," he said.—*Addison Bartush Collection*

One of approximately 4,500 survivors of the infamous *Black March*, after the war Paul Lynch obtained a PhD degree in bio-chemistry and physiology at Cornell University and had a long scientific career with the Beltsville Agricultural Research Center in Maryland. Many decades later, reflective over the suffering he experienced and witnessed in World War II, Paul commented: "War is not man's greatest achievement." This photo was taken after Paul entered basic training in the fall of 1943. —*Paul Lynch Collection*

Cadet Addison Bartush mastered twin-engine flight in this model trainer and affectionately referred to it as the "Beaverboard Bomber" since much of the plane was made from pressed wood to conserve metal for real bombers. Circa winter 1943–44, George Field, Lawrenceville, IL.—Addison Bartush Collection

Co-pilot Addison Bartush in the cockpit of a B-17 during crew training at Gulfport Army Airfield, Gulfport, MS, circa August 1944.—*Addison Bartush Collection*

Waist gunner Paul Lynch exiting a B-17, Gulfport Army Airfield, Gulfport, MS, circa August 1944.—*Addison Bartush Collection*

B-17s in the flight line, Army Airfield, Gulfport MS circa August, 1944.
—*Paul Lynch Collection*

The Bishop Crew at Gulfport Army Airfield, circa September 1944. Enlisted men standing from left to right: Robertson, Cumings, Monkman, Sheen, Lynch, Kendall. Officers kneeling left to right: Peacock, Miller, Bartush and Bishop.—*Addison Bartush Collection*

Arial photo of USAAF Air Station Bassingbourn taken by Addison Bartush. 1955 RAF
photo (inset) shows proximity of hangers and other facilities.—*Addison Bartush Collection*

Maj. Immanuel J. Klette (smiling at camera) with Brig. Gen. Gross and Maj. Hudson.

Prepping for a mission at Station 121 USAAF Bassingbourn, UK. As the armorers load bombs, a mechanic works on an engine without the protection of a ramp. In 1944–45, 91st aircraft markings were red.—*Marion Havelaar Collection (Ethell)*

Father Michael Ragan

B-17 flying through a flak alley.

Left: This photo was taken in March 1943 before Charles Cumings of Neenah, Wisconsin trained to become a top turret gunner. Later as flight engineer/gunner for the Bishop Crew while training at Gulfport, MS, Cumings was the one who inadvertently got his plane commander Dave Bishop into trouble over the increased carburation incident. Sergeant Cumings perished on this, his first combat mission.—*Paul Lynch Collection*

Center: The Wild Hare was shot down on a November 26, 1944 mission to the Altenbeken Viaduct with nine men aboard, including the six men from the Bishop Crew whose photos appear on these pages. The three non-Bishop crewmembers that also flew this mission were: Lt. Robert J. Flint (POW), S/Sgt. Daniel V. Hiner (KIA), and S/Sgt Bartolomeo Zanotto (KIA)

Below: Although they had an altercation while training to become crewmembers, waist gunner Paul Lynch and radioman John Kendall put their differences aside for the good

of the team. This photograph was taken at the end of their training in Gulfport, MS just before the crew flew to Maine. Lynch would witness Kendall cut down by Luftwaffe gunfire. —*Paul Lynch Collection*

First pilot Dave Bishop takes charge: a training mission flown out of Gulfport Army Airfield, Gulfport, MS circa August 1944. Bishop was captured and became a POW after the crash of The Wild Hare.—*Addison Bartush Collection*

Non-complaining and extremely well liked, tail gunner Owen Monkman was killed on the mission to Altenbeken. His parents in Montana endured the agony of long-term hope quashed: the U.S. Army Air Force changed Owen's status from "missing in action" to "killed in action" in August 1946. This portrait was likely taken during or after basic training.—*Paul Lynch Collection*

The survivor of a harrowing parachute jump after being wounded, Navigator/Flight Officer Robert J. "RJ" Miller wanted few reminders of what he endured during the war. He had little contact with former Bishop crewmates. Photograph taken Gulfport Army Airfield, Gulfport MS, circa August 1944. Former Gulfport crewmate Ray Peacock wrote to Addison: "Tell RJ to stay out of the crap games." — *Paul Lynch Collection*

Kriegsgefangenenpost

Postkarte

GEPRÜFT
An
1

Mr. = Mrs. Roger Lynch

Empfangsort: 59 Grand St.
town
Land: Leominster, Mass.
country
Landesteil U.S.A.
(Provinz usw.)
county

Gebührenfrei!

12309
U.S. CENSOR

Dulag-Luft Germany

Date 7, Dec. 1944

(No. of Camp only; as may be directed by the Commandant of the Camp.)

I have been taken prisoner of war in Germany. I am in good health — slightly wounded (cancel accordingly).

We will be transported from here to another Camp within the next few days. Please don't write until I give new address.

Kindest regards

Christian Name and Surname: Glenn Paul Lynch
Rank: S/Sgt.
Detachment: U.S. Army Air Force

(No further details. — Clear legible writing.)

The "Postkarte" that POW Paul Lynch mailed on December 7, 1944 to his parents in Massachusetts from the Dulag Luft interrogation center near Frankfurt. Such notification was a requirement of the Geneva Convention.—*Paul Lynch Collection*

Below: A POW formation at Stalag Luft IV. Sergeant Paul Lynch and the other POWs experienced this twice daily, in the mornings and afternoons. "It was a head count," Paul explained. This warm weather photo was taken prior to Paul's arrival at the camp. —*Donald Kremper Collection*

Perspective of Lager "A," and barracks I, 2, and 3 photographed from a guard tower. The "warning rail" running near the barracks was as close as POWs were permitted to approach the fences without being fired upon. The outer fence was electrified; note the shadow of the guard tower.— *Donald Kremper Collection*

Winter in northern Poland was severe as attested by this photo of four U.S. airmen relaxing and posing on a large snow bank at Stalag Luft IV. Note the smiles, no gloves and open flight jacket. This photo was taken in 1944 but the month is unknown —*Dawn Trimble Bunyak Collection*

"Mist, fog, snow, frost, and drizzle," precludes air operations by the Eight Air Force for days on end in mid December 1944. U.S. troops besieged in the Battle of the Bulge could not be assisted from the air. Taken at USAAF Air Station Bassingbourn, vehicles used for towing bombs, servicing and fueling B-17s sit idle.— *Marion Havelaar Collection (Harlick)*

Soon to be famous Rhapsody in Red B-17 #297959. Photo by Addison Bartush, USAAF Air Station Bassingbourn, UK, circa February 1945.—*Addison Bartush Collection*

Twenty-six bombers appear in this photo taken through a radio hatch of a bomber flying with a lower formation. On a typical mission day the 91st would put up a total of approximately 36 B-17s, representing three squadrons.— *Marion Havelaar Collection (Harlick)*

Coming back from a bombing mission and no longer in danger, Addison enjoys male entertainment in the February, 1945 edition of *Esquire* magazine. At this point in the war his confidence has returned. Note his dress for cold conditions.—*Addison Bartush Collection*

A strike photo from the February 3, 1945 raid on Berlin that commenced Operation Thunderclap. Wind driven smoke rising from earlier bombings obscures whole city blocks. Templehof airdrome is centered in the photo.—*Marion Havelaar Collection*

Operation Thunderclap continues—Dresden after aerial attacks of 13–14 February 1945. The sculpture "Gute" ("Goodness") by August Schreitmüller.

February 6, 1945: the start of the 500-mile, three-month *Black March* from Stalag Luft IV. Approximately 6,000 POWs made the march, mostly American airmen, and 1,500 died. Per POW Paul Lynch, the marchers divided into groups of approximately 200 each, and six guards, three to a side, escorted. A number of marchers carried improvised tin can-laden backpacks that soon caused spinal or shoulder problems. The groups were kept apart to prevent massing for a rebellion. Note a lead group in the distance.—*Donald Kremper Collection*

Douglas A-20A, similar to the three planes Paul witnessed in action the morning of April 24, 1945. Forty-nine percent of the planes supplied to the Soviet Union through Lend-Lease were A-20s.

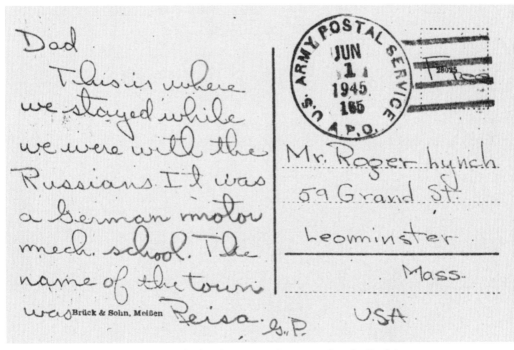

Dad

This is where we stayed while we were with the Russians. It was a German motor mech. school. The name of the town was Reisa. G.P.

Brück & Sohn, Meißen

Mr. Roger Lynch
59 Grand St.
Leominster
Mass.
USA

Postcard showing the technical school in Riesa, Germany that the Red Army used as a collection center for U.S. citizens (former POWs of the Nazis) per the Yalta agreement. Paul was held at this center from May 12 to May 25, 1945, when he and approximately 160 other Americans were repatriated to U.S. military control. As indicated by its postmark, Paul mailed this card home on June 1, probably from Camp Lucky Strike in France.— *Paul Lynch Collection*

April 25, 1945, the last strategic mission for the Eighth Air Force in World War II—airport attack, Pilsen, Czechoslovakia. Note part of a cumulous cloud that impeded visibility. Photo source: Headquarters 1st Air Division newsletter First Over Germany, Vol. 1. No. 4 dated May 5, 1945.—*Addison Bartush Collection*

A group of unidentified American G.I.s at their moment of liberation May 2, 1945. Sergeant Paul Lynch and his fellow escapers were "liberated" by the Red Army on April 24 but not returned to U.S. military control until over a month later.—*Donald Kremper Collection*

Jack, Addison & Chuck—guests of their father Stephen J. Bartush at the Rotary Club of Detroit, Summer, 1945.—*Addison Bartush Collection*

Left to right: Paul Lynch, Dave Bishop and Addison Bartush at the 1998 reunion of the 91st Bomb Group. Dave and Addison saw each other occasionally following the war, but this was the first time the three had reunited since 1944. "One can imagine the incredible emotion that we experienced that day," Addison recalled. They joked about again flying together as a team. Dave Bishop lives in Spartanburg, SC, Paul Lynch in Union Bridge, MD, and Addison in Grosse Pointe, MI—all still "unstoppable."—RA 2014.—*Paul Lynch Collection*

Treblinka death camp who were brought in for their expertise in the disposal of human remains. They estimated that another 10,000 non-residents had also perished, as Dresden was packed with transients who were attempting to flee the advancing Soviet army.[8] The non-resident figure may be low; the true number of humans consumed by the super hot fires will never be known. A number of sources—some done objectively and credibly—give varying figures for casualties.

Addison had been especially shocked over what he saw at Dresden, there is no doubt about that. Dresden had been his 14th mission; he had seen enough by then to be battle-hardened. He may have thought he had seen it all, but Dresden changed that perception.

A commentator had this to say about America's participation in the Dresden raids: "By this time the Americans, in the aftermath of the Battle of the Bulge, seemed to have lost their earlier squeamishness about bombing whole cities."[9] *Time-Life Books* noted the British and American ground forces were stalled at the time of the Dresden bombing and that, "Blasting Dresden and other cities in eastern Germany from the air would give Stalin tangible proof of the effort of the British and the Americans on Russia's behalf. . . . Not incidentally, the raids would also remind Stalin of the awesome air power possessed by Britain and the United States."[10]

Asked how he felt about the Dresden bombings today, Addison responded: "I don't think Adolf was of a mind to quit," he noted, "but I cannot justify in a moral sense what I observed that day."

Addison and his wife, Marion, took a boat trip on the Elbe River sometime in the 1990s and ended up visiting Dresden. "You could see that it had been rebuilt," he remarked. "And rather drably so," he added, referring to the years of Communist occupation. Asked if he told anyone about his personal history involving Dresden, he responded in the negative. "They were still anti-American," he said.

The bombing of Dresden was not a one-time event but rather the continuation of *Operation Thunderclap* implemented earlier over Berlin. An encyclopedic reference states the *Thunderclap* plan called for "attacks against cities in the communication zone of the Eastern Front, through which key routes to the east converged. . . . The cities designated as chokepoints where the bombing would be most effective were Berlin, Dresden, Chemnitz and Leipzig."[11] The intent behind *Thunderclap* was to compel Nazi capitulation by inflicting horrendous casualties on the German civilian population[12] and hindering Nazi troop movements at the Red Army front. The casualties were inflicted, but the German soldiers fought on and capitulation was not achieved.

Addison was fortunate that his first mission as pilot had been scrubbed. He never bombed Dresden, but he was a witness to the horror. What he could not appreciate at the time this happened was the debate that the bombings would spark at the highest level of the Nazi government about what might be done in the way of a wartime response.

At the time Dresden was bombed, Paul Lynch was deep inside and travelling through the enemy country.

CHAPTER TEN

Swinemünde to Halle, Nazi Germany

Having survived the critical first ten days of the march, Paul fell into a daily routine involving keeping pace and searching continuously for food. "The longer we stayed on the march, the less frequent those Red Cross packages arrived," he observed. "Once in a while we would arrive at a farm and a few packages would be waiting, but in most instances it was three or four persons to a package. This food didn't last very long." Some of the marchers who smoked cigarettes from the parcels did so for a reason, Paul recollected. "It helped to lessen one's appetite, or so I was told." As hungry as he may have been, Paul resisted that temptation.

"We began looking for alternative sources of food," Paul continued. The POWs succeeded in locating a type of food that had 48 calories per serving, with 2 calories of fat; not sufficient to replace the number of calories burned each day on the march, but enough to keep them from starving to death.[1] "We found that most every farm had rows of kohlrabies covered with a layer of dirt to prevent freezing," Paul explained. "These kohlrabies are root crops that look somewhat like turnips and are used to feed livestock. Most farms had some piles close to the barn, so as soon as we arrived a scouting party would go out and bring back several kohlrabies."

As unappetizing as a continuous diet these tubers must have become to the men, kohlrabies were a traditional food on the European dinner table. They were a good source of dietary fiber and also high in vitamins C and B6. Paul told of the preparation: "We would cover slices of kohlrabies with German ersatz butter grease, fry it on a piece of metal and it would be our bread at night and our toast in the morning."

It was a long, cold winter and the weather was unrelenting. At least one storm temporarily halted the march. "I remember a large German cooperative farm and we stayed there a couple of days," Paul said.

The Chesterfield cigarette wrapper that Paul used to record the names of German cities that he passed through reveals the route that he and his group took through central Germany. From Swinemünde on the Baltic Sea to the north the group proceeded inland, first in a southwesterly direction through the cities of Anklam, Malchin, Waren and Parchim, there making the first of four crossings over the Elbe River, and then in the same direction to the cities of Uelzen and Hannover. At Hannover his column made a sharp left turn and headed in a southeasterly direction passing through Wittenburg and Halle, following roughly the upstream track of the Elbe River. From Halle, Paul would cross the Elbe a final time and make good his escape through the Soviet battle line. The odyssey lasted three months.

Viewing a map, Paul's approximately 500-mile trek through Nazi Germany could be loosely termed "the big circle route" around Berlin. His captors directed the POWs to places where it was perceived, or at least hoped, that the Allies would not be.

"I saw considerable bomb damage in a number of the cities I passed through," Paul said, "but after all these years I cannot remember which cities." When he passed through Anklam, he had no knowledge that the first bombing attack there had been the notorious gunfight at 12,500 feet that the 91st Bomb Group participated in on October 9, 1943, a little over a year before he arrived in England.

As Paul passed through or near to this city, he had no idea that Adolf Hitler and his advisors were then actively weighing the fate of all British and American airman POWs. Without daily BBC news reports, Paul and the other POW marchers were unaware of the firebombing of Dresden. Nor did they know that this event might have changed the German conduct of the war.

On February 19, 1945 Reich Minister Goebbels recommended to the Führer that Hitler publically renounce the Geneva Convention and order the immediate execution of all British and American airmen POWs, upwards of 30,000 men. Apart from being a reprisal for the bombing of Dresden, Goebbels reasoned, such an action would have the additional benefit of so enraging the British and American armies in the field that no white flags of surrender, whether waved by members of the Wehrmacht or by German civilians, would be honored. This, Goebbels argued, would bring about "total war" on both fronts. At the time, the Nazi leadership was concerned that German resistance in the West was not stiff enough.

Hitler ordered the man who would eventually succeed him, Admiral Karl Doenitz, to weigh in on the issue which Doenitz did the following day. A transcript made of the meeting reveals that Doenitz said: "The disadvantages would outweigh the advantages." To this dispassionate but arguably sensible response, however, Doenitz added chillingly: "It would be better in any case to keep up outside appearances and carry out the measures believed necessary without announcing them beforehand."[2]

Hitler took no action.

Had Hitler issued an execution order, it would have been an easy matter for the SS to carry it out on small, remote columns of POWs such as the one Paul Lynch marched in. Many prisoners from Stalag Luft camps had been relocated by this time to other camps or were, like Paul, on the move. Only the large Luftwaffe Stalag Luft I near Barth Germany stood intact at this time with approximately 10,000 airmen-officer POWs. The Allies made contingency plans to put up a fight at the first sign of trouble at this camp, and also a few others of the lesser camps where spy information might be gleaned. Nothing could be planned, however, to attempt to save those POWs being marched.

Oblivious to all of this, Paul and his POW companions trudged on.

"When we passed through cities, guards were on the alert for possible civilian trouble," Paul indicated. "We didn't stop to view sights. Of course we saw bomb damage." Paul elaborated about something important: "We were very careful and wanted to have good communications with our guards at all times because when we went through a city that had been bombed," he said, "the civilians threatened us. Our guards would not let these people come in close."

Paul used the word "hostile" to describe these encounters, and told how thankful he and his fellow POWs were for their guards who "ran them off."

There are a number of documented incidences of Allied POW airmen being murdered by enraged German civilians. There exists also a famous photograph of a withered old man, looking terrified, standing next to a priest and a U.S. Army M.P. He was about to be hanged in a town square for murdering a U.S. airman.

There was one instance along the march that really scared Paul and it did not involve civilians. "One day we were plugging along at a slow pace," Paul related. "I happened to be in the first group and we could see some sort of camp ahead. A little farther down the road we saw it was an SS training camp. We knew it was SS when a group of young, black-shirted boys came storming out of a building and charged us. They came at us with clenched fists, shouting. The guards became very nervous and shouted, 'Snell, snell,' urging us to go faster. The situation was getting ugly."

Paul explained that the SS were approximately 15 to 20 in number and all young males. The camp they came from was a group of buildings surrounded by a perimeter fence and it looked like a school. "I noticed ahead of me that one of the fellows in our group was making a slow move towards the nearest guard. I caught his intentions. He was going to get the guard's gun if possible."

Paul indicated that the gate of the camp was approximately 100 yards from the road that the POW column was on. "I think they were in a class and spotted us through a window," he said. "They came at us on a full run and we did not know if they were armed with pistols."

Paul continued: "I suspected with the first shot from the SS, the guards would fade into the landscape. I looked at the guard nearest to me, and what he carried in his hand, and I figured one flying tackle might put him over and I could get his gun. I started my move and positioned myself only a few feet away from him. I think I had a good chance even though I was weak. He was quite old. I didn't intend to be cut down by a group of fanatic SS without a fight. I looked back and saw others [POWs] making their moves. The guards were so intent on watching the SS that they couldn't see what was taking shape. I hoped that none of us would make a premature move."

As the SS got closer Paul saw there were no officers or noncoms in the group, only boys. When it was discerned that this would only be fist waving and shouting and nothing more, the crisis defused. "Our guards signaled for us to move along quickly and quietly," Paul said. "The line kept moving and the SS kept shouting and threatening but no guns appeared. Our first group got past the SS, then the next group got past and finally we all made it. We breathed a sigh of relief. It could have been bloody if guns had been introduced."

Paul was quite certain that the SS command had put the boys up to this antic. "I suspect these kids were encouraged to hassle us by their instructors who remained in the building watching," he opined. "Again, once we realized they weren't armed it became a different situation. We were used to fist waving and shouting by that time, believe me. When the POWs that followed us saw us get through unharmed, well, that was a big boost for them."

Paul and the other POWs had been fortunate. An irony about this incident is that as terrifying as it must have been, from a danger perspective it was probably less risky than the encounters with enraged civilians in the bombed-out cities. Even though these "boys" were likely tall, as the SS recruited from the largest and strongest specimens of German youth, the SS behaved not as a mob but rather as a robot: killing when ordered to do so. In the Third Reich the execution of U.S. and British POWs needed the approval of Hitler.

By the time Paul reached Hannover, he had completed close to two-thirds of his march and the weather was moderating. This city had been a major industrial center and it was bombed 88 times during the war. Ninety percent of the town center was destroyed.[3] Reading about the systematic demolition of this city, one cannot help think of Addison's comment: "When it came to bombing cities, they were all bad."

All Paul said about Hannover was: "To be honest I can't recall going through it. I suspect it would have stuck in my memory with all that destruction. It is on my list of cities, yes." It was at Hannover that the column doubled back towards the Elbe River. "We kept moving south at a slow but steady pace," Paul related. "I think we were in the Magdeburg area [located between Hannover and Wittenburg] and the Red Cross packages came less frequently. Transportation in Germany was almost non-existent."

The International Red Cross made an effort during this timeframe to truck in emergency aid from Geneva to Allied POWs on the move. The Reich's POW Administrator, SS General Gottlob Berger, granted permission for a fleet of trucks to enter and travel throughout Germany. The trucks were flatbed and painted white, and each had a white canopy bearing large Red Cross markings.[4] The trucks traveled in convoy over assigned routes known to Allied pilots and they were so clearly marked that only once were they mistakenly strafed.

Paul never saw these trucks but made an insightful observation about them: "I expect this would have been a difficult project to work," he observed. "Civilians and displaced persons would have given them trouble."

Paul agreed that another problem with the relief effort was the fact that at that time POW columns were fanned out all over Germany. Finding them or coordinating locations for food delivery to them was difficult to near impossible.

"The feeling of hunger was always with us," Paul said. "The civilians were being pinched quite badly also, but at least they didn't have to march every day. We were not getting any news from the outside world so things looked bleak and discouraging. The old guards were being replaced so frequently with more old guards that it was difficult to get much information from them. I didn't think they liked the situation any better than we did and probably resented doing the job."

Paul told of a meal he would never forget: "I can recall the evening when we pulled into a farm for the night and were almost mixed with the occupant-residents. Our guards didn't seem to care. A young girl came close to me and a friend from Arkansas and I said "Guten Abend." She smiled. I had a thought and dug out the only thing I had that most Germans wanted and that was a bar of Ivory soap. It was still in its wrapper, never opened! She recognized it immediately. "Haben sie zwei eier fur ein Stuck Seife," I said in my fractured German. It worked. She ran into the house and brought two eggs in her hand and we swapped. That night my friend and I each ate an egg along with the ersatz coffee and fried kohlrabi."

Paul passed through the historic city of Wittenberg where Martin Luther in 1517 nailed his 95 theses to the door of All Saints', the Castle Church, initiating the Protestant Reformation. The Allies had spared the Wittenberg city center from bombing. "I was not aware of the town's historic significance at the time," Paul said, then added caustically: "History wasn't of much importance."

Paul learned of President Roosevelt's death on April 12, 1945, ". . . from the rumor line. We wondered if it was true and how it might change our conditions, if at all."

Towards the end of Paul's march he observed a long line of U.S. P-47 fighter planes, or Thunderbolts, performing a dive-bombing mission. He described them as peeling off and coming straight down, dropping their bombs and then returning straight up, gracefully "hung by their props." Paul was proud at the professionalism displayed by these USAAF pilots. "We were far away from what they were attacking," Paul explained. "We did not see the target." Paul heard the bombs go off but there was no follow-up strafing.

Passing through the last city on his cigarette paper log, Halle, the food situation became desperate, and they marched for a week without much food. Their pace was down to a shuffle. Paul made a special prayer one night, promising to always believe if God would provide some food. Later that same evening some Red Cross packages finally did get through. They were delivered by the "thinnest living horse I have ever seen," he remembered. The POWs consumed these rations, "ten persons to a box."

Paul described what it was like crossing over the Elbe River the last time on his forced march, this time heading east: "We crossed it and were in a fairly large-sized town that was loaded with displaced persons. There was no destruction, but it seemed like there were a lot of people who didn't have anything and didn't know where to go." Paul added: "I remember going across a long bridge and seeing all those people." The Germans Paul observed undoubtedly very much hoped to cross that same bridge only going in the other direction. After four crossings he was again on the same side of the river as the Red Army.

Paul could not have known it at the time but a couple of months earlier at the Yalta Conference the Elbe River had been agreed upon as an East-West dividing line. Also, there was this agreement:

> . . . all United States citizens liberated by the forces operating under Soviet command will, without delay after their liberation, be separated from enemy prisoners of war and will be maintained separately from them in camps or points of concentration until they have been handed over to the United States authorities, as the case may be, at places agreed upon between those authorities.[5]

A reciprocal provision (identically worded) was in place for the return of Soviet citizens liberated by the forces of the United States.

The pact also contained an unusual stipulation:

> Hostile propaganda directed against the contracting parties or against any of the United Nations will not be permitted.[6]

CHAPTER ELEVEN

The Left Echelon

O n March 1, 1945, Addison's mother wrote him a letter, stating, "Just 15 days and you will be twenty-three years old!" She also reported on one of the four 'M's:

While in Saks shoe department, [I] spoke to a girl who lives in the same home as Marion Maxwell in Ann Arbor—her name is Barbara Strong. She likes Marion very much. I told her Marion went with you and she said I wonder if he is the boy she gets letters from? What say you?

In 1948 Marion Maxwell would become Addison's wife.

The fact that Addison may have been from an affluent family did not buy him favor in the United States Army Air Forces. On March 6, 1945, he was issued a *European Theatre of Operations Male Officers' Uniform, Clothing & Accessory Card.* This slip of paper authorized Addison a "yearly allowance" to purchase one pair of "Gloves, wool," one pair of "Leggings," one "Scarf," etc., and as he purchased these items, an Army clerk noted on the reverse side of the card by strike-out what items he acquired. This card is a testament to how controlled resources were in World War II. Lose an item of clothing and one would be out of luck for a year.

As the months progressed the letters that Addison received from home became increasingly positive in anticipation of the war ending in Europe. In early March, Addison's mother wrote of the radio broadcaster Drew Pearson reporting on the air: "Any day now should bring good news." She would later write: "Dad tried hard to have me select a white orchid ($20). I said [to Dad] when you boys get home I'll splurge then!" Indeed, the news from

155

the European theatre of operations was encouraging. On March 7, 1945, a detachment of the American 9th Armored Division captured intact a bridge over the Rhine River opposite the little town of Remagen.[1] The last major natural defensive barrier of the Third Reich in the west had been breached.

Addison continued to pound on the Nazis, flying five more missions in March to places named Chemnitz, Ulm, Vlotho, Oranienburg and Spandau. By the end of the month he had, including a tally for recalls, 27 combat missions to his credit. With each passing day it was becoming more probable that Addison would survive the European war by reason of either completing his "tour" of 35 missions or by the surrender of Nazi Germany. Still, to paraphrase a latter-day pundit: it would not be over 'til it was over.

Of the 65 heavy bomb groups in the Eighth Air Force, the 91st had the most POWs. The status of former Bishop crewmembers was no longer unknown to Addison except for tail gunner Owen Monkman, who remained missing in action. Dave Bishop and RJ Miller were reported to be POWs at Stalag Luft I and Addison knew just where that camp was, since Barth, Germany was on the not-to-be-bombed list. With respect to Paul Lynch, Addison had learned of the reports of Stalag Luft IV closing and the march to the west. Maybe Paul was tucked away in another camp by now, Addison hoped, riding it out like Dave and RJ.

Addison had learned nothing through the official chain-of-command that caused him to be concerned for Dave and the others. The press furor over the Dresden bombing had settled down and, as Addison recounted, none of the adverse publicity about that mission caused him or others at Bassingbourn to believe that this raid might result in negative consequences for POWs. "The question did not come up," Addison said.

The tragedy of November 26 had receded in Addison's mind by then. He now accepted that Kendall and Cumings were killed as official confirmations on this had been made; he hoped that some good news might yet arrive about Owen, a person he regarded as a close friend, but in his mind he knew this was not likely to happen.

Addison believed strongly that the most positive thing he could do for his POW and MIA friends was to do his best to help win the war as quickly as possible. But prayers for intercession also helped, Addison knew, and he made them faithfully. Father Ragan continued to give him spiritual support.

In early April, Addison was promoted to first lieutenant and his mother wrote him a congratulatory note. She made reference to his letter to her dated April 6. "This is the first time any of your letters had been opened," she wrote. She told her son that his letter bore the rubber stamp of Army Examiner #1082, a censor.

Addison flew four missions in April, including a mission to Rochefort, France, where he served as first pilot. This was a tactical mission "against a pocket of German troops located on the mouth of the Gironde River."[2] The Nazi holdouts there denied the use of the port of Bordeaux to the Allies. Photos taken after the strike revealed that the target as a whole had been hit "on the head."[3] Addison's squadron, however, was unable to spot its assigned target—that being four high-caliber casemate guns. Smoke from an earlier strike covered the area.[4]

Addison's friendship with Lt. Goldberg, the first pilot from Detroit, continued to grow, but a special situation came up with this officer. Addison came to believe that Goldberg was being discriminated against by certain squadron first pilots because he was Jewish. "They gave him holy hell," Addison averred.

Asked to explain, he did: "They would often put him in the most difficult flying position," he said. "The left echelon."

"Some positions in formation flying are not easy," Addison continued. "There is a lead plane and one on the left and one on the right," he said. "The one on the left is in the worst position." Addison explained that a pilot in the left position constantly had to look across his co-pilot in order to see out the window to where the other airplanes might be. It was "hard to stay in" on the left, he indicated, and added that this meant increased "danger of collisions."

Convinced that there was no reason for Goldberg to constantly draw the left echelon assignment other than prejudice, Addison went to bat for him. At a pilots' meeting, one not attended by Goldberg, his friend again got volunteered to fly this more hazardous position. Addison objected strongly: "I told some people to get off his back," pointing out to them that what they were doing was "not right."

"He [Goldberg] is a good pilot. He does what he is told to do."

Asked if Goldberg had ever been insulted behind his back or even to his face, that is, called derogatory names, or denied association with Christian pilots, Addison responded "No." Addison remained adamant, however, that prejudice was what it was.

The Greatest Generation had strong physical courage, a deep love of country, a willingness to sacrifice and the ability to recognize and confront evil, but it was not without its flaws. This generation harbored significant racial prejudice. In 1942, Alistair Cooke, later to become famous for *Masterpiece Theatre* on PBS, traveled across wartime America by automobile on assignment to report on what he observed. On a number of occasions in both the North and South he related episodes of blatant anti-Semitism.[5] The author Joseph Heller, himself Jewish and a veteran World War II USAAF combat airman, addressed this issue in *Catch-22*, where the command leadership wanted to "lynch" a young airman because they perceived him to be Jewish.[6]

Addison's plucky defense of Goldberg, a full pilot, may have served him well within his squadron. It is an adage that an associate in a law firm must stand up to the partners in order to himself become a partner. Addison stood up and asserted leadership in a ticklish situation. Around this time Addison was selected to become a first pilot. That Addison defended Goldberg was telling not only about Addison, but also likely how he had been raised.

When Addison flew to Pilsen, Czechoslovakia, on April 25, 1945, he knew it would be his last mission. Pilsen proved to be a memorable way for him to finish out the war indeed!

The mission had aspects to it far different from other combat missions Addison participated in. The day before Addison and his fellow airmen were ordered to fly to Pilsen, Supreme Headquarters Allied European Force (SHAEF) made known to the enemy when and where the air strike would take place.[7] The targets were the never-before-bombed Skoda Armament Plant and a nearby airfield where Nazi fighters had been spotted, including a few jets. In announcing the targets publicly beforehand, SHAEF hoped to avoid massive civilian casualties such as had occurred at Dresden. Tens of thousands of civilians worked at the Skoda factory.

The 91st Bomb Group was detailed to attack the airport. In the bomber stream, which consisted exclusively of 1st Air Division units (seven bomb groups), the 91st would be the last in, flying the exposed tail-end Charlie position.

This airstrike had another aspect to it that made it stand out from many others—there was a very significant operational screw-up.

Finally—extraordinarily—on his 91st and final mission, the famed Lt. Col. Manny Klette would experience the unthinkable: most of his first pilots would fail to obey his direct order!

Addison was asked whether he ever knew that the day before the mission was to take place, a flight of P-51 Mustangs dropped leaflets over the target area warning those below that the attack was coming the following day.[8] Addison answered: "No, I did not."

In 2001, historian Lowell Getz wrote an account of this mission. Getz pointed out that the 24-hour advance notice to the enemy had no parallel in World War II and it arguably endangered those who flew the Pilsen mission by allowing the Nazis a full day to position their mobile flak guns. The leaflets announced that Allied bombers would attack the Skoda Armament Plant, and that people should stay away from it. According to Getz, the BBC also broadcast the same message the night before.[9]

Addison did not recall knowing Getz, nor had he read his book, but he perked up upon hearing the claim of an advance 24-hour warning. Of the Pilsen raid, he noted: "The flak was really thick."

One of the documents Addison brought home was a newsletter published by *Headquarters 1st Air Division* on May 5, 1945. An article appearing in the newsletter had this to say about the Pilsen mission:

> *In an unprecedented move, the Eighth Air Force revealed the objective of the heavy bombers more than an hour before the Fortress formations were due to arrive at the target area. The BBC overseas broadcast warned Czechs working in the Skoda plant to stop work and seek shelter.*[10]

Asked if he remembered hearing the BBC broadcast the warning while he was on the way to Pilsen, as purportedly did a number of upset B-17 radio operators, Addison replied, "No, but I remember talk about the factory being bombed to keep it out of the hands of the Russians."

Addison's recollection about the Russians was in sync with the history. There existed yet another reason that made the Pilsen mission unique: its purpose had little to do with fighting the Nazis. At this late juncture in the war there was no way that the Germans could deploy the heavy weapons being turned out at Skoda. They lacked usable rail and highway conduits and the fuel necessary to make the shipments. Also, when Skoda was bombed, on April 25, the war in Europe was almost over. Hitler would be dead only five days later and hostilities ended a little more than a week after that.

The Pilsen mission was not part of *Operation Thunderclap*. It was not designed to interrupt communications or inhibit troop movements to the front. But like *Thunderclap* it had much to do with the Soviet Union. Not only would this raid deny the Soviets the Skoda weapons and the use of the plant, it would show them firsthand just how much destruction a relatively small U.S. heavy bomber raiding force could inflict. SHAEF of course could never admit any of this publicly.

As stated, the Eighth Air Force launched strategic operation #958, "the final heavy bomber mission against an industrial target"[11] on April 25, 1945. Of the 307 B-17s sent into Czechoslovakia, Addison's plane and 77 others were assigned to hit the airfield and the rest were sent to destroy the arms factory.

Addison described the only thing good about the Pilsen mission from his perspective: "I remember the long flight in. It was 90% over friendly territory and that was nice," he recalled.

Upon reaching "IP" or the "Initial Point" for the bombing run, Addison observed, "We had the best seat in the house to view the action ahead," referring to the fact that his squadron was in the absolute tail-end Charlie position. "We were ordered to attack visually," Addison continued, pointing out that radar bombing might have killed Czechoslovakian civilians living near the airport. "And we were in the lowest position."

Per information submitted by the 324th after the attack, the bombing altitude for the mission was only 21,100 feet.[12] The fact that other squadrons from the 91st flew ahead of and above the 324th that day could have spelled trouble for Addison and his squadron mates in the melee that happened. There exists a famous photograph of a B-17 with its left stabilizer missing because of a "friendly" bomb dropped from above. Additionally, about the tail-end Charlie position, a commentator wrote:

> *To be at the end was to be without the protection of other planes. To be at the end was to be the last one over the target when the enemy gunners manning the antiaircraft artillery on the ground were sure of their range. To be at the end was to be the last home, if you got home at all.*[13]

When Addison approached the target area he knew immediately that something had gone very wrong. "I remember the clouds," Addison said, and then added: "They weren't supposed to be there." Like all mission plans that called for visual-only bombing, fast flying fighters were supposed to canvas the target area as the bomber force was midair and radio in the signal for "all clear" or "poor visibility" weather. If clouds obscured a target, then the bomber force would divert to a secondary target.

What had gone wrong?

"It was wild," Addison remembered. "Planes were everywhere circling to find their assigned targets through the cloud cover." He continued: "It was a three-ring circus, and the rings were the planes circling. They looked for holes in the cloud cover so they could drop visually and not kill civilians."

Addison did not see bombers shot down that day due to the heavy flak but he was aware that it happened. One of members of Addison's squadron, however, Flight Officer Schafts reported "Observed 4 B-17s going down."[14]

With Klette in the lead, the 324th entered last into the fray. "It was mass confusion," Addison said. "There were planes everywhere. I never saw anything like it. Flak was going off all over the place and there was danger of collisions. Suddenly I saw bombs falling, we all saw it, and just assumed it was bombs away. We toggled our bombs, lots of bombers did, and expected to go home."

Addison continued: "The next thing we see is Klette not turning. He ordered the squadron to tighten up behind him for a second go-around. With no more bombs to drop, the first pilots balked. When they got the chance they turned for England and kept going."

Asked if he was aware that Klette was angry on the return flight, Addison smiled and simply replied, "Oh, yes." Apparently some of Klette's radio traffic had not been friendly, but Addison did not recollect the details of what his commanding officer said. In any event, it was a long, tense flight back—over four hours worth—and all Addison knew was that he was overjoyed for two specific reasons.

Landing at Bassingbourn, Addison learned that the fighter planes that reported the weather had been lost when they signaled, "Clear skies" for Pilsen. This snafu explained part of what had happened. The other part did not involve human error as much as bad luck. One of the squadron's "up front" B-17s (not Klette's) dropped its bombs early as the result of being hit by flak. The bombardier on that ship intently watched and waited for Klette, who had his doors open to release his bomb load. When the flak hit, the jolt caused this man to yank his toggle switch. Seeing bombs falling, other bombers of the 324th released their bomb loads. "I can't say how many planes in our squadron dropped their bombs," Addison said, "but I think it was most all of them."

Flying in the lead Klette could not see any of this of course. Klette closed his bomb bay doors, ordered another pass and expected his squadron to follow him. When Klette saw his subordinates heading for home in defiance of his direct order, he became dumfounded and furious.

"We did not make that second bomb run," Addison confirmed.

"Some people caught hell," Addison continued. "I was at the de-briefing and he raised holy hell there." Asked if Klette used pejoratives, Addison was unsure after all the years. "It was his wrath that I remember most," he said. "Klette was a scary guy when he was mad and he was really worked up that day. I remember him calling several plane commanders 'yellow' to their face. I also remember hearing the word 'court-martial.' " Addison smirked: "Klette didn't care if they had dropped their bombs or not. He had been disobeyed."

Addison explained it was "the senior pilots and the echelon leaders," who experienced Klette's fury, and that he, Addison, had been really glad when this happened to have been a second pilot. The other thing he was overjoyed about was surviving the war.

Addison agreed completely with the plane commanders who disobeyed Klette's order and turned back. "Why risk getting killed on a second run without bombs when the war is already won?" he reasoned, adding: "We needed to get the hell out of there. If I'm not mistaken, I also think there was a false armistice about this timeframe."

One can have no difficulty visualizing what this session and other sessions must have been like; that is Klette screaming, "Pull wings in, lieutenant!" and "Ride the beam!" whenever a head might turn or an eye might wander in search of sympathy and support. It is a universal USAAF axiom that an angry commanding officer is, well, a serious and not seri*ass* proposition. And Klette, being a lieutenant colonel, had the rank to make those before him quake.

Addison recollected that the brouhaha blew over in a couple of days when the realization sank in that the best way to celebrate a victory in war is with joy and not punishment of those who had served so nobly and so often in the past. Addison did not know whether the chain-of-command got involved in the cooling of Klette's temper, but he agreed that court-martials would not be, after all, a storybook ending for the "first group of the first wing of the first division" and also the squadron made famous by *Memphis Belle.*

Reliving this event so many years later, Addison had a good chuckle. He believed Klette was not one to carry a grudge; that the man was simply an out-and-out, driven by-the-book military perfectionist. Also Klette was smart enough not to make the second bomb run without his squadron, Addison pointed out.

Addison viewed this as one of the scariest missions he had ever participated in. There were casualties. Six of the 307 attacking B-17s were lost owing to flak. The advance notice to the enemy had arguably been deadly for USAAF airmen. Equally telling about how dangerous this last mission of the war was—out of the 307 B-17s that flew it, 180 came back damaged.[15]

The accidental bomb drop apparently turned out to be productive. A strike photo in the *1st Air Division Newsletter* showed the airport hit. The Havelaar history of this mission reported, "The bombers . . . struck with very good results."[16]

As an aside, *Rhapsody in Red,* the only B-17 that Addison returned from England with a photograph of—the airplane that had that tastefully drawn yet suggestive nose art—the bomber that Earl Sheen saved a life aboard—ended the war with panache. Lowell Getz noted humorously in his well-written chapter about this mission that the shot-up airplane managed to land at Bassingbourn without brakes, lost control, went across the grass and finally stopped with a section of a tent dangling off her radio antenna.[17]

Asked what Addison did following the Pilsen raid, he quipped: "Apart from enjoying the Officers Club you mean?" Earlier he mentioned how much he had grown to like English beer, but not the way the English did. "We chilled ours," he said.

Addison would fly one more time over Germany but never again over Nazi-controlled territory. "I was co-pilot on a trolley run," he recollected. "We took our ground crew for a ride over some of the targets that we had hit. We flew low, maybe 5,000 feet, maybe lower, I can't remember. Addison paused then added. "Not only did we see the extensive battle damage but we flew over POW camps full of German soldiers who were our prisoners. The camps were large and we could see them standing there looking up at us." That mischievous smile, that look of childish joy, then came over his face. "We dive bombed them!"

He explained himself: "We . . . teased them a bit by opening our bomb bay doors and coming in on them at an angle." His smile grew wide at the memory, which would cause any reasonable person to think, after a period of reflection: what the hell, the Germans started it!

A few days after Addison completed his final mission he received a letter from his mother. "We are proud of you," she wrote. The war was not quite over yet and she had no way of knowing that her son was no longer in jeopardy, but her letter did hint that the world might be getting back to normal. She wrote of "Lattie" and a friend using "our seats" at the Tiger baseball game the day before and that how the men sitting behind them broke a bottle of liquor, badly soiling Lattie's "large shawl with fringe." Addison had to have had a hearty laugh when he received this tidbit of civilian news from home. Oh, for the joy of little travails and at Briggs Stadium, no less!

Earlier in April, Addison's father had mailed him a commemorative booklet published by the Rotary Club of Detroit, entitled "A Tribute." The tribute read: "To the hosts of our sons and daughters on embattled fronts of land and sea and in the skies, we of Rotary would bring a tribute of pride and affection . . ." The ninth, tenth and eleventh names on the list of 145 sons and daughters were the three Bartush boys, Addison, Jack and Chuck.

That Addison and his brothers would be coming home to a hero's welcome there was no doubt. On May 7, the day before V-E Day, a Mr. Chic Sayles from The Procter & Gamble Distributing Co., Cincinnati, wrote Addison the following: "Addison, I wish there was a way of conveying to you splendid chaps our feeling regarding the marvelous work you are doing. I'm afraid our appreciation even then would fall short of what it actually should be ..."

On that same day his mother wrote about the excitement building in Detroit: "The radio has been on all a.m. awaiting the 'good news.'" She briefly considered going downtown to witness the raucous celebration but changed her mind. "Dad thought I should probably stay at home," she wrote.

On May 11, 1945, the European war having been won only three days earlier, Addison's mother wrote the same letter as millions of other mothers:

"No doubt you may go to the Pacific?" she asked. "I hope I am wrong."

Asked about this, that is, whether he had been concerned over the prospect of more war, Addison laughed. "No," he replied. "I was too busy partying at the Officer's Club."

The hope expressed in Addison's graduation booklet from twin-engine school a little over a year earlier had come into fruition: ". . . none of us will have a feeling of satisfaction until our enemies have been blasted into submission." Addison and his buddies had earned the right to feel satisfied and to celebrate. The submission they achieved, unlike the armistice that ended World War I, was complete.

And as for that young lady's prediction, one of the four M's, that Addison would make first pilot? Addison proved her correct: his official USAAF service record reflects him separated from active duty as a pilot. Under the category "Military Occupation," the typed words read, "As a pilot was in command of ship and crew."

That Addison and his squadron mates had to have been ecstatic at having survived the European war, there can be little doubt, but in the exuberance of the celebration, Addison had fallen back into a bad habit. On May 14th his mother scolded him: "Dear Addison: Don't tell me you are in the Pacific? We haven't heard from you since April 30th."

One thing for sure, there was going to be recognition. And there was.

CHAPTER TWELVE

A Red Army Horseman

On the ground in Germany the POWs' Black March progressed, "Four of us decided that we had had enough and
would escape at the earliest opportunity," Paul said. Asked if the fear of
execution played a part in the decision to flee, Paul's response was unequiv-
ocal: "No. Several of us were watching and we hadn't seen any SS men in
quite a while. Also we were going into the territory where the Germans had
evacuated because of the advancing Russians. It was kind of a no man's land."

At this late juncture in the war it was still possible for Hitler to order
the killing of POWs, but whether such an order would or could be carried
out was another matter. Hitler did not accept Goebbels February recommendation to execute all of the Western Allied airmen, but apparently he
did order that captured U.S. and British air officers be exposed as hostages
(i.e., used as human shields) "in downtown target areas of Berlin and other
major cities" to deter the further bombing of these sites.[1] This draconian
order was not carried out due largely to the fact that there was no barbed
wire available with which to pen-up the POW officers. Still, even at this late
date, and as mentally unstable as Hitler was, he could have changed course
and issued a general execution order.

The three men who accompanied Paul on the breakaway were not part
of a group that he marched with regularly. "We couldn't see any future in
just traveling back and forth. There was no system or reason for what we
were doing. It probably wasn't a good decision, but we made it." Paul stated
that the lack of food was an important consideration; that the Red Cross
packages were no longer coming through.

The decision to slip away on April 22 had been spontaneous, that is, not planned in advance. The column of POWs halted for a break and the guards had gone to the front of the line, "probably to drink coffee," Paul opined. He and the three others—men not well known to him—seized the moment to slip quietly into the woods. "It was a risky thing to do," Paul acknowledged, adding that the German guards at this juncture may have been in the same circumstance as the POWs, that is, hungry, exhausted and discouraged. He did not know what food was available to them. "They were older," he emphasized again. "It was a struggle for them to keep up." Undoubtedly these guards probably also feared an encounter with a Soviet patrol. They were on the wrong side of the Elbe River, after all. How might they escape?

Paul pointed out that more than four men could have possibly escaped that day, but that his little group of four was a manageable number. "One can't hide, say, 30 men," he observed. There were rumors to the effect that other POWs had previously escaped from his column, but he did not know this.

"Our opportunity came with the mid-morning break as we were next to a patch of woods and the guards were not paying the slightest attention to us," Paul said. "We made our break and kept going until we felt safe from pursuit. After that we just wandered south looking for a farm and food."

"We traveled in daylight," Paul related, responding to a question whether he and the others hunkered down in the deep woods until darkness set in. "We wanted to find shelter and locate food. We looked for a farmhouse. We were also afraid of being pursued." He chuckled and then added: "But I don't think we were. I don't think they even missed us." During this late and very chaotic period of the war it is doubtful that the guards followed up on missing POWs, or even took periodic head counts. The hopelessness of the situation for them had to be very much on their minds.

"We knew we were travelling south because of where the sun came up in the morning and went down in the evening, so we knew what general direction we were heading. We had no map, it was just guesswork." They headed south because there was little alternative. As much as they would like to have advanced in a westerly direction towards where they thought the Americans might be, the Elbe River blocked such a route to American controlled areas. Although they didn't know it, the Allied powers had agreed to meet at the Elbe. "We didn't have any idea where they [the Americans] were," Paul emphasized. "From day to day, we didn't get any reports."

One of the major waterways in central Europe, 1,000 feet wide in places, Paul and his escaper companions would have needed a boat or a bridge to cross the Elbe, and obviously at the end of World War II neither was accessible. There exist film records of thousands of Germans, both military and civilian, desperately struggling on hand and foot to cross over this river on wrecked and even partly submerged bridges, to put the river between themselves and the advancing Soviets. These damaged bridges were populated choke points. To get to one Paul and his companions would have had to expose themselves to many enemy combatants, including SS units. They had been wise to keep a distance between themselves and the Elbe.

This small group of Americans hoped they might be in no-man's land, that is, a completely empty area between opposing armies. With each passing hour on the move—seeing no human activity whatsoever—that impression grew. "It was completely evacuated," Paul said about his rural surroundings. "The Germans in the area did not want to get captured by the Russians."

"Some of us had canteens and others, metal containers," Paul remembered. "We were careful not to drink out of streams, only well water."

Asked if they had been spotted, would they be recognized as escaped American POWs, Paul replied: "Not necessarily. We wore old [U.S.] Army uniforms without any insignias." Paul elaborated that the Germans could only recognize him as a POW when he marched in a long, guarded, column. "In a small group," he said, referring to himself and his companions, "we might have passed as displaced persons." To drive his point home, Paul added: "Later, the Russians did not know who we were."

As an aside, the Luftwaffe guards could have easily and inexpensively avoided this potential recognition issue by simply painting a large letter "K" (for Kriegsgefangener) on the backs of POW greatcoats, but this was not done.

"It was cold but we did not encounter storms those first days," Paul continued. Avoiding roads, the band of four "crossed fields and went through woods." Paul added: "I do not recall seeing many roads."

Cognizant that their slow movement could make them an easier target for an enemy rifleman, the POW escapees nevertheless lacked the energy to cross an open field on the run. They were bone tired and weak. Coming out of a woods, they stopped and surveyed an open area as best they could. The men were also fully aware of what would happen to them if they ran into an SS patrol.

Paul did not know any of the names of the men that he was with or even where they hailed from in the United States. "We were only concerned about making the right moves," he said, indicating that the conversations he had with the other Americans were business-like. "We did not want to be discovered or tracked down. Also, again, we were after food. We decided things together."

"About evening we came to an abandoned house and barn," Paul related. "There seemed to be no prospects there on first look until we heard a hen in the barn. We peeked in and there she was. We had to corner her in the barn or she would outrun us. Very detailed plans were made to capture that hen. We all took our positions armed with sticks and began to close in. She made her break for the open door and the fellow at that position got her with one swipe. One of the fellows found some small carrots, some kohlrabi in back of the barn and a few cull potatoes in the cellar of the house. They all went together with the chicken into an old bucket we found in the barn. That night we had chicken soup for dinner. How lucky we were!"

Paul and the others had been so elated with finding food that they forgot to check for booby traps on the premises. The house was "old and with four or five rooms," Paul said. "It wasn't big and was not furnished," he continued, suggesting that the previous occupants had had enough time to cart out their belongings.

The four men felt secure enough to maintain an outside fire for a period after nightfall. That night they slept in the house on the floor, thankful to have a roof overhead; they did not bother to set up a guard-watch. "We were pooped," Paul said. After a decent night's rest, the men had the remains of the soup for breakfast and moved on.

Paul elucidated that the four of them felt the need to do something affirmative in order to make contact with friendly forces. Reflecting, he added: "Considering the direction we moved in it is doubtful we would have encountered Americans." He also explained, however, that he and his companions did not give up hope that the U.S. Army might find them. Later Paul would opine: "We had no grand plan. We were impatient youth who managed to luck out. The Russians or the SS could have shot us all."

"That afternoon we came to a bombed-out brick building so we looked around inside and found that it had been a Focke Wulf factory as parts and plans were scattered all around. Across the road from the factory were two large fuel tanks that seemed to be intact. We decided to sleep in the area that night."

The factory was three or four stories high and made of brick. Part of the factory had been destroyed and the windows had been blown out. The long side might have been a hundred yards in length. They entered it from the narrow side. "There were no pulleys or machinery to speak of but rather a lot of discarded [airplane] parts," Paul remembered. "Partially built wings and fuselages, mostly damaged, but we could recognize Fw-190s."

The Nazis produced 20,000 of these airplanes. With a 34-foot wingspan and a service ceiling of 37,000 feet the Fw-190 could do over 400 mph and was regarded as the best piston driven fighter in the Nazi inventory.[2] It would be irony indeed if the fighter planes that shot down *The Wild Hare* had been built at this manufacturing plant, the one that provided temporary shelter for Paul and his companions. The likelihood of this was slim however, as scores of such small manufacturing plants were disbursed throughout the Third Reich.

Paul confirmed that the plant was not in an industrial park, but rather surrounded by countryside. "It was by itself," he said, referring to the plant and the fuel tanks across the road. "An open area." The fuel tanks were "probably a couple hundred yards" away from the factory and not camouflaged. They were exposed to view and were metal colored; Paul could not venture a guess as to their capacity or size, other than to note that they were large.

"Early that evening we heard a rumbling sound from down the road. We slipped up behind a knoll and saw that the rumbling was from German Tiger tanks! We were quite concerned, as we did not want to be in the middle of a battle. Where would we go? We decided to stay as the Germans were moving away from us and toward the west."

The tanks were "probably 300 yards" away when Paul and the others first saw them. "We didn't know what it [the noise] was. We snuck out [of the building] and took a look. It was twilight but we could clearly recognize them."

Paul recollected spotting "maybe four" tanks and he got a good look at them—he could clearly see the painted white crosses. "The hatches were buttoned down," Paul observed, meaning there were no panzer crewmen visible. Moving in his general direction, the tanks did not carry soldiers on top and stayed on the road. "They were moving right along. In my opinion they were trying to get out of there as fast as they could. This was a retreat," he observed. "We feared troops were following and we hid as fast as we could."

"We didn't go back into the building but rather found that knoll and also some nearby brush to hide behind." Paul related as to how the tanks were spread out in a column maybe 50 yards apart on the road that passed between the factory and the fuel tanks. Asked if there was infantry anywhere, he replied: "No, thank goodness" and pointed out that the tanks were doing 20 or more miles per hour and that infantry would not be able to keep up. "We peeked over the knoll without being seen but I don't think they would have stopped even if they spotted us, as they seemed intent on moving out," Paul said. The tanks passed within "a couple hundred yards" of the POW escapees.

That Paul and the others correctly identified the German tank model there can be no doubt. The Nazi Tiger tank, with its long 88mm flak gun, massive 60-ton displacement and 21-foot length, was unique by World War II standards. Also, Paul's estimate of the speed was close: the Tiger Tank had a maximum speed of 24 mph. In addition to its big weapon, a Tiger sported two machine guns.

The tanks probably used the twilight to escape; there was enough light to see a bit outside but too dark for Soviet air operations. At this end-stage of the war these panzer troopers had to have been desperate to get out. They were the last line of the Nazi defense.

The tanks passed close by but not so close that Paul could smell their exhaust fumes. Paul admitted to having the daylight scared out of him: "We were very concerned for what might be coming behind them. We didn't know what was going on." The escapers realized immediately that they were not in a no-man's land as they had previously assumed. "We feared we might end up in a middle of a battle," Paul repeated. "We spent the night outside, watching." That night he told of no warming fire and little sleep. The need for food had been temporarily supplanted by the more immediate need for security. "We had canteens, but I can't remember how full they were," Paul said.

Asked if there was an agreed upon plan if enemy infantry showed up, Paul replied: "Not really. Run away." He added: "We'd probably retreat back in the direction of the farmhouse." Asked if there was anything in the factory that the escapees might use as a weapon, Paul replied: "If we possessed anything that looked like a weapon, it might cause us to get immediately shot."

The four men determined to stick together, that is, not split up no matter what. "We stayed in control," Paul recollected, a tone of gratification in his voice. "We were very worried, but no one had a nervous breakdown. We remained quiet." Paul said that none of the escapers fruitlessly whined and second-guessed their decision to escape, and no disagreements erupted. Paul prayed to God for deliverance that night and undoubtedly the others did also. "Yes, quite often," Paul said about his prayers. The men supported each other by talking. There was no need to whisper. "It wasn't necessary, no one was near," he explained. This would be a night that Paul would always remember. No German troops appeared. The escape plan to the southeast remained intact.

"Next morning we were sitting along the bank by the old factory when we heard the sound of planes," Paul remembered. "Three A-20 attack bombers were making a bombing run at about 2,000 ft. on those fuel tanks. I ran to the factory and flattened out by the back wall. Suddenly, I looked up and saw that the wall had no support and probably it would come down with a small blast so I ran as fast as I could to the nearest ditch and slid in. The bombs hit the tanks but no fuel explosion occurred. They were empty and probably contained diesel fuel at one time."

"They were rockets," Paul elucidated about the attack. "They weren't big bombs." When the planes appeared, "the other fellows scattered in different directions," Paul explained. He indicated he was a couple hundred yards away from the explosions, but wasn't positive about this distance. Asked about the number of rockets fired, he responded: "Two or three. Maybe one from each plane." Paul did not cover his ears, but this did not present a problem for him. The ground shockwave was not that powerful, he recollected, and he reported that the wall that he originally took cover under remained standing. Paul and his companions were not injured and the attack was over quickly.

"I jumped up and waved to the planes as they circled back to see what damage had been done," Paul said. "I don't know that they saw me but if they did, it was my hope they might report the possibility of American soldiers in the area."

Paul offered that he might not have been so enthusiastic in waving at the planes had he been aware that the pilots could have been (and probably were)

Soviet. "I did not see markings," he confessed, referring of course to national insignia. Paul was unaware at the time that the U.S. had supplied the Soviet Union with approximately 3,000 Douglas A-20 Havoc Bombers; he assumed when he saw these American-built aircraft that the pilots were also American. The A-20 was a twin-engine tactical bomber designed for low altitude bombing and strafing runs. The model had fixed forward cannons. One or more of these pilots circling back might have squeezed a trigger.

There was no question but that these pilots were competent. "They did hit those storage tanks," Paul observed. "I saw it after the explosions." The Soviet Air Force had 7,000 airplanes, most of them low-level air-to-ground attack models, not unlike the A-20, and they were effective against ground targets.

Paul and his companions had been lucky. First they had been lucky no German infantry showed up. Then they had been lucky at not being injured or killed when they "sat" in close proximity to a military target. That these storage tanks might be struck from the air by the Soviets was foreseeable, and those trained in infantry tactics would probably be alert to this danger and take defensive positions accordingly. Lastly, they had been lucky not to be strafed. From the air, how would a pilot or pilots know that a man with his arm waving on the ground might not be attempting to distract them while other men shot at them?

Would their luck hold?

After the planes left Paul and his companions decided to stay another day in the vicinity of the factory. "We didn't have any real options," Paul indicated. "We didn't want to follow the trail west with those Tiger tanks, but there wasn't any food here and that chicken soup had been eaten long ago. We had no maps and we really didn't know where we were or which way to turn. We suspected that the Americans might be west of us, in the direction of the Tigers, but we had no assurance of that. We were getting very discouraged."

The escapers made a good decision: "We just sat quietly and watched," Paul said. They would sit peacefully in clear view and let the Red Army come to them.

"Mid-morning April 24th we spotted a lone figure coming up the road and we thought he was on a mule, and suddenly we realized it was a Russian soldier on a Mongolian Steppe horse. He didn't look up or down but just plodded slowly until he went out of sight. We wondered if he even observed us. If he did, we didn't worry him much. Well, the Russians were on the way so we decided to sit tight and see what happened."

Despite not knowing for sure whether they had been spotted, the men sensed that maybe they had, and their spirits soared in anticipation. "Someone made the crack that the Russians had sent that fellow out to destroy those Tiger tanks; since we didn't look like Tiger tanks he kept on going," Paul related, chuckling at the memory.

Seeing the Russian horseman, it occurred to Paul that perhaps his frantic earlier hand waving at the airplanes had paid a dividend. "I expect the pilots probably reported that we did not look like [German] soldiers," he opined proudly, and rightfully so.

Paul reported that he could not see if the rider had a radio, which would have appeared as a box-like contraption. "I didn't even see a rifle," he said, "but he must have had some weapon on him."

"No, he just plodded along on the road," Paul recollected. "He did not wave or signal in any manner." Again, Paul and his companions had been fairly certain the rider had spotted them. They had seen the Soviet horseman clearly and there was no reason for him to have missed seeing them. The closest point of approach was a couple hundred yards—the same distance as with the Tiger tanks, only this time without concealment on the part of the POW escapees.

The Red Army was known to probe in this manner. A horse would be quieter than a motorized vehicle and give its rider some degree of extra speed if needed. More important, only one soldier's life—the scout's—would be at risk. In the movie *Schindler's List* there is a scene somewhat like what Paul and his companions experienced. At war's end, a solitary Soviet rider casually approaches hundreds of Jewish refugees, approximately half women, and announces that they are liberated. In the case of Paul and the others, the rider did not approach probably because the four men could still be part of a Nazi trick.

"Later that day we saw a patrol of Russian soldiers coming up the road," Paul continued, "and we got a little tense because we might not be able to convince them we were Americans. If we ran they would become more suspicious so we just sat and waited. They came to investigate us but guns were not drawn and they didn't seem too concerned. They understood the word "American" but not much else. We showed them our dog tags and they motioned us to follow, so we did." The Soviet patrol consisted of only a handful of men, undoubtedly done this way to preclude the possibility of an ambush of a larger number of Red Army soldiers in an open area.

Thinking back on this moment of liberation on April 24, 1945, Paul expressed pride that he and his companions had decided to break away. "I found out, however, that the column we came from was liberated by the British several days later," a fact that he learned many years after the war at a reunion of the 91st Bomb Group.

Asked if meeting the Red Army soldiers was a highly emotional thing for him, Paul reflected before responding. "No," he said. "They were friendly yes, but . . . this was not like meeting . . . Americans." Paul admitted that he did not know what the future might hold. When might he be repatriated? How would he and his companions get across the river? Paul was relieved to be finally out of the reach of the dreaded SS, but a new set of anxieties quickly arose.

The small Soviet patrol led the Americans through their battle line: "Soon we joined a larger group lead by a sergeant whose right hand had a thumb but no fingers," Paul related. "We drew pictures in the dirt to let him know that we were fliers and had been shot down. Then we told him we were prisoners and had escaped from the Germans. We could see that he was very impressed by the escape. He stopped to tell all the Russian soldiers and they seemed to change their attitude."

Paul clarified what he meant by change of attitude: "I think initially the soldiers who picked us up thought we were just more displaced persons. They did not appreciate the significance of our dog tags. When their sergeant explained we were shot down U.S. Army Air Forces members who escaped the Nazis, the men looked favorably upon us."

Paul concluded the story of his liberation day: "The Russians asked what we wanted. Food of course! They offered us some very course, heavy bread. It didn't even look good but we ate all that was offered and gave our 'Thanks' in return. Now I understood how the Russian soldiers could fight for so long. Two or three pounds of this bread, soaked by a bottle of vodka in the bottom of their stomachs, would last about a week."

Asked if he and his fellow escapers were offered vodka, Paul replied, "No, but we sure saw them drink it." Paul would see more of this excessive drinking in the weeks to come and also an evil that it facilitated.

CHAPTER THIRTEEN

Watching the Soviet Army Sweep

O n April 25, the day after Paul was liberated to Soviet control, a significant event happened not far away from where he was. Westward thrusting elements of the Soviet First Ukrainian Front linked up with the eastward moving U.S. First Army at a town named Torgau on the Elbe River. It was approximately 40 miles east of the city of Halle, and 20 miles northwest of the city of Riesa, where Paul and his companion escapers would eventually end up in a Soviet-run collection center for U.S. citizens. Traveling in a southeasterly direction, they had to have been very near to Torgau, the place where Nazi Germany was split in two. He learned of the link-up from his Soviet liberators.

Asked if the word of this event generated excitement, Paul responded: "I remember it was a good feeling to know that the war was about to be over. But there was no big celebration about it. The Russians were pleased that they had joined the Americans, yes, but the link-up wasn't rejoiced."

Paul's group had joined a Red Army patrol that had an established daily routine. "We tagged along with that unit for a couple of weeks," he said. "They were sweeping the area for German soldiers and it was interesting to watch them work." The Americans observed a phenomenon that had happened since the dawn of civilization; that is, watching a conquering army advancing over enemy territory. Asked what was interesting about it, he responded: "The way they approached a town. The way they went into buildings. They did it with a mechanical precision, no fuss. The sergeant was good. He'd get together with his men every morning and explain to them what needed to be done. It was all planned out. Some would go in one direction and others in another direction."

There was little, if any, disagreement on patrol. The Soviet soldiers knew their assignments and carried them out in a professional manner. When they entered a building, some would remain outside to provide cover if the enemy appeared. The Americans were not able to observe as much as they might have liked, however. While the sweeps were carried out they were instructed, or rather motioned, to stay put in areas that the Soviets deemed safe.

This procedure went on for many days, and no contact was ever made with German soldiers or others, as this area had been completely evacuated. There were no white flags hanging out of windows, and weapons were never fired. Asked to estimate the number of hamlets, villages and towns that the Soviet soldiers swept, Paul answered: "About one a day, I think, except for near the end when there was a larger town not too far from Riesa. We stayed in that one for a couple of days." No natural obstacles were encountered such as rivers or ridges; it was mostly countryside interspersed with small population centers.

Paul did not remember seeing the Soviets search for landmines but indicated that they may have. He never heard an explosion, and the Soviet soldiers didn't seem concerned.

Asked if the Red Army soldiers positioned snipers in advance, Paul replied: "No. I think at this point the Russians were not worried about being attacked. They were being cautious, yes, going through towns thoroughly one at a time. They wanted to make sure there were no surprises." The four Americans had indeed been fortunate. The Nazis had not yet surrendered but for all intents and purposes, the war was over in this area.

The Red Army sergeant had about 30 infantry soldiers under his command. "Things were very informal and the soldiers had a great deal of respect for the sergeant," Paul said. "I imagine they had been fighting together for some time." Paul communicated with the sergeant on several occasions by drawing pictures in the dirt or sharing a few basic German words that they both knew. "He had a very pleasant, happy personality. I found out that in one of the big battles in Russia a German soldier threw a grenade at him and he picked it up to throw it back; it exploded in the air and he lost his fingers. I think he was lucky that the injury was not more serious but he seemed very casual about the loss."

Paul came to sense that this sergeant, with his positive outlook on things, was a natural leader. On the flip side, over the weeks they spent together the sergeant may have made a similar assessment of Paul. In any event, the two got along well together.

Asked how old the sergeant was and what "big battle" he had been wounded in, Paul answered, "late twenties" and "I believe it was Stalingrad." Digesting this response, one can envision that the Red Army sergeant was akin to an infantry version of Manny Klette. Like Klette, he was probably a few years older than most of the men he commanded, had extensive combat experience and was not prone to make mistakes.

Some individuals simply stand out in the art of war.

Hitler had been unwise to invade the Soviet Union, and doubly so while being engaged in a war with Great Britain. The corporal-turned-Führer should have read what Peter the Great did to all-powerful Sweden or what the Russians did to Napoleon's army after it reached Moscow. The "jovial" Red Army sergeant was about as robust a warrior as ever stalked the earth, and the Red Army was full of men like him. No doubt SHAEF appreciated this.

"They never offered us weapons to use nor did we ask for any," Paul said. "I think we were considered to be guests. I imagine if they had gotten into a bind we would have pitched in to help. We sort of tagged along and kept out of their way so they could do their job."

The Red Army unit that the escapers travelled with moved in a southerly direction. Paul consistently referred to these soldiers as Russian but in reality many were Ukrainian. As stated, the Soviet Union referred to its forces south of Berlin, in the area where Paul's escape took place, as the First Ukrainian Front."[1] The southern spearhead was commanded by Field Marshal Koniev, himself a Russian. Koniev competed with Marshal Zhukov (in the field and also for the world press) who commanded the northern spearhead then nearing center city Berlin. About Ukrainian nationality, Paul said: "Maybe they did mention this but we didn't get it."

"Evenings were agreeable because we tried to communicate as much as possible," Paul related. "They were very interested in things we had in America. In spite of the language barrier, we seemed to be able to get a picture of what they had in Russia and it wasn't much." Asked how he sensed these Red Army soldiers came from poverty, Paul's response was telling. "It was what the soldiers did not say," he explained. "They didn't mention schools, automobiles or even their homes. We got the impression that there wasn't much there."

At this stage in the conflict the Red Army was the most powerful ever assembled in history. It had 6,250 tanks, 41,600 guns, 7,000 aircraft and almost 2.5 million hardened front-line combat troops.[2] Asked to comment on this, Paul said: "All I remember is those 30 men. And later those assigned to take care of us at Riesa." He added: "Most there were women."

Paul was also asked to give his impression of a comment made by a victorious commanding general about his troops' behavior during the closing days of a different, earlier war: "Nothing seemed to fatigue them. They were ready to move without rations and travel without rest until the end."[3] Paul opined that the Russians were as pleased as he was at the prospect of surviving the war and going home. He added nothing more, however, suggesting there existed no special enthusiasm on the part of the 30 Red Army soldiers to experience more combat.

Finally, Paul was asked to comment on this:

The men of the Red Army, advancing relentlessly westward showed no mercy. "You are now on German soil," they'd been told as they crossed the border. "The hour of revenge has struck!" Each regiment was encouraged to keep its own "revenge score." One battalion carried with it across eastern Germany a hand-lettered poster that read: WE ARE NOW GETTING OUR REVENGE FOR 775 OF OUR RELATIVES WHO WERE KILLED, FOR 909 RELATIVES WHO WERE TAKEN AWAY TO SLAVERY IN GERMANY, FOR 478 BURNT-DOWN HOUSES AND FOR 303 DESTROYED FARMS.[4]

Paul made clear: "The villages that we walked through were not looted or burned." He would later witness the infliction of a ruthless revenge extracted on a surrendered people, however.

"One day we came to a German village, and as the Russians checked for soldiers we went into an attractive home previously occupied by the Burgermeister," Paul said. "Things were not damaged so the place had been lived in recently. We checked all through the house and then went down into the cellar. What a surprise, there was a huge pile of discarded parts of Red Cross packages strewn all over the floor. He had been stealing our food on a grand scale."

He continued: "About that time one of the other fellows called us from outside. There was the fat Burgermeister in full uniform stretched out on the floor of the chicken house with a self-inflicted bullet hole in his head. None of us wasted much sympathy on him."

This proved to be the only corpse that Paul Lynch and the other Americans viewed. "We got permission from the Red Army soldiers to stay in this house," Paul explained. "The Russians did not know he [the Burgermeister] was in the chicken coop, they had left the area. There were no Russians with us when we found the body." He added: "There wasn't any aroma or decay."

"He was stretched out on a bench-like bed of sorts, with his arms to his side. He shot himself with his left hand I do believe." Paul opined that if the Soviets had shot him his body would not have been laid out in an orderly fashion. Also, Paul heard no shots ring out in the village that day. Paul did not recollect seeing the weapon used, however. "We did not really look," he said.

Surprisingly, while in the field Paul did not learn of Hitler's suicide that was announced on Nazi radio on April 30. Paul offered: "The ordinary Russian soldiers were not as well clued in as the Americans soldiers on world happenings. They lived from day to day and one bottle of vodka to the next, one loaf of bread to the other, and that was their life." Paul reemphasized that there had been considerable drinking. "Not while they were on duty, but yes, when they could do it, there was," he said.

The Soviets declared V-E Day on May 9, a day later than the other Allies, because of a separate surrender they took from the Nazis, and on this date Paul and the other Americans were still on patrol with the 30 Red Army soldiers. "The war simply ended," Paul related. There had been no firing of weapons into the air, arm waving or even time given off for rest and relaxation. This may have been so because the 30 soldiers needed to complete the sweep of the area they had been assigned to clear before returning to a place where they could get a hot meal—the good sized city of Riesa.

"When we came to Riesa, we were put into an abandoned German technical school," Paul related. "It was rather sad to part company with this group as we seemed to get along well together. I think the Russians felt the same way. The sergeant came up to me and put his hand on my shoulder and his expression told me that he was sad to leave us here. I have often thought of him."

They arrived at the technical school on May 12, 1945, and were housed in a dormitory complex that had been turned by the Soviets into a "collection center" exclusively for U.S. citizens per the Yalta agreement. The war had been over for three days when they arrived, and Paul's group would remain there for almost two more weeks, finally returning to U.S. military control on May 25. Paul was again on the west side of the Elba River, which the Soviets occupied at the time.[5] In 2012 while being interviewed for this book Paul would learn something significant relating to his stay at the collection center, something that he said U.S. government representatives never told him about in 1945 or that he learned from newspapers, newsreels or radio broadcasts after his return to U.S. military control.

Per the Yalta agreement, repatriation teams from the United States and the Soviet Union were supposed to have ". . . immediate access into the camps and points of concentration where their citizens are located"[6] U.S. authorities should have had access to Paul and the other Americans on the very day they arrived at the Riesa collection center; that is, May 12, yet that did not happen. Paul and the other Americans in Soviet custody did not know what the Yalta agreement provided for or what was actually going on at the time.

When he was a POW, Paul regarded himself as a "bargaining chip" for Hitler. He did not know until 2012 that when he entered that collection center at Riesa, he had become a bargaining chip for Stalin. Paul viewed the Russians as allies, and he had been protected by the Red Army sergeant and his men. And asked if he had been treated well by the Russians while at Riesa, Paul replied: "Yes, I was. We all were."

"I was assigned a small room on the second floor of the dorm with a single cot," Paul said. He described in specific detail the view from his window: "The back side of an apartment building with long balconies on each floor running the length of the building."

"My room was littered with papers and textbooks. I found some post cards with a picture of the dorms and decided to take several to show where I stayed." Referring to the picture of the dormitory appearing on one of the post cards, Paul said: "My room was on the back side, left corner of the center dorm."

"We hadn't been there very long when a large group of U.S. infantry soldiers came in to stay," Paul continued. "They had been captured by the

Germans at the Battle of the Bulge and liberated by the Russians." They were all privates, and there were about 160 of them.

Paul described the food at Riesa as "plain but adequate" which, although perhaps was faint praise, also meant it was a big step up from a steady diet of kohlrabi and ersatz butter-grease! "The Russians sent a crew to work in the kitchen. Most were rather husky women but very friendly. One day I saw one lift a full garbage can off the ground and throw it on a truck as if it was filled with feathers. At first, I thought she might be exceptionally strong but later I saw several others do the same thing. Don't think I wanted to tangle with those gals. One thing that did impress me was that they seemed to be happy while they worked." Paul expressed a similar opinion for most of the male Red Army soldiers he observed.

Paul told of another memorable encounter with a different kind of Russian woman. He was selected to take what he thought would be a physical examination, and when he reported to the medical section: "There stood a petite, cute, female Russian Army doctor," he effused. "I thought, 'Oh no, she is going to have me drop my pants and cough.' She didn't, but asked about my age, my unit, family back home, where I was shot down and how I happened to be here in Riesa. She was very interested in my story and told me I was lucky to have made it all this way."

The doctor ended the session cordially, Paul reported, that is without requiring a salute. "She extended her hand for a shake and told me I seemed as well as expected," he said. Asked if other Americans got the same interview with the cute Doctor, Paul responded: "I don't know if they did or not."

"Soon, the Russians got us all together and had us give our name, rank, outfit, last unit address and home address," Paul related. "Since I was one of the highest ranked Americans, the Russians put me in charge of a platoon but didn't tell me what was expected at the time." Asked how big his platoon was, Paul responded, "About a third of the G.I.s," suggesting 50-plus men. "I can't say why I was picked," Paul said, "just a matter of chance, I guess." Asked whether any of his other USAAF sergeant-escapers were selected for platoon leaderships, Paul answered: "Not that I know about."

"The next thing that happened," Paul explained, "was that I was called in to see a Major in the Red Army. He spoke very correct English and his uniform was immaculate. He was very friendly, informal and cordial. He was very concerned for the conditions and well being of the men. He told me the U.S. Army would be contacted immediately and given a list of Americans and the location of this place. We would be informed as soon as the Americans set up a date to pick us up. That was the best news I heard in months. Then came one demand or order; we were not to leave the area of the school. That worried me some at first because this might be one more prison, but soon I would understand why that order was given."

Paul did not have to wait long. In his "small room on the second floor" that evening, Paul heard a commotion outside. He looked out his window at the building across the street, the one with the "long balconies on each floor running the length of the building." The building housed tenants and Paul said he saw, "the Germans running out the back door of one apartment, along the balcony and into the door of another apartment."

Paul continued: "I assumed the Russian soldiers were coming in the front door of each successive apartment looking for women. I suspect the soldiers were drunk because many drank Vodka like water. Several times I heard screams and often shots."

Paul did not use the words "rape" or "murder" but he left little doubt about what he thought was happening across the way. "I really felt sorry for these people but I didn't dare intervene. Now I understood why we were restricted to the school grounds."

Paul and the other U.S. servicemen internees were still dressed in the filthy uniforms they had worn as POWs, and if they had left the campus and gone into the town of Riesa they might well have been mistaken for displaced persons and shot for no other reason than malevolent sport by blindly intoxicated, marauding, vengeful Red Army soldiers. The Red Army Major had been correct to issue his "one demand or order." Paul agreed: "The drunks might have taken us for Germans and shot us," he observed.

The horror lasted three or four days, and then tapered off. By the day of his repatriation, May 25, the behavior had pretty much stopped.

There was another, additional reason that the Red Army Major issued his order, and Paul would learn about it in 2012. The Major did not want any of the U.S. soldiers in his custody to attempt to flee to their own countrymen. Asked what distance the U.S. Army was from him while he was at the collection center in Riesa, Paul replied: "Four miles."

A daily routine set in at the collection center, albeit an uncomfortable one owing to what happened nearby to the school at night. There were no showers available, but the G.I.s were fed hot meals and were well treated. Paul proved to be an easygoing platoon leader. Chuckling at the memory, he elucidated on his military wisdom: "I decided there would be no mind-numbing marching to pass the time. We had roll call, sick call and about twenty minutes of calisthenics a day in the morning and that was it. I even got a fellow to lead the calisthenics so he would take the gripes."

With each passing day, however, Paul and his fellow Americans became more anxious about repatriation. The distance to the American line was minimal, so why the delay?

On or about May 18, about a week before his release, representatives of the U.S. Army showed up on the campus. "An American jeep drove in carrying three chaplains," Paul related. "They were on a visit to determine our location, see how many of us were there, how we were doing and to let us know what was happening. They explained that we would be going out across bridges and that there was only one U.S. controlled pontoon bridge over the Elbe River and 'military traffic' had first priority. Trucks would be sent as soon as there was an opportunity—in other words a delay."

Paul and the other American internees took at face value what the chaplains told them about "military traffic" tying up the pontoon bridge and causing a delay in their return to U.S. military control. Asked if he ever questioned what that "military traffic" might have been between the Americans and the Soviets, whether it be food, equipment or supplies, Paul responded, "No." Asked if he ever thought about why the U.S. Army chose to send in chaplains, as opposed to say, infantry or staff officers, Paul again responded in the negative. In short, Paul and the others accepted the delay as customary U.S. Army bureaucratic inefficiency and nothing more—"red tape" of course!

Paul learned in 2012 that these U.S. Army chaplains had participated in a well-meaning obfuscation. It was human traffic going over that pontoon bridge, and no doubt other bridges, that caused the delay in his repatriation process. The U.S. government was both contractually obligated by the Yalta agreement and compelled by circumstances to repatriate Soviet citizens. If Stalin did not get his citizens back, then U.S. citizens under Soviet control would not be returned—it was that basic. If the chaplains had attempted to explain this on May 18, it undoubtedly would have created apprehension, and done absolutely no good. Paul was being held hostage, but he did not know it.

In 2012 Paul learned of a World War II incident described by *Time-Life Books*, in a chapter entitled, appropriately, *The Anxious Deliverance*:

> *Prisoners in German camps relieved by the Red Army often had to endure delays of a month or more under Soviet guard before they were turned over to the Allied forces. For example, the Red Army arrived at Luckenwalde on April 23 when the U.S. Ninth Army was just west of the Elbe River, less than 50 miles away. Because of red tape and Soviet truculence—on one occasion Russian soldiers actually fired shots above a convoy of U.S. trucks sent to fetch the prisoners—it was May 20 before all the Allied prisoners were evacuated to safety behind U.S. lines.*[7]

The U.S. Army likely selected three chaplains to go to the collection center at Riesa because they were non-combatants and if Soviet forces fired upon them or took them hostage, it would undoubtedly spark an international outrage.

"The defectors?" Paul asked when being interviewed. "We returned them to the Russians, is that it?"

Yes, it was the defectors that created a huge moral crisis for the governments of the United States and Great Britain. It was a crisis that was resolved with minimal publicity attributable to the desire to keep as quiet as possible actions taken by democracies under duress that violated basic tenets of human rights, the most fundamental being the denial of asylum for those being persecuted for political reasons. It was also because of the Yalta mandate for no adverse propaganda.

Underneath the story of the collection center at Riesa—one that impacted the lives of approximately 160 Americans—lays a much larger story. The source of much of what follows comes from a lecture presented in the fall of 1988 at Hillsdale College by Nikolai Tolstoy, heir to the great writer, entitled, *Forced Repatriation to the Soviet Union: The Secret Betrayal*.[8]

When Germany invaded the Soviet Union in 1941, millions of Russians, including a large number of soldiers, mistakenly hailed the swiftly advancing Nazi armies as liberators. They welcomed the defeat of the detested Stalin and in some instances Russian military units marched to their surrender with their bands playing. German propagandists recorded scenes of these defections on film.[9]

After surrendering, the Nazis threw these Russian soldiers into unsheltered barbed-wire stockades on the exposed steppe and millions died of starvation and the elements during the severe winter of 1941–42.[10] With this horrible act the Germans made clear their intention to wage a war of territorial conquest followed by population "resettlement." This was the implementation of *Lebensraum*, the plan to acquire additional living space for the German "Master Race." Hitler had chillingly foreshadowed this years earlier in his book *Mein Kampf*."[11]

The Soviet Union, never a signatory of the Geneva Convention, did not lift a diplomatic finger to ease the plight of its suffering, imprisoned and dying countrymen. Indeed, the Tolstoy account describes some POW camps where Russians "were forced to watch [through a barbed wire fence] their British, French and American counterparts receive food parcels, clothing and letters from home."[12] The International Red Cross was barred "except on a few rare occasions" from visiting Russian captives. Anthony Eden, the British foreign secretary, was quoted as saying, 'Well, for some reason which we know nothing about, Stalin is determined that nothing should be done for the Russian prisoners.'[13] The unstated "reason," obviously, was that Stalin viewed these men, having willingly surrendered, as traitors to the Soviet Union.

The Soviet captives who survived were turned into slaves of the Third Reich and many were impressed into military service. At war's end several million Soviet citizens were displaced in Central Europe and a million actually fought in the German Army. Tolstoy states: "During the D-Day invasion in June 1944, British and American military authorities estimated that one out of every ten German soldiers captured was in reality a Soviet citizen."[14] After the war, it seemed no one wanted these people from the East, and no country volunteered asylum.

At the conclusion of the war in Europe, Stalin, being a dictator paranoid over the prospect of losing power, determined to get these men back so that he could either liquidate them or "re-educate" them in his Siberian labor camps, where the chance of survival was slim. Stalin appreciated that such a large number of ex-communist countrymen could, one way or another, create a problem for him in the future and he determined to deal with this possibility quickly and ruthlessly.

There are documented accounts of Stalin's treachery. In December 1944, a British ship carrying Soviet citizens to be repatriated arrived in Murmansk. Many of the former POWs were "sent to the *educational* camps," an observer recorded, but approximately 150 were selected for special processing. These men were marched by the Soviets to sheds on a nearby quay. Automatic gunfire was heard. Afterwards a covered lorry was seen leaving one of the sheds, and later, a "floor stained dark" was spotted by an observer who got a chance to glance into this shed.[15] Following the war the British forcibly returned to Soviet control some 40,000 Cossacks who were arguably not Soviet citizens since they had fought with the White Russians during the Revolution and managed to escape to Austria. *Pravda* owned up that the leaders of these Cossacks had been hanged by Soviet authorities; the other Cossacks were never heard from again."[16]

There are many verified accounts of Soviet crimes against their own people. There is a reference to Russian prisoners being executed by their own kind in a quarry near Riesa. There were eyewitnesses, "who gave statements on this."[17]

Before the Yalta Conference the American policy was that no Soviet POW would be repatriated by force. At Yalta this policy changed.[18] Why did Roosevelt agree to this? Roosevelt backed away from providing asylum to victims of political persecution in exchange for Stalin's promise that the Soviet Union would join the war against Japan within three months of the conclusion of the war in Europe. He also did so to get American POWs back. There were 90,000 U.S. POWs in Germany at war's end and the Soviets picked up approximately a third of them.

Soviet prisoners reportedly hanged themselves in, of all places, the notorious Dachau Concentration Camp near Munich where the Americans set up a collection center for Soviet citizens. Supposedly there is "a rare American Army film that showed a POW stabbing himself 56 times to avoid being taken into custody by SMERSH officers."[19] Things reportedly got so bad that the military leaders Eisenhower, Montgomery and Alexander revolted against their own governments and unilaterally issued orders outlawing forced repatriations.[20] In the end, however, the forced repatriations went forward as agreed upon at Yalta. And Stalin, true to his word, declared war on Imperial Japan August 9, 1945, three months to the day after VE-Day and three days after the atomic bombing of Hiroshima. This was the same day Nagasaki was bombed. In the weeks remaining before Japan surrendered, the Soviet Union occupied Manchuria and later ended up with half of Korea. The formula for the next war had been set at Yalta.

Undoubtedly each side, East and West, broke its reciprocal promise given at Yalta to allow "immediate access" to the collection centers. There were many heated discussions with Soviet representatives over the repatriation issue, and much of the talking, or rather haggling over human lives, took place in the city of Halle, the last major city that Paul marched through. Also at times the Americans and the British were in disagreement over what the repatriation policy ought to be. Per Tolstoy, "Two million Russians—including White Russians, Cossacks, Slovenians, Croats and Serbs who were POWs or simply living in exile—were forcibly repatriated to the Soviet Union."[21] What resulted was a human tragedy of epic proportion.

"I didn't hear a word about it," Paul said, referring to the subject of prisoner swapping. He reiterated that he never learned about it while he was at Riesa or later when he waited at the port of Le Harve to board a ship bound for home. Asked specifically if he had ever heard of the phrase "forced POW repatriation," Paul replied emphatically, "No, no."

Per his response, one can reasonably infer that Paul was not supposed to know, just as he was not supposed to know about the 7,000 African-Americans stationed on the same military base with him at Biloxi, Mississippi. The press had been selective in reporting during this era, or perhaps more accurately stated, controlled.

U.S. newspaper reports from the period immediately following the Nazi surrender support Tolstoy's contention of secrecy. A major *New York Times* headline dated May 11, 1945 declared "Freedom of the Press Curbed in Europe—SHAEF and Russians Keep Iron Censorship in Occupied and Liberated Areas." Other news articles discussed "new censor rules" regarding press stories,[22] the barring of "Alien" (foreign) news media from "distribution in Germany"[23] and disciplinary actions taken by the U.S. government against six U.S. correspondents who violated rules—three cases of "suspension" and three cases of "shipped back to the United States" (several violations involved attempted entry into the Soviet-occupied zone to find out what was going on).[24]

Then there was this, appearing on May 13, 1945:

SHAEF ASKS RUSSIANS ABOUT FREED PW'S

ADVANCE HEADQUARTERS, *Reims, France, May 12 (AP)— Nearly half of the estimated 200,000 British and 76,000 American pris-*

oners of war still in Germany are believed to be within the Russian zone of
occupation, and Supreme Headquarters has twice requested a meeting or an
agreement to arrange for their return.

This article provided the names of the senior Soviet and U.S. military officers involved. It concluded: ". . . and it cannot be foreseen what arrangements the Russians may approve—the last of these men might be on their way to Britain and the United States within two weeks to a month."

The article says nothing adverse or alarming about the Soviet Union, paints U.S. authorities in a proactive mode, makes no reference to the Soviet POW situation, and foreshadows up to "a month" for the return process to happen.

Some G.I. POWs actually witnessed the prisoner trading. The writer Kurt Vonnegut experienced it and wrote about it in his novel *Slaughterhouse 5*. What he witnessed likely was not filmed.

The rain was coming down. The war in Europe had been over for a couple
of weeks. We were formed in ranks, with Russian soldiers guarding us—
Englishmen, Americans, Dutchmen, Belgians, Frenchmen, Canadians,
South Africans, New Zealanders, Australians, thousands of us about to stop
being prisoners of war.

And the other side of the field thousands of Russians and Poles and
Yugoslavians and so on guarded by U.S. soldiers. An exchange was to be
made there in the rain—one for one.[25]

Not all Western Allied POW camps liberated by the Soviets became bargaining chips, and a notable exception was Stalag Luft I near Barth, Germany where Dave Bishop and RJ Miller were held. The Red Army liberated this camp on May 1, 1945 and within a few days following the Nazi surrender on May 9 the Americans and British were permitted to implement an airlift evacuation of approximately 10,000 POWs. Stalin retained enough Americans and British POWs at other locations, however, to achieve his twisted political objective.

It is difficult to blame President Truman for what happened as a result of the POW repatriations, having played from a deck dealt to him by Roosevelt at the Yalta Conference. When Truman assumed the presidency in

April 1945, he looked to the future course of the war with Japan and hoped to lessen its cost in American lives. The atomic bomb had not been tested yet. Truman also very much wanted the tens of thousands of young American POWs like Paul to be returned safely home. The last thing he needed was a much-publicized dispute with the Soviet leader, a supposed ally.

"I can clearly recall the day that the American trucks rolled into that school," Paul said. "We were in formation when we loaded the trucks," he explained. "Everyone let out a big cheer and we didn't have any trouble getting the guys into those trucks." No roll call was needed, Paul related, for no one would miss this movement! "Shortly we crossed over and crossed back the Elbe River, and when we rolled back onto the west bank we knew we were in American territory and really liberated."

Awaiting Paul and the others was a U.S. Army field mess hall. "My first thrill was to see pitchers of milk," Paul said. "The second stop was the delousing unit." Paul told of "steamy showers, new uniforms" and removing "a Nazi blood-filled tick hidden between my legs." Paul had worn the same uniform for six months. He reported he weighed 126 lbs.; that he had lost 60 lbs.—representing a 32% weight loss over a six-month period, and this measurement was done a month after being fed by the Soviets. The average weight loss for an American POW in the European Theatre was 35 to 45 lbs. Paul lost more weight because he made *The Black March*.

Paul related that he went through several medical examinations upon his return to U.S. military control and that there was initial concern for his vision. "The lack of food could have impacted my ability to see, or so I was told," he said. Fortunately for him this was not the case. Paul had no recollection of ever being examined by a military psychiatrist or psychologist.

Paul was sent along with other liberated POWs to Camp Lucky Strike, a tent city near the port of Le Harve where he awaited priority transportation home along with 48,000 others with his status. The U.S. Army came up with an acronym for these men—they were called "RAMPs"—"Recovered Allied Military Personnel."

After a week or so in camp Paul and thousands of other RAMPs embarked aboard the large Coast Guard ship the USS *Alfred H. Mayo*, where the major activity was waiting in a chow line twice a day. Underway he was thrilled to learn that his port of arrival would be Boston, only 40 miles from his home.

"I called them," Paul said, referring to his family of course, "and then took a bus to Worcester where my parents picked me up."

Like Addison, Paul would be treated special. "The parade through Leominster for the veterans was a thing to behold," he recollected fondly. "There were so many times I thought that I would never have the opportunity to be home again."

In Memoriam: Conversations with Addison Bartush and Paul Lynch

F ormer ball turret and waist gunner Billy Robertson of Philmont, NY, lost no time in experiencing the joys to be had in a world at peace. Among Addison's memorabilia is a short letter postmarked April 16, 1946. The note thanked Addison "for your wonderful present" and the envelope contained snapshots explaining the reason for Addison's gift. A happy couple proudly displayed their newborn to the camera; the baby boomer generation had begun.

On Sept. 2, 1946, Mrs. Gordon Monkman of Bynum, Montana, mailed Addison a letter. "We no longer have the sheep Owen used to speak of," she wrote. "We couldn't get reliable help and sheep are temperamental creatures." She enclosed a lengthy local newspaper obituary about Owen. The War Department had officially changed Owen's status from missing to killed in action, and this prompted a news article in the local paper. Addison had written the Monkmans a letter of condolence over this event and she responded. "Dear Mr. Bartush," she wrote. "Thank you for your very kind letter."

The obituary described the considerable efforts that Mr. and Mrs. Monkman had made to learn anything they could about their son's disappearance.

Last August [1945] his father, Gordon Monkman, made a trip to Nevada, Mo., to interview F/O Robert Miller, navigator. Then he traveled to Columbus, Ga., where he met Lt. David Bishop, co-pilot of the plane on the bombing mission. In November, Sgt. Paul Lynch, waist gunner from Leominster, Mass., visited the Monkman's. None of these men could give any information concerning the son's whereabouts.

Owen Monkman was 20 years old when he disappeared. In addition to his parents, Owen was survived by a brother who also had served in the armed forces. Mrs. Monkman wrote to Addison, "Some day we hope to meet the other boys of the original crew," meaning of course, Billy Robertson, Earl Sheen and Addison. She also posed a question to Addison that would be asked of him six-plus decades later at the conclusion of my interview.

"Addison, did you ever see Mr. and Mrs. Monkman?"

"Yes, Dick, I did," Addison responded. "She called me one day and said she and her husband would be driving through Detroit, and asked if we could meet. We agreed to meet at the Ambassador Bridge and I took my son Jay with me, who was a youngster at the time. This would have been in the early fifties, I believe. I remember waiting and waiting, and finally they arrived."

"There was not much that you could say to them, was there?"

"No there wasn't," Addison said, beginning to choke up.

"Are you OK?"

"Yes, go on, please." Addison picked up a Kleenex, removed his glasses and dried his eyes.

"They just wanted to meet you, correct? They wanted to meet the man that their son had written home about." There was no need for Addison to reply and he did not. "This was closure for them? Another member of the Bishop Crew?"

"Yes."

"And Owen had been one of your favorites among the enlisted men?"

"I regarded him as a friend," Addison confirmed. "I still do."

"Did you have any stories to share with them about Gulfport or Bassingbourn?"

"I suspect I did, but I can't remember them. It was so long ago."

"Were you glad you waited for them?"

"Absolutely."

"Did you ever see them again?" Addison shook his head, indicating no.

Other than meeting Mr. and Mrs. Monkman once, Addison never met the parents of his other lost Bishop crewmembers. Addison told me that he had had no contact with waist gunner/lifesaver Earl Sheen and that he remembered little about the, "tall, thin person." After the war Addison informed me that he made a few attempts to get in touch with his former navigator RJ Miller, but Miller did not reply to Addison's letters. When Addison called, Miller's phone always rang off the hook. Addison told me he surmised that Miller, who had been seriously wounded and recovered in a German hospital before being placed in a POW camp, may have been so traumatized by his experience that he wanted no reminders of what he had endured. Addison added, however, "I don't know this, Dick." From the many stories I have read about aircrews of World War II, I knew that the passage of time often did not serve to sooth one's psyche; that in some cases the result was exactly the opposite—i.e., growing anger at the realization that one had been compelled to do things against one's will and perhaps even one's conscience. I expect this is what may have happened to author Joseph Heller; in Miller's situation it is impossible to know. When I later interviewed Paul Lynch, I learned that Miller died in 1988 of cancer. Paul could tell me no more than Addison about Miller's attitude.

When war broke out in Europe in 1939, President Franklin Roosevelt pleaded publicly in the name of decency for the combatants to refrain from bombing cities.[1] Of course the Nazis paid no attention to Roosevelt, and they were the first to target civilians with the terror bombing of Warsaw. Rotterdam and London soon followed. In January 1943, with America a little over a year into the war, Roosevelt met with British Prime Minister Winston Churchill at Casablanca. The Nazi-started carnage had hardened these political leaders—they issued a joint statement to undertake "the heaviest possible bomber offensive against the German war effort."[2] Six months later, the massive Allied air raid was conducted over Hamburg, the first of what would become a continuous operational military pattern. The British bombed by night and the Americans by day.

By the end of the war the German civilian death toll from bombing was 600,000, "including 75,000 children under 14."[3] When one thinks of this, whatever might be one's views on the British and American air war strategies, one cannot help but be saddened.

Did the massive Allied air attacks on Nazi Germany destroy German industrial capacity and shorten the war? Much has been written about this subject, pro and con. One thing is certain, however: German leaders, both civilian and military, thought that it did. Alfred Krupp, the arms manufacturer, admitted after the war that the air attacks destroyed 60% of his industrial capacity; his plants were nestled in heavily populated cities. Another industrialist said: "The virtual flattening of the steel town of Düsseldorf contributed at least half of the collapse of the German effort." Field Marshal Albert Kesselring perhaps said it most succinctly: "Allied air power was the greatest single reason for the German defeat."[4] And Kesselring was in a position to know—he was arguably the most efficient German to don a military uniform, having held the Allies to a slow crawl in Italy with almost no airpower and desperate fuel shortages.

In 1944, the last full year of the war, U.S. aircraft production was 96,318, UK production 26,461 and the Soviet Union, 40,300 for a grand total of 163,079 aircraft. Most of the aircraft constructed were warplanes destined for the European Theatre. By contrast, Nazi Germany produced 40,593 aircraft that year, all of them warplanes.[5]

World War II resulted in a loss of human life that has no parallel in history. By war's end, an estimated 72 million humans had been killed.[6] The Soviet Union had the largest number of total deaths at 23.6 million (13.5% of its population) followed by China at 20 million persons. Germany suffered 7.5 million total deaths representing 11% of its wartime population. The death count in Eastern Europe and the Pacific are also high. The United Kingdom and the United States suffered fewer deaths—450,000 (1%) and 417,000 (0.3%).

Undoubtedly World War II ended for the German people any attraction to blind militarism. To what extent the USAAF and RAF heavy bombers may have played a part in what today might be termed a "culture change" I am not prepared to argue—but I like to think that some positives resulted from what Addison and many others did. A monster needed to be slain and the airmen did their part. The sacrifice of these strategic Allied air warriors was not futile.

And at Addison's level, what was that sacrifice?

A review of the casualty reports prepared by the 91st Bomb Group during the period that Addison served at Bassingbourn reveals the following statistical information: 132 men killed in action, 3 killed in accidents, 14 missing in action and 133 prisoners of war. Thirty-three B-17s were lost while Addison was assigned to the 91st. Of the 163 days that Addison served in a combat command, this accounts for airplane losses at an average of one every five days. Of course this average is skewed by the loss of 13 bombers on one day, November 2, 1944—the *Massacre at Merseburg,* at a time when Addison was training for combat flying status. Addison's squadron did not fly this tragic mission; nevertheless, Addison was then part of the "91st team"; he was there at Bassingbourn and had to endure this tragedy along with the rest of his bomb group.

Of Addison's squadron, the 324th, or "Klette's Wild Hares," eight bombers were lost while Addison served as a member of this squadron. Thirty-four men were killed in action, one killed in an accident (in the P-47 Thunderbolt fighter plane accident described at the beginning of this book) four were missing in action and twenty-eight became prisoners of war.

"Addison, let me mention some names of officers that you served with in the 91st who did not make it, men who were killed on missions that you yourself flew, were in your squadron, or you might have otherwise known. I want to see if any of these names brings back memories. If this will upset you and you don't want to do this, let me know and we won't do it. I will only write what you want me to write and then only as a tribute to these brave men. Nothing will be sensationalized."

Prior to this session I had decided not to read the names of the officers killed on the November 2 Merseburg raid, as I assumed Addison, being a new arrival at the time, would not remember them, and I also assumed the same for all enlisted men for all missions flown while Addison was at Bassingbourn. The enlisted men would have berthed and messed apart from Addison and would have had little, if any chance to interact with him. I started out with a big one—Addison's second mission to Zeitz, November 30, 1944—four days following the loss of his crewmates on *The Wild Hare*.

"Ralph Stoltz, second lieutenant and Bernard Goldstein, second lieutenant? They were the pilot and co-pilot and they went down on November 30, 1944, near Leipzig." I added: "These officers were from your squadron Addison and you were on this mission flying with them. The target was Zeitz."

Addison looked at me blankly and I continued: "The description from the casualty reports reads, 'This B-17 was observed to pull out of formation at 24,000 feet at about 2 minutes after bombing [as the result of] a direct flak hit. It exploded in mid-air and disintegrated completely with wings on fire. All were killed except the navigator, 2nd Lt. George Minich, who ended up a POW.' "

I looked at Addison. "Do you remember witnessing this?" I asked. "Do you remember these officers?"

"No recollection," Addison replied.

The fact that Addison could not remember anything about this happening reinforced my opinion about his mental condition during this timeframe. Had he subconsciously blocked this painful memory out? I expected Addison not to remember many, if not most of the names I was about to read to him because they were from different squadrons. But for sure he would have known Stoltz, Goldstein and Minich. To go out with 12 planes and come back with 11, well, one would remember that, unless . . .

"Howard Mitchell, first lieutenant? December 5 at Berlin. He was a pilot from the 322nd and flew an unnamed B-17G No. 43-38693. Four including Mitchell were killed and five taken prisoner."

Addison shook his head indicating a "No."

"Pilot Earl Jeffers and co-pilot John Welch? They crashed January 1 while flying *Heats On*. Also navigator Clyde Harlow. On the start of a mission to Kassel, the plane developed engine trouble and Jeffers tried an emergency landing at a nearby fighter base. He crashed into parked P-51s and everyone was killed. This crew was from the 401st Squadron."

"I remember the event," Addison recalled. "But I did not know these men. If one is taking off, not at full altitude and loses power, as happened here, it can be a very dangerous situation. This was a tragedy that could have happened to any aircrew."

"Donald Williams? A flight officer and navigator and Alan Hillman a second lieutenant listed as bombardier. From the 323rd. They went down from flak over Gerolstein, Germany, on January 6, 1945. The plane was named *Jeanie*. You did not fly this mission."

"They were acquaintances," Addison confirmed. "I remember them but I can't tell you anything about them."

As I looked down the list I tried to visualize what it must have been like being in one's early twenties, waking up on any given non-flying-day morning, showering and shaving, putting on one's uniform, perhaps enjoying a first cigarette, strolling over to the 91st Bomb Group's Officer Combat Mess, looking at the others there and asking oneself: *who is going to die this week?* This had to have been a gladiatorial existence, no doubt.

The next event was the one that Addison told me about earlier that he had witnessed firsthand. "Frank Adams, the first lieutenant pilot and Lt. Col. Marvin Lord, the co-pilot and bomb group leader from the 324th. You saw this happen, Addison, on your February 3 mission to Berlin, *Operation Thunderclap*. All were lost including Capt. Nando Cavalier, the bomb group bombardier and two other officers, lieutenants Arthur Ebarb and Stanley Sweitzer. The plane was B-17G No. 42-97632 and unnamed."

Addison now provided detail that had escaped him in an earlier session. "It was a direct hit from a big [caliber] flak gun behind the wing and it broke the airplane into two pieces," he said. "Being the lead plane it was equipped with H2X Mickey Radar, that meant that there was a big black curtain in the radio room to keep it as dark as possible for the radar operator. I remember seeing the four engines, which were still running, take the front section of the plane up and up while the black curtain fell out and floated gently down. It was an unbelievable sight. We flew past them and there were no chutes spotted."

Addison confirmed that he knew these men well, remembered them and that they had undoubtedly been especially targeted by the German flak battery because they were flying the always most dangerous lead position. "Lord was very young to hold the rank of lieutenant colonel," Addison added respectfully, "and I remember the morning of that mission standing next to him to receive the blessing from Father Ragan."

"Was he Catholic?" I asked.

"No, he was not." I looked over at my friend and saw him sobbing. "He was a special person, Dick, they all were," Addison whispered, tears flowing from his eyes. In addition to Lord, the others killed had been Klette's crew. Of course Addison remembered.

"Addison?"

"I'm OK." Looking at my friend I could not help thinking of something out of the ordinary that I had seen in Marion H. Havelaar's excellent historical reference book, *The Ragged Irregulars of Bassingbourn—The 91st Bombardment Group in World War II*—a full-page color photograph of Marvin Lord dressed in his flying gear. Lord was the only pilot so distinguished in the extensive volume. I also thought: my concept of "closure" is invalid. Sixty-three years had gone by when I did this session with Addison and in his mind it was as if this tragedy had happened yesterday.

Addison motioned for me to continue and I did so.

"Eddie Knight, first lieutenant and pilot and Bruce Becker, second lieutenant bombardier? It was a direct flak hit over Burnberg on February 20 aboard B-17G No. 42-102490. You did not fly this mission, Addison, but these men were from your squadron, the 324th. Six men were killed and three ended up as POW's."

"Yes," Addison answered, looking away. His voice quivered: "That's all I can say."

"Peter Pastras, a Michigan man, first lieutenant and pilot. Robert Morris, second lieutenant and co-pilot, George Latches, second lieutenant and bombardier. 401st. A flak hit at Stendal on April 8. The airplane was named, *Times-a-Wasting*. Seven KIA and two POW."

The only recollection Addison had was the name of the bomber. "I may have flown that airplane," he said.

"Woodrow Lien, second lieutenant and co-pilot. A flak hit on the same mission over Stendal, but on a different airplane, *Wee Willie*. Four KIA, four MIA and one POW. From the 322nd." Addison confirmed that he had flown aboard *Wee Willie* but did not know Lien.

"Hollis Forbes, also from Michigan. He was the second lieutenant pilot. Everyone was killed in a crash landing at Weston, approximately 24 miles from Cambridge on April 12, 1945. From the 401st. Forbes dragged a wing tip of *The Peacemaker* on the ground. The other officers aboard were the co-pilot, 2nd Lt. Henry Maximovich and Flight Surgeon Maj. John Walker."

"I remember that crash near Cambridge, "Addison responded. "But I did not know these men. Flight surgeons occasionally went for rides," Addison added, "to see what it was like."

"The *Skunkface III* crew over Dresden on April 17, from your squadron. 1st Lt. pilot Harry Camp, 2nd Lt. co-pilot William Heath and 2nd Lt. Richard Penner, who was the navigator. You were not on this mission."

"Heath was from Kentucky, I believe" Addison said, "a fellow co-pilot. A buddy of mine and a good guy. I recollect Camp and Penner, but I was not close to either." I looked at Addison and sensed him trying hard to control his emotions. These were names that he had not heard in . . .

"And finally, Maj. James Griffin, who crashed trying to roll the Thunderbolt at 1,000 feet on May 5, 1945, the last casualty of the 91st. "What can you tell me about Major Griffin, Addison?"

"Well, I was in the Officer's Club celebrating the end of the war in Europe, and we heard him roaring outside. Then we heard the loud crash. He had gone down where two of our runways on the base intersected."

"Did you know him?"

"Yes. He was from my squadron. He was a great pilot but performed a maneuver too low. Also a BMOC, most definitely. He was well-liked."

"What was he doing flying a P-47?"

"I don't know."

―――――

IN MEMORIAM
Tribute to a Sense of Duty
A CONVERSATION WITH PAUL LYNCH

―――――

"From my readings, Paul, I believe it is fair to state that there is a significant amount of commentary put out by former American aircrew POWs that is highly critical of the way Luftwaffe personnel administered the stalag lufts and handled *The Black March*. In regard to the stalag lufts, their general complaint is that the Germans could have put forth a better effort with regard to food, sanitation and shelter. Also, the Nazis didn't have to be so mean with their gorilla-like sergeants. Trust me on this, Paul, following the war a large number of former POWs expressed strong resentment over how they had been treated."

I continued: "All the stalag lufts had certain elements in common: increasing hunger, cold, filth and endless roll calls in the open elements. Also, interestingly, each of the three major stalag lufts had a hidden radio."

"My question for you, Paul, is this: thinking back, did you harbor any resentment over how the Germans treated you while you were at Stalag Luft IV?"

"I wasn't at Stalag Luft IV very long," Paul observed. "But I did harbor some resentment. A friend of mine worked at Fort Devens, Massachusetts, and he made me aware of how well the German POWs there were treated. These POWs had first call on rationed food items over American citizens. Having said this, I will again state that I believe Germany tried to live up to the Geneva Convention."

Always the contrarian, I shot back: "If Boston had been laid in ruins by the Luftwaffe I suppose the German POWs at Fort Devens might have received different treatment, do you agree?"

To which Paul deflected: "As I believe I may have said earlier, Dick, war is not mankind's greatest endeavor."

"Would you like to learn the fate of the other major stalag lufts?"

"Yes."

"Every camp has its own story, Paul. At Stalag Luft III near Sagan, Poland, 10,300 American and non-American airmen POWs, including officers and noncoms, were force-marched over a two-day period in January 1945, some 55 miles to a railroad station. They ended-up in various POW camps across central Germany, to be liberated on a catch-as-catch-can basis."

I added: "As an aside, the 1960 movie *The Great Escape* was based on a March 1944 event at this camp. Seventy-six POWs, mostly British, made it out through a tunnel, and three actually made it to freedom in neutral countries. Hitler had the SS execute 50 British POW officers in reprisal."[7]

Paul remained silent but I could sense what he was thinking. "Yeah, Paul, Hitler took a dim view of escapers."

"On May Day the Red Army overran Stalag Luft I near Barth where Dave Bishop, RJ Miller and 10,000 other officer POWs were confined, the same camp that Gabreski wrote about. Of all the camps holding U.S. and British POWs, this one got the swiftest repatriation result. It happened that there was a workable airport nearby that the Soviets allowed the Americans and British to use. The airlift started May 12 and was completed by the 15th, only six days after Soviet V-E Day."

"And Paul?"

"Yes?"

"I don't know if this speedy return resulted from preferential treatment or not." I observed: "These officers may have just been lucky. They may have gotten out before the real haggling started. I did not locate anything addressing this issue, but I have to confess I didn't look that hard either."

As I uttered this, I mentally cackled: R.H.I.P.—rank has its privilege!

"As I said earlier, Stalag Luft IV has no counterpart, Paul. *The Black March* from Stalag Luft IV stands alone in the history of the Second World War in Europe."

Paul did not respond.

"I came across a book published by the University of Oklahoma Press in 2003 entitled *Our Last Mission*.[8] It contains a personal account of a Black Marcher who started from Lager "C". I mention the academic publisher because institutions of higher education invariably apply high standards to what they put out. Anecdotes and references are fact-checked. Scholarship is the goal."

"Paul?"

"Yes."

"While this Black Marcher expressed some sympathy for the suffering of his over-age captors, overall he had a distinctly different recollection about them than you did. What I am about to read to you is a coalesced selection of his comments taken from 16 pages of that book."

In the first thirty days of the march guards handed out less than one loaf of bread to each prisoner . . . At first the Germans threatened to shoot any prisoner caught trading for food with refugees or peasants . . . . . . Terror coursed through his limbs when a firing squad of German soldiers lined up thirty feet away . . . . . . "You have fifteen minutes to replace the stolen bread from my pack or I shoot these men . . ." . . . the bread ration was replaced . . . . . . There were some reports that when an ill prisoner dropped out of formation a guard fell out and a shot was heard . . . . . . guards abandoned feeble and ailing prisoners along the road . . .[9]

"This individual also marched past that city made famous by Martin Luther. He took a different route but ended up near to where you were."

"Care to comment, Paul?"

"That's not how I remember it, Dick."

"Looking back, what do think is the most remarkable thing about your story? Take a moment and think about it, please." I added: "After you tell me, I'll tell you what I think is the most remarkable thing. It came to me after I read and re-read your wartime memoir, *The Great Warrior*."

"That I got home again," Paul replied after reflecting. "Lucking out."

"That's a good answer. Now here is mine."

"You were on the march for over three months and not once do you report hearing the sound of gunfire, not even the sound of Allied warplane strafing. You walked through the heart of Nazi Germany, Paul, and the only time you heard gunfire was after VE Day when you were no longer, technically speaking, a POW. I find this circumstance astonishing."

Paul chuckled.

"Paul, why do you think Hitler refrained from executing you and the other POWs? Do you have ideas on this? I have an idea of my own, but I want to hear your thoughts before I express it."

"I believe the German general staff was in control of the war at that time so we were not destroyed."

"That may be, but I didn't find anything indicating that Hitler ever issued an order to exterminate American or British aircrew POWs. It is difficult to look into the mind of a psychopath, but everything I've learned about Der Führer points to him being racist. My hunch is he viewed you guys as Aryan."

When I said this to Paul, I thought again about what historian William L. Shirer wrote in *The Rise and Fall of the Third Reich* about that macabre conference on February 19, 1945—the day Hitler ordered Admiral Doenitz to weigh in on Goebbels recommendation to renounce the Geneva Convention and execute all U.S. and British airmen.

Paul did not agree. "We were not German Aryans," he said, adding: "We had good trading potential."

"I could be wrong, Paul. But I do think Hitler made major decisions based upon racial considerations. I recall seeing a *History Channel* presentation where a lady who knew Hitler from childhood came forward after the war and stated that Hitler told her that the Jews were being eliminated to preserve the biological balance in Europe, that is, to compensate for the high losses of German soldiers.[10] I believe the truth is no one will ever positively know what criteria Hitler weighed when he determined your fate."

I continued: "I did find a Nuremberg judgment that supports your opinion, Paul, that the German general staff prevented your destruction. The subject matter related to 'War Crimes and Crimes Against Humanity— Murder and Ill-treatment of Prisoners of War.' The court made the following finding of fact:"

> *In March, 1944, the OKH issued the "Kugel" or "Bullet" decree, which directed that every escaped officer and NCO prisoner of war who had not been put to work, with the exception of British and American prisoners of war should on recapture be handed over to the SIPO and SD. . . . These escaped officers and NCOs were to be sent to the concentration camp at Mauthausen, to be executed upon arrival, by means of a bullet shot in the neck.[11]*

"OKH stands for 'Oberkommando des Heeres,' the high command of the German Army. Apparently the Nazi generals did have a soft spot for the Brits and Americans, Paul, or did not order them murdered because of the Geneva Convention. How much Hitler may have had to do with this I could not determine." When I said this, I thought, incredulously: Would U.S. Army Chief of Staff General George C. Marshall attach his name to such a policy? Murdering prisoners and specifying a firearm execution not instantaneous is beyond the pale.

"Paul, did you ever make an attempt to contact any of the former POWs that were with you at Stalag Luft IV, on the march, or at Riesa?"

"No."

"Why not?"

"During the march I made a mental decision that if I ever got home I would put this entire rotten experience out of my mind. That is exactly what I did with the exception of the loss of my friends on the crew. I did make a trip to Montana to see Owen's family. Mrs. Monkman and my mother were in close contact through it all." Paul added: "It was a difficult trip for me to make, and not easy for the Monkmans either."

"So you repressed *The Black March*?"

"Yes, pretty much. Many years passed with no attempt at recollection on my part."

"Have you viewed website memorials for Stalag Luft IV POWs?"

"No."

I asked a question I knew the answer to. "What motivated you to write *The Great Warrior* in 1998, Paul, your 34-page war memoir that I quoted so heavily from?"

"It was at the strong urging of a cousin and my sister Eleanor. They thought I should preserve a record for the family."

Indeed, I thought. Paul opened *The Great Warrior* with this:

Never in the ten-million-year history of mankind on this planet has a person been so put upon by the very people he loves so dearly, namely Barry and Eleanor. Nixon had his Watergate, the Clintons their Whitewater-gate and I have my Naggers-gate. In spite of this burden, I will attempt to marshal my meager strengths and abilities to describe the portion of my life devoted to my tour of England and Germany as a special representative of the U.S. Army Air Forces.

"Paul, you earlier mentioned that you had a trip to Germany after the war. Tell me about it, please."

"I was invited to a research conference in 1978 to present a paper I had written about lead poisoning. Everyone was very friendly and there was no mention of the war." Paul added: "It was held at a technical college near Munich."

"Did you visit any of the places that you marched through?"

"No."

"Were you curious to do so?"

"Not really."

"And your reunion with Addison and Dave Bishop?"

"The three of us got together for the first time in 1998 at the 91st Bomb Group reunion in Savannah, Georgia. It was wonderful to see them after so many years. So much time had passed and we were still in good shape!"

Hearing this, I imagined how I would have felt if I were in Paul's shoes. I knew that Addison and Dave had seen each other now and then after the war, but Paul had not seen either man since late November 1944. I thought: wow.

I moved to a new topic.

"Paul, you may be correct in your assessment that your camp commandant was not out to make the lives of POWs miserable. Bombach was in a tough spot. When the Great Escape took place in 1944, Hitler seriously considered executing a number of Luftwaffe officers who he held responsible for letting it happen, including the camp commandant of Stalag Luft III. In the end Hitler didn't murder his turnkeys, but rather inflicted his maniacal wrath on POWs in violation of international law. My point is, Bombach and all the camp commandants had to be forever mindful of who they worked for and the fact that the SS might show up at any moment unannounced. The absence of atrocities at Stalag Luft IV, however, apart from the gauntlet run should count for something I suppose."

I added, "On the other hand, Bombach was a senior officer in the Luftwaffe, in a position of command and had the non transferable responsibility under the Geneva Convention to diminish the unavoidable rigors of prisoners of war and also mitigate their fate. Approximately 1,500 POWs under his charge died during his watch. Given what I have learned about quite a number of these deaths, I don't feel one bit sorry for him for having been arrested, detained and subjected to a rigorous criminal investigative process. The fact that he was not prosecuted does not, in my opinion, make him a good guy." I added: "*The New York Times* on May 14, 1945 ran a story on the bitterness of released American POWs who endured the 500-mile march. Their anger seemed to be focused on the commandant. One of them said to a reporter, and I quote from the article, '. . . [he] spelled out slowly the name of the German officer who left standing American prisoners to die on the roadside.' "

"And Paul?"

"Yes."

"I wish to pay you a compliment."

Paul waited for me to continue. "You did not find fault with your guards even though I gave you every opportunity to do so. You viewed these Germans as human beings not unlike yourself, that is, people trapped in an inextricably bad situation. In fact, you expressed gratitude for the protection they offered when you encountered angry civilians and SS Cadets. I salute you on this. I also believe that you have been blessed to return relatively unscathed by this amazingly traumatic ordeal; being able to live a happy and productive life in spite of what you went through. You married, had a family, pursued higher education and enjoyed a long professional career.

After a pause I continued: "Paul, you chose to end *The Great Warrior* with the following statement:"

> *At this point the reader should realize that, in reality, I was no great warrior but I was indeed a very, very lucky survivor.*

"I'm not sure that I agree with your self-assessment, Paul, and I'll tell you why." After another, more pregnant pause, I did the talking, practically all of it.

"Four years ago when I started this project Addison told me that you were smart."

"What does that have to do with anything?"

"You were that NCO, Paul, the one selected for Norden bombsight training." As I said this I thought: also brave, strong and disciplined.

"So?"

I ignored Paul and continued: "You fired your machine gun."

"As did others."

"You jumped when ordered and saved yourself. You made your parachute fall as instructed."

By now Paul sensed where I was going and that it would be useless for him to try to stop me from saying what I intended to say. "You did not display fear while at Dulag Luft."

"You survived the march, and without nourishment due to a theft, I might add, during that first critical week. You experienced no racking shoulder pain from carrying your bedroll and gear. You drank only boiled water and slept in the extreme cold with other men, like that British pharmacist instructed. How did Senator Warner put it? '. . . forced to do something that would be difficult for well nourished, healthy and appropriately trained infantry soldiers to accomplish . . .' You found those kohlrabies, Paul, you did not starve to death. You did instinctively what today is taught at the U.S. Air Force survival school."

"You had an action plan for the SS. You weren't about to be put down without a struggle."

"And Paul?"

"You escaped and passed through a battle line. You figured out how to do it." I added: "And in doing so you earned the respect of members of a Red Army combat unit."

"And about that Red Army Sergeant, Paul?"

"Did it ever occur to you that maybe he put in a good word about you with that Russian Major? And the Major ordered his good-looking doctor to interview you to assess your leadership suitability?"

"Well it occurs to me," I said. "Of the four escaper-sergeants, you were the one selected, Paul."

"Finally, you got yourself and the men in your charge out alive. Things could have gone very wrong in Dodge City. I expect you told your men to hunker down and this was a smart thing to do."

"Was luck an element in your survival? Absolutely. Did Addison have luck when that 88mm shell passed cleanly through his wing? I could go on, Paul, but no. Like Addison you are a hero and a great warrior. You are both great warriors, in fact as good as America has ever produced."

"Don't say a word, Paul, I'm about to conclude. I'm glad you suggested to me that we do this, for as I interviewed you it dawned on me that the war annals of the 91st Bomb Group are as much about what happened on the ground as in the air."

"When I did this *In Memoriam* session with Addison, I used in his account *real names* of airmen from the 91st who died, men that he might have flown with and known. The details of their deaths are published."

"Paul, I cannot do the same with you because practically all the men who perished on *The Black March* disappeared without a trace. Unlike with Addison, I have no specific information about individuals to provide to you. I have nothing with which to refresh your recollection."

"I have no doubt that the U.S. Air Force today has a fairly complete listing of names of the 1,500 Americans who perished during *The Black March*. In my research I located the names of seven who did not make it. They died of disease. They marched from Lager "C" and were tended to by Flight Surgeon Dr. Leslie Caplan. I found their identities in Caplan's deposition."

I finished: "The names of these men can serve to solemnize what could have happened to you, Paul. I believe war stories should include the actual names of those who gave . . ." I paused and added: "How did Lincoln put it? 'The last full measure of devotion.' "

"Yes," Paul said. "Yes."

"These American heroes are casualties of a just war. They aren't from the 91st but that doesn't matter. Let them stand for all."

George E. Briggs	39 193 615	S/Sgt
John C. Clark	33 279 680	S/Sgt
Edward B Coleman	12 083 471	S/Sgt
George F. Grover	16 066 436	S/Sgt
William Lloyd	18 217 669	S/Sgt
Harold H. Mack	17 128 736	S/Sgt
Robert M. Trapnell	13 068 648	S/Sgt

Addison Bartush (continued)
"Addison, it occurs to me that America today in many ways is a far different society than it was during World War II. I'm referring to the ideological component. Would you agree with that?"

"Absolutely."

"Let me show you something." I pulled from the pile two letters that had been mailed to him while he flew combat; both were from Gesu Conference—St. Vincent De Paul Society. "It's printed here proudly in the headline of the *Gesu Newsette*, '1,000 U of D. High Grads Serve.'" I handed Addison the *Servicemen's Edition*. "Look."

"Do you think you would see such a headline today in an American high school newspaper, even if it were only five serving in the Middle East?"

"No, I do not."

"Let me read to you something else from the newsletter. I don't expect that you knew the young man mentioned but he has nothing to do with the point that I am making."

Pro Dio; Pro Patria
A memorial mass was offered in Gesu church this week for Pfc. Robert Phillips, 20-year-old son of Mr. and Mrs. Philips of Tuller Avenue. Pfc. Philips died for his God and his country during the invasion of the Peleliu islands.

"We believed, back then, that we were doing the morally right thing, do you agree?

"Yes, and I feel bad about what is going on in America today," Addison responded.

There was no need for him to elaborate.

When I thought back to my sessions with Addison while working on this book, I had no doubt that the members of the 324th had a great deal of respect and even outright admiration for their military leaders—Klette, Terry, Lord, et al. I asked myself: is this the fabric of mainstream American society now? Today, some might casually dismiss such loyalty as a subtle form of fascism; ironically the very thing Addison and his cohorts fought against and many of them lost their lives over. This dismissal of the special bond between the men and their leaders, I expect, gives little regard to the enormity of the historical record of Adolf Hitler and the Nazi regime.

"Addison, I know that you and your brothers received an incredible amount of support from your parents, loved ones and friends going through this ordeal. I mean there are those hundreds of letters. Your mother wrote you when there was nothing else for her to report other than a menu item.

She wanted you to have something to open up and read from home, for you to know that she was thinking about you."

I looked over at Addison and saw that he was holding back tears.

"And I want to pay you and your family a compliment, Addison, for it occurs to me that your father had enough money to probably have pulled some strings for his sons. I don't know that he didn't try, but my sense is from reading his letters that he was a 'duty, honor, country' guy down the line."

Addison could not speak but rather nodded agreement.

"A final complement, Addison, and this time it is to you and to all of your same age friends who wrote to you. I read their letters. There was a lot of humor and some complaining, yes, but I did not see anything inappropriate regarding subject matter, language, or prejudice.

"Addison, do you think young Americans today have any appreciable knowledge of World War II?"

"They probably know it happened, but that's about all."

"Do you think young people should study the history of this war?"

"I think it would help them immensely."

"Why?"

"It could happen again. Human nature has not changed." When I heard Addison say this I could not help adding mentally: You are correct Addison. The only thing that has changed is technology, and in regards to war, not for the better. Weaponry today is more lethal than ever.

"What have you told your only grandchild, Stephen, about your war experiences?"

"Stephen's mother has told him that I was in the war. I have not talked to Stephen about it."

"What would you want Stephen to know? After all Addison, your military experience is ultimately being preserved for him, is it not? Isn't this the reason that you wanted to be interviewed?"

"Is it?"

"Yes, I believe it is. Stephen is a teenager now and as such this probably won't mean that much to him. But many years from now I think this might mean a whole lot to him, particularly if he becomes a father and he views his children in the same light that your father viewed you and your siblings. What would you want Stephen to know about your experience in this horrible world-wide event?"

"That World War II did not make us secure," Addison said. "That it worked for a while, then the peace that was achieved fell apart."

"And you are sorry for that?

"I am very sorry for that."

"Addison, circling back to Mrs. Monkman, when she wrote you in 1946, she asked you a question and I am going to now ask you the same question again." I withdrew the old letter from its envelope; it had been badly stained by acid leaching from the newspaper clipping of her son's death. The top of its pages had a photograph of the Grand Teton mountain range taken from the Montana side. I read slowly to Addison the words that she had written 62 years earlier.

"Do you feel the war and the sacrifice of millions was worthwhile?"

"Well, Addison? What say you?"

Addison looked at me and pondered a response. After a moment he answered in the only way that in my opinion, anyway, made sense.

"Yes and no," he uttered. "Yes and no."

"Would you like to hear how Mrs. Monkman answered her own question? I think it is appropriate to let her have the last word, don't you?" Addison nodded for me to proceed. "This is what a grieving mother wrote in answer to her own question so long ago:"

Somehow I am doubtful for all we still hear is war, and there is an armament race on. You boys who were in it—I do hope you will speak out, now and loudly, and ever more loudly—against war—and all its trappings.

The Altenbeken Viaduct today.

Notes

CHAPTER ONE

1   *The History Place, World War II in Europe*, as reported at http://www.historyplace.
    com/worldwar2/timeline/posen.htm (date accessed 1/28/2011)

2   *History of Keesler Air Force Base*, as reported at http://keesler.af.mil/library/factsheets/
    factsheet.asp?id=4881 (date accessed 2/11/2011). "Generally unknown to most
    was the role that the Tuskegee Airmen and other black troops played on Keesler.
    In fact, more than 7,000 were stationed at Keesler Field by the autumn of 1943.
    These soldiers included pre-aviation cadets, radio operators, aviation technicians,
    bombardiers and aviation mechanics."

3   Ambrose, Stephen E., *The Wild Blue.* New York: Simon & Schuster, 2001, p. 65

4   Headquarters, Department of the Army, Washington DC, *Field Manual 23-65,
    Browning Machine Gun Caliber .50 HB M2,* Chapter 1-7 Table 1-1 General Data, as
    reported at http://m2hb.net/manuals/fm23_65.pdf (date accessed 12/27/2013)

CHAPTER TWO

1   National Museum of the US Air Force, *Norden M-9 Bombsight*, as reported at
    http://www.nationalmuseum.af.mil/factsheets/factsheet.asp?id=8056 (date ac-
    cessed 12/27/2013). The bombing raid mentioned was an attack on ball-bearing
    factories at Schweinfurt.

2   Obituary of Owen Monkman, August 1946 (newspaper clipping—publisher un-
    known)

3   Nichol, John and Rennell, Tony, *Tail-End Charlies—The Last Battles of the Bomber
    War, 1944–1945.* New York: Thomas Dunn Books, an imprint of St. Martin's
    Press, 2006, p. 243

4   *Combat Chronology*, op. cit., October 1944, as reported at http://paul.rutgers.edu/
    ~mcgrew/wwii/usaf/html/Oct.44.html (date accessed August 4, 2013)

CHAPTER THREE

1 DiGeorge, Pat, *Liberty Lady, a B-17 Bomber Crew, the OSS and a Wartime Love Story*, as reported at http://libertyladybook.com/2009/04/14/schweinfurt/ (date accessed 12/29/2013)

2 Havelaar, Marion H. with Hess, William N., *The Ragged Irregulars of Bassingbourn— The 91st Bombardment Group in World War II*. Atglen, PA: A Schiffer Military History Book, 1995, introduction by Roger A. Freeman, p. 7

3 Havelaar, op. cit.,p. 59 (Chapter 6 pp. 55–62 relates the BG history of the Schweinfurt raid)

4 Havelaar, op. cit., p. 71

5 Havelaar, op. cit., p 71-75

6 BBC Home—WWII People's War as reported at http://www.bbc.co.uk/history/ww2peopleswar/stories/54/a4841354.shtml (date accessed 3/20/2012)

7 Addison's mission list reflects 27 combat missions. The other four missions represent credited recalls and are not shown.

8 Havelaar, op. cit., p. 169

9 Havelaar, op.cit

10 Havelaar, op. cit., p. 161

11 Spartacus Educational, *The Blitz*, as reported at http://www.spartacus.schoolnet.co.uk/2WWblitz.htm (date accessed 12/28/2013)

12 Frisbee, John L., *Air Force Magazine*, May 1986, Vol. 69, No. 5, as reported at http://www.afa.org/magazine/valor/0586valor.asp

13 Frisbee, op. cit., p. 1

14 Frisbee, op. cit.

15 Frisbee, op. cit., p. 2

16 Getz, Lowell L., as reported at http://www.91stbombgroup.com/chapter_1.htm p. 17 (date accessed 3/24/2008)

17 Frisbee, op. cit., p. 2

18 Frisbee, op. cit.

19 National Geographic, *The Wings: How the Yanks of the Eighth Air Force Helped*; March 1994; insert about Father Ragan at p. 100; also see *History of Father Michael S. Ragan*, as reported at http://frragan.com/albums/08FrRagan/frraganblesses91stbombgroupinbassingbourneengland.html (date accessed 08/10/2013)

CHAPTER FOUR

1 Bailey, Ronald H. and the Editors of Time-Life Books, *The Air War in Europe*. Alexandria, VA: World War II Time-Life Books, 1981, p. 183

2 *Combat Chronology of the US Army Air Forces* November 1944, as reported at http://paul.rutgers.edu/~mcgrew/wwii/usaf/html/Nov.44.html (date accessed 3/18/2008)

3   World War 2 Headquarters, *WWII German 88mm Anti-aircraft, Artillery Gun*, as re-
     ported at http://worldwar2headquarters.com/HTML/weapons/german/88gun.
     html (date accessed 12/28/2013) "Over 18,000 (including all variants were built
     during the war." Note: including other calibers and pre-war production figures,
     total AA guns equated to approximately 25,000.
4   Grant, Rebecca, "Twenty Missions in Hell" *Air Force Magazine*, April 2007, p. 75
5   U.S. Army Technical Manual TM E9-369A: German 88mm Antiaircraft Gun Ma-
     terial, June 29, 1943, as reported at http://www.lonesentry.com/manuals/88mm
     antiaircraft-gun/88mm-antiaircraft-gun-introduction.html (date accessed 12/28/
     2013) "Rate of fire: 20 rounds per minute (practical rate at an aerial target)"
6   Grant, op. cit., p. 74
7   Grant, op. cit., p. 76
8   Halpert, Sam, *Mission List, 324th Bomb Squadron, 91st Bomb Group* as reported at
     http://www.b17sam.com/misionlist.html (date accessed 2/27/2008). Also see
     Halpert, Sam, *A Real Good War.* St. Petersburg, FL: Southern Heritage Press 1997.
9   *History, The 91st Bomb Group (H) Section One,* prepared by the 91st Bomb Group
     Memorial Association (undated) p. 2 (note: no author shown; this reference book-
     let is a 91st BG reunion handout provided to the author by J. Addison Bartush)
10   Havelaar, op. cit., p 161 The author describes the planning for the disastrous
     November 2, 1944, raid on Merseburg as follows:

     For some weeks Luftwaffe opposition had been almost nil and air-
     crews were beginning to believe that it had been defeated and would
     no longer be a large threat to them. However, the Germans had been
     carefully conserving their fuel until they could make a massive inter-
     ception of the bombers and extract a crippling number from their
     formations. November 2nd was the day chosen for the Luftwaffe to
     put up over 500 single-engine fighters to oppose the bomber stream
     of the Eighth Air Force.

     The 91st Bomb Group put thirty-seven B-17s in the air for the mission and thirty-
     six of them would drop their bombs. The course to the target was as if a ruler had
     been used and it went directly to the target. There was no zig-zag or any deviation
     that would tend to pull any aerial opposition away from the target area.
11   Frisbee, op. cit., p. 2
12   Bailey, Time-Life Books, op. cit., p. 184
13   Bailey, Time-Life Books, op. cit., p. 183
14   Bailey, Time-Life Book, op. cit., p. 182
15   Bailey, Time-Life Books, op. cit., p. 184

CHAPTER FIVE
1   Havelaar, op. cit ., p. 173.

2 Stout, Jay A., *Unsung Eagles*. Philadelphia & Oxford: Casemate, 2013, p. 234

3 Ask: *How Fast Does a Skydiver Fall?* as reported at http://www.ask.com/question/how-fast-does-a-skydiver-fall (date accessed 12/28/2013)

4 Letter from Pearl Bishop dated January 17, 1945

5 Havelaar, op. cit., p. 189

6 Army Air Forces Statistical Digest, World War II, *Battle Casualties in all Overseas Theaters* as reported at http://www.usaaf.net/digest/t34.htm (date accessed 12/28/2013)

7 *Accident-Report.com Military Aviation Incident Reports*, as reported at http://www.accident-report.com/crews/alpha/namep_phif.html (date accessed 10/26/2013); also *Eighth Air Force Historical Society, Aircraft Groups*, as reported at http://www.8thafhs.com/db/get_one_acgroup.php?acgroup_id=47 (date accessed 10/26/2013)

8 *Combat Chronology*, op. cit., November 30, 1944

9 Havelaar, op. cit. p. 174

10 Royal Air Force RAF Wyton *Heritage Center Pathfinder Collection* (see tactics section), as reported at http://www.raf.mod.uk/rafbramptonwyton/history/thepathfinderforce.cfm (date accessed 12/30/2013)

11 Havelaar, op. cit., p. 175

12 Letter from Miss Mary B. dated December 10, 1944.

13 V-Mail letter by Lt. John M. Antes dated February 13, 1945

14 US Air Force National Center for PTSD as reported at http://www.ptsd.va.gov/apps/aboutface/service-branches/usaf.html (date accessed 12/30/2013)

15 World War II Database, *Battle of the Bulge 16 Dec 1944–28 Jan 1944*, as reported at http://ww2db.com/battle_spec.php?battle_id=42 (date accessed 12/30/2013) "The Allies suffered 76,890 casualties (with 8,607 Americans killed)"

16 *Dailies of the 324th Squadron*, as reported at http://www.91stbombgroup.com/Dailies/324th1944.html (date accessed 8/11/2012)

17 Nichol, op. cit., p. 245

18 Havelaar, op. cit., p. 176

CHAPTER SIX

1 Yale Law School, *The Avalon Project—Documents in Law, History and Diplomacy*; *War Crimes and Crimes Against Humanity—Murder and Ill-treatment of Prisoners of War; Opinion of Parker, John J., Alternate Judge, Nuremberg Trial of Major War Criminals*, as reported at http://avalon.law.yale.edu/imt/judwarcr.asp (date accessed 7/31/2012)

2 American Prisoners of War in Germany—*Dulag Luft*—Prepared by Military Intelligence Service War Department, 1 November 1945—Compiled and presented by Greg Hatton, as reported at http://www.b24.net/pow/dulag.htm (date accessed 12/30/2013)

3   Simmonds, Kenneth W., *Kriegie* (published 1960), as reported at http://www.merkki.com/new_page_2.htm (date accessed 05/16/2012)

4   Gabreski, Francis, *Gabby—A Fighter Pilot's Life* (Orion Books, a division of Crown Publishers 1991) p. 188, commenting on his stay at Oberursel: "The following day I was taken from my hot box, allowed to shower, and then introduced to my interrogator . . . I decided to come on strong, so I started right in to complain about the heat in my cell . . . Smooth as silk . . . [he] apologized for the thoughtless treatment. It must have been an accident, he said. He would take care of it immediately. So now he took on the role of the good guy."

5   Gabreski, op. cit., p. 193

6   International Red Cross Inspection Report, Stalag Luft IV, January 1945, as reported at http://en.wikipedia.org/wiki/Stalag_Luft_IV (date accessed 05/18/ 2012)

7   For information on the French POW experience in World War II see Helion, Jean, *They Shall Not Have Me: The Capture, Forced Labor, and Escape of a French Prisoner in World War II.* New York: Arcade Publishing, 2012.

8   Schumacher, John C., *Story of WWII Shoot Down and POW Experiences*, as reported at http://www.rb-29.net/html/79SchumacherSty/07.01shcum.html (date accessed 05/30/2011). Chapter 7 *"Camp Life—The Good, The Bad, The Ugly."*

9   Gabreski, op. cit., p. 194

10 O'Donnell, Joseph P., *POW 1414*, as reported at http://www.remember-history.com/my-heroes/sgt-joseph-p-odonnell-pow-1414/ (date accessed 07/12/2012)

11 Gabreski, op. cit.

12 Report of the International Committee of the Red Cross Visit of October 5 & 6, 1944 by Mr. Biner, Stalag Luft IV, as reported at http://www.b24.net/pow/stalag4.htm (date accessed 6/12/2012) p. 3 of 6

13 Report of the International Committee of the Red Cross Visit of October 5 & 6, 1944 by Mr. Biner, Stalag Luft IV, op. cit., pp. 1 and 2 of 6

14 Report of the International Committee of the Red Cross Visit of October 5 & 6, 1944 by Mr. Biner Stalag Luft IV as reported at http://www.b24.net/pow/stalag4.htm (date accessed 08/28/2013)

15 Bunyak, Dawn Trimble, *Our Last Mission—A World War II Prisoner in Germany.* Norman, OK: University of Oklahoma Press, 2003. P.105 "A German at the camp took this photograph and the rest of the photographs at Stalag Luft 4. The guard traded the photographs for contraband. Sgt. Frank Paules, camp spokesman, carried the photographs back to the United States after liberation"

16 Hillenbrand, Laura, *Unbroken.* New York: Random House, 2010,.p. 263

17 Frisbee, John L., Valor: Lest We Forget, airforce-magazine.com, Vol. 80, No. 9, September 1997 as reported at http://www.airforce-magazine.com?Magazine Archive/Pages/1997/Sep (date accessed 5/22/2011)

18 Congressional Record, Proceedings and Debates of the 104th Congress, First Session, Vol. 141, Washington, Monday May 8, 1995, No. 75 Senate Commemorating the 50th Anniversary of the Forced March of American Prisoners of War from Stalag Luft IV

19 Bunyak, op. cit., see Chapter 13 "The Gauntlet" pp 127-132

20 Caplan, Leslie, M.D., *Testimony Regarding Mistreatment of American POWs at Stalag Luft IV (given 31 December 1947)* as reported at http://www.rb-29.net/html/79 SchumacherSty/07.01shcum.html (date accessed 05/30/2011).

21 The sadistic Luftwaffe guard was nicknamed "Big Stoop" by the POWs after a bad character in the comic strip *Terry and the Pirates*. See Schumacher, op. cit., Chapter 7: Schumacher states that he lost his hearing in his left ear as a consequence of being attacked during an inspection by Big Stoop who was "about 50 years old." Also Krebs, William A., *Testimony for the Judge Advocate War Crimes Investigation*, as reported at http://www.stalagluft4.org/krebs.htm (date accessed 05/30/2011) Krebs testified on 10 June 1945 that Big Stoop, ". . . a man by the name of Schmidt . . ." along with other Germans went through his barracks and stole " . . . watches, rings and other objects . . . " Additionally see, Caplan, op. cit. "Big Stoop was the most hated of the guards." In regard to ear cuffing POWs, Dr. Caplan testified, "This would cause pressure on the eardrums which sometimes punctured them." Also see: "*Big Stoop*" at http://www.feldgrau.net/forum/viewtopic.php?f=26&t=14175 (date accessed 6/6/2012). "Big Stoop the giant from Stalag Luft IV . . . had come with the prisoners all the way to Moosburg. He could not have realized how hated he was . . . There are various accounts of his death . . . head in a bushel basket . . . a pickaxe in his head . . ."

22 Bunyak, op. cit., p. 137

23 Deposition of Capt. Henry J. Wynsen for Judge Advocate General's Investigation, 20 July 1945, as reported at http://www.b24.net/pow/stalag4.htm (date accessed 6/6/2012).

24 Gabreski, op. cit., pp. 196-197

25 Mrazek, Robert J., *To Kingdom Come: An Epic Saga of Survival in the Air War Over Germany*. New York: New American Library, a division of Penguin Group, 2011, p. 288

CHAPTER SEVEN

1 *324th Squadron Dailies from 1945*, as reported at http://www.91stbombgroup.com/Dailies/324th1945.html (date accessed 8/11/2012)

2 USAAF Chronicles, op. cit., January 1945

3 Getz, op. cit., p. 25

4 Wikipedia, *V-1 and V-2 Rockets*, as reported at http://en.wikipedia.org/wiki/V-1_

flying_bomb and http://en.wikipedia.org/wiki/V-2 (date originally accessed 7/20/2009)

5 *V-2* as reported at http://en.wikipedia.org/wiki/V-2 (date accessed 10/2/2012)

6 *V-2*, op. cit.

7 Door, Robert F., *B-24 Units of the Eighth Air Force, Osprey Combat Aircraft #15*. Oxford: Osprey Publishing, 1999, p. 74

8 Letter from Eileen Kircheson of Purley, Surrey to Addison dated March 20, 1945.

9 *West End at War*, as reported at http://www.westendatwar.org.uk/page_id_224_path_0p28p.aspx (date accessed 10/9/2012)

10 Havelaar, op. cit., Appendix 2, Aircraft Assigned

11 Havelaar, op. cit., p. 221

12 Schaffer, Ronald, *Wings of Judgment—American Bombing in World War II*. New York & Oxford: Oxford University Press, 1985, p. 96

13 Salmaggi, Cesare and Pallavisini, Cesare, *2194 Days of War*. New York: Barnes & Noble Books, 1977, p. 666

14 *Stars and Stripes*, London Edition, Wednesday January 3, 1945, p. 1

15 For details on British heavy bombing of German cities see http://en.wikipedia.org/wiki/Sir_Arthur_Harris,_1st_Baronet (date accessed 6/25/2012)

16 Wikipedea, *Operation Gomorrah*, as reported at http://en.wikipedia.org/wiki/Bombing_of_Hamburg_in_World_War_II (date accessed 6/28/2012)

17 Schaffer, op. cit., pp. 96–97

18 Ibid

19 Havelaar, op. cit., p. 179

20 Schaffer, op. cit., p.97

21 Bailey, Time Life Books, op. cit., p. 188

22 Havelaar, op. cit., p. 179

23 Allen, Thomas B., *The Wings of War: How the Yanks of the Eighth Air Force helped turn the Tide in World War II, National Geographic*, March 1994 p. 94

24 *324th Squadron Dailies from 1945* op. cit

CHAPTER EIGHT

1 Paris, John "Pappy," *Pappy's War, A B-17 Gunner's World War II Memoir*. Bennington, VT: Merriam Press, 2004, as also reported at http://www.398th.org/History/Veterans/History/Paris/Paris_March.html (date accessed 4/13/2011). This compelling personal account begins: "The Black March! I choose this title. Some went so far as to call it the Death March. Many were marked for life, while others died along the way. I prefer to reserve that infamous title for my comrades who suffered the obscenities of the Japanese bayonet on the infamous Bataan 'Death March.' The dirt roads were rutted, water filled, and with a crust of dirty ice on top."

2   Air Force Magazine, *Valor: Lest We Forget* Vol. 80, No. 9, September 1997

3   Bailey, Ronald H., and the Editors of Time-Life Books, op. cit., *Prisoners of War World War II*. Alexandria, VA: Time-Life Books, 1981, p. 170, reporting that on January 27, 1945 at 10:00 p.m., "The German guards gave them [the 10,300 airmen POWs at Stalag Luft III] an hour's notice to pack and prepare to march west." The forced march lasted approximately one week; crowded railroad cars were used for part of the travel.

4   Yale Law School, *The Avalon Project—The Yalta Conference—Agreement regarding Japan* as reported at http://avalon.law.yale.edu/wwii/yalta.asp (date accessed 3/31/2012)

5   Yale Law School, *The Avalon Project: Agreement Relating to Prisoners of War and Civilians Liberated by Forces Operating Under Soviet Command and Forces Operating Under United States of America Command: February 11, 1945*, as reported at http://avalon. law.yale.edu/20th_century/sov007.asp (date accessed 10/17/2011)

6   *The Herald Tribune*, February 15, 1945

7   Wikipedia, *Stalag Luft IV* as reported at http://en.wikipedia.org/wiki/Stalag_ Luft_IV "On February 6, 1945 some 8,000 of Luft 4 set out on what would be called The Black March" (date accessed 1/11/2011); also the American National Red Cross POW Bulletin Volume 2, No. 12, issued in December 1944 reported Luft IV as having "40 barracks, each housing 200 men" which supports the 8,000 figure.

8   Air Force Magazine, op. cit.

9   Air Force Magazine, op. cit.

10 Stupak, Steven, *Veterans History Project*, Central Connecticut State University; Center for Public Policy and Social Research, interview conducted December 18, 2003, as reported at http://contentlibrary.ccsu.edu/cdm4/item_viewer.php?CISOROOT =/VHP&CISOPTR=2757 (date accessed 05/20/2011)

11 Air Force Magazine, op. cit., refers to "sub-zero weather" at the beginning of the forced march.

12 Paris, op. cit., p. 5-6

13 Paris, op cit. The material quoted is from the 398th Bomb Group Memorial Association website. The published book version is: Paris, John "Pappy," *Pappy's War, A B-17 Gunner's World War II Memoir* (Merriam Press 2004)

CHAPTER NINE

1   PBS: The War: *Dresden, Air Attack On (13-15 February 1945)*, as reported at http:// www.pbs.org/thewar/detail_5229.htm (date accessed 12/30/2013); History: *February 13, 1945 Firebombing of Dresden* as reported at http://www.history.com/this-day-in-history/firebombing-of-dresden (date accessed 12/30/2013) "Eight square miles of the city was ruined." Also see http://en.wikipedia.org/wiki/Bombing_of_

Dresden_in_World_War_II (date accessed 7/20/2009)

2   Nichol, op. cit., p. 264

3   Nichol, op. cit., p. 364

4   Havelaar, op. cit., p. 179

5   Nichol, op. cit., p. 274

6   Fowler, George, editor, *Holocaust at Dresden* Article from *The Barnes Review*, February 1995, pp. 3-13. *The Barnes Review*, 645 Pennsylvania Ave SE, Suite 100, Washington D.C. 20003, USA; "U.S. Chief of Staff George C. Marshall announced publicly that Dresden had been attacked at Stalin's specific request, although after the war the Soviets and East Germans repeatedly referred to the raid as a 'diabolical plan' of Churchill's 'to kill as many people as possible'."

7   *Combat Chronology*, op. cit.—February 14, 1945

8   Nichol, op. cit., p.274

9   Nichol, op. cit., p. 278

10 Bailey, Time Life Books op. cit., p. 188

11 Wikipedia, *Thunderclap Plan*, as reported at http://en.wikipedia.org/wiki/Thunderclap_plan (date accessed 10/3/2012

12 Davis, Richard G., *Operation 'Thunderclap': The U.S. Army Air Forces and the Bombing of Berlin* (Journal of Strategic Studies, Volume 14, Issue 1, 1991)

CHAPTER TEN

1   *Kohlrabi, cooked, boiled, drained without salt*, as reported at http://nutritiondata.self.com/facts/vegetables-and-vegetable-products/2467/2 (date accessed 3/21/2012)

2   Shirer, William L., *The Rise and Fall of the Third Reich.* New York: Simon & Schuster, 1960, p. 1428

3   Wikipedia, *Hanover World War II*, as reported at http://en.wikipedia.org/wiki/Hanover#World_War_II (date accessed 3/25/2012)

4   Bailey, Ronald H. and the Editors of Time Life Books, *Prisoners of War.* Alexandria, VA: World War II Time-Life Books,1981, p. 175

5   Yale Law School, *The Avalon Project: Agreement Relating to Prisoners of War and Civilians Liberated by Forces Operating Under Soviet Command and Forces Operating Under United States of America Command: February 11, 1945*, op. cit., Article 1

6   Yale Law School, *The Avalon Project*, op. cit., Article 2

CHAPTER ELEVEN

1   Salmaggi, op. cit., p. 689

2   Havelaar, op. cit., p. 189

3   Havelaar, op. cit., p. 189

4   *324th Squadron Dailies from 1945* op. cit

5   Cooke, Alistair, *The American Home Front 1941-42*. London: Allen Lane, The Penguin Group, 2006. p. 56: Louisville Doctor distrusted Roosevelt "because he listens too much to the Jews" and a Jewish "syndicate" took over the businesses in town; p. 61: Q: "If you live in Atlanta what is the first thing you ask of anybody?" A: "Are you an air-raid warden or a Gentile?"; p. Chicago: ". . . the all too human itch to relieve the sense of guilt for this honeymoon by blaming it on the Jews."

6   Heller, Joseph, *Catch-22*. New York: Borzoi Book published by Alfred A. Knopf, 1995, pp 100-101

7. Getz, Lowell L. *"Mary Ruth Memories of Mobile, Chapter 8. Pandemonium Over Pilsen: The Forgotten Final Mission,* p. 2

8. Getz, op. cit., p. 2

9. Ibid, p. 2

10. Headquarters, 1st Air Division, *First Over Germany,* Vol. 1, No. 4, May 5, 1945 p. 1 (document provided by J. Addison Bartush)

11. *CombatChronology,* op.cit—April 25,1945

12. Statement of Lt. Darling, 25 April 1945 as reported at http://www.91stbombgroup.com/Dailies/324th1945.html (date accessed 08/02/2014)

13. Nichol, op. cit., p.5

14. Statement of Flight Officer Schafts, 25 April 1945 as reported at http://www.91st bombgroup.com/Dailies/324th1945.html (date accessed 08/02/2014)

15. *CombatChronology*, op. cit—April 25, 1945

16. Havelaar, op. cit., p. 189

17. Getz, op. cit., p. 11

CHAPTER TWELVE

1   Bailey, Time-Life Books, op. cit., p. 171

2   Focke-Wulf Fw190, as reported at http://www.aviation-history.com/focke-wulf/fw190.html (date accessed 2/12/2012)

CHAPTER THIRTEEN

1   Pitt, Barrie, Consulting Editor, *The Military History of World War II*. London: Aerospace Publishing Limited, 1986, p. 294

2   Swanston, Alexander and Swanston, Malcolm, *The Historical Atlas of World War II*. Edison, NJ: Chartwell Books, Inc., 2007, p. 334

3   Grant, Ulysses S., *Memoirs*. New York: Library Classics of the United States, Inc., 1990, p. 728

4   Ward, Geoffrey C. and Burns, Ken, *The War.* New York: Alfred A. Knopf, 2007, Ward, p. 392

5   Green, Philip, Sequel to: Liberated by Cossacks, as reported at http://www.bbc.co.uk/history/ww2peopleswar/stories/07/a3194507.shtml (date accessed 09/06/

2014). "The town of Riesa was under Russian control and we were told to keep strictly within town limits, the war was still going on in sporadic outbursts, this was at the end of April 1945, the end came on May7th. Meanwhile it was made known to the ex 'Kriegies' (from Kriegsgefangener-Prisoners of War) that we would remain at Riesa until an EQUAL number of ex-Russian prisoners plus civilian slave workers had been assembled from the American and British sectors."

6   Yale Law School, *The Avalon Project: Agreement Relating to Prisoners of War and Civilians Liberated by Forces Operating Under Soviet Command and Forces Operating Under United States of America Command: February 11, 1945,* op. cit., Article 2, Paragraph 1

7   Bailey, Time-Life Books, op. cit., p. 177

8   Nikolai, *Forced Repatriation to the Soviet Union: The Secret Betrayal,* reprinted by permission from *Imprimus,* the monthly journal of Hillsdale College, December 1988, Vol. 17, No. 12, as reported on http://www2.hillsdale.edu/news/imprimis/archive/issue.asp?year=1988&month=12, (date accessed 10/05/2013)

9   Ibid, p. 2

10 Ibid

11 Holden, Herbert T., *The Continuing Relevance of Clausewitz: Illustrated Yesterday and Today,* p. 17, as reported at http://www.globalsecurity.org/military/library/report/1991/HHT.htm

12 Tolstoy, op cit., p 2

13 Ibid, pp 2-3

14 Ibid, p 3

15 Ibid, pp 4-5

16 Ibid, pp 7-8

17 Vercoe, Tony, *Survival at Stalag IVB: soldiers and airmen remember Germany's largest POW camp of World War II.* Jefferson, NC and London: MacFarland & Company, Inc., 2006, Vercoe, p. 181

18 Tolstoy, op. cit., p 5

19 Ibid p 6

20 Ibid

21 Ibid, p. 1

22 *New York Times,* May 12, 1945 *"NEW CENSOR RULE PROVOKE DISPUTE"*

23 *New York Times,* May 11, 1945, *"ALLIES IN GERMANY BAR FOREIGN PRESS"*

24 *New York Times,* May 14, 1945 *"SHAEF SHOWDOWN ON PRESS IS LIKELY"*

25 Vercoe, Tony, op, cit., Kurt Vonnegut quoted p. 174

EPILOGUE

1   Stephens, Bret, "Waterboarding and Hiroshima," *Wall Street Journal,* November 6, 2007, p. A18

2   Stephens, op. cit., quoting essayist Algis Valiunas

3   Stephens, op. cit.

4   Nichol, op. cit., pp 356-357

5   http://en.wikipedia.org/wiki/World_War_II_aircraft_production (date accessed 9/4/2012)

6   Wikipedia, *World War II casualties* as reported at http://en.wikipedia.org/wiki/ WWII_casualties (date accessed 7/20/2009)

7   Wikipedia, *Stalag Luft III*, as reported at http://en.wikipedia.org/wiki/Stalag_Luft_ III (date accessed 7/1/2012) Additional note: The Judgment at Nuremberg noted of the 50 executed British POW officers: "It was not contended by the defendants that this was other than plain murder, in complete violation of international law." See Yale Law School, *The Avalon Project*, op. cit; http://avalon.law.yale.edu/imt/ judwarcr.asp (date accessed 7/31/2012)

8   Bunyak, Dawn Trimble, *Our Last Mission—A World War II Prisoner in Germany.* Norman, OK: University of Oklahoma Press, 2003. see Chapter 16 "The Black March" pp 165-181

9   Bunyak, op. cit.

10 Jones, Bill Treharne, *The Fatal Attraction of Adolf Hitler*, a BBC centenary biography, broadcast April 1989. Henrietta Von Schirach, who had known Hitler since childhood, stated that she had confronted Hitler after witnessing Jews being rounded-up in Amsterdam. "Herr Hitler, you ought not be doing that," she reported saying to the Führer. Hitler's heated response, per her statement, was: "Every day 10,000 of my best soldiers die on the battlefield while others carry on living in the camps. That means the biological balance in Europe is not right anymore."

11 Yale Law School, *The Avalon Project*, op. cit; http://avalon.law.yale.edu/imt/jud-warcr.asp (date accessed 7/31/2012)

Selected Bibliography

Ambrose, Stephen E., *The Wild Blue.* New York: Simon & Schuster, 2001.

Bailey, Ronald H. and the Editors of Time-Life Books, *The Air War in Europe and Prisoners of War.* Alexandria, VA: World War II Time-Life Books, 1981.

Bunyak, Dawn Trimble, *Our Last Mission—A World War II Prisoner in Germany.* Norman, OK: University of Oklahoma Press, 2003.

Cooke, Alistair, *The American Home Front 1941–42.* London: Allen Lane, The Penguin Group, 2006.

Door, Robert F., *B-24 Units of the Eighth Air Force, Osprey Combat Aircraft #15.* Oxford: Osprey Publishing, 1999.

Grant, Ulysses S., *Memoirs.* New York: Library Classics of the United States, Inc., 1990.

Halpert, Sam, *A Real Good War.* St. Petersburg, FL: Southern Heritage Press 1997.

Havelaar, Marion H. with Hess, William N., *The Ragged Irregulars of Bassingbourn—The 91st Bombardment Group in World War II.* Atglen, PA: A Schiffer Military History Book, 1995.

Heller, Joseph, *Catch-22.* New York: Borzoi Book published by Alfred A. Knopf, 1995.

Helion, Jean, *They Shall Not Have Me: The Capture, Forced Labor, and Escape of a French Prisoner in World War II.* New York: Arcade Publishing, 2012.

Hillenbrand, Laura, *Unbroken.* New York: Random House, 2010.

Johnson, Richard Riley, *Twenty Five Milk Runs and a Few Others.* Victoria: Trafford Publishing, 2004.

Logan, Edward F., Jr. *Jump, Damn It, Jump!* Jefferson, NC and London: Mc-Farland & Company, Inc. Publishers, 2006.

McLaughlin, J. Kemp, *The Mighty Eighth Air Force in WWII, A Memoir.* Lexington, KY: The University Press of Kentucky, 2000.

Mrazek, Robert J., *To Kingdom Come: An Epic Saga of Survival in the Air War Over Germany.* New York: New American Library, a division of Penguin Group, 2011.

Meurs, John, *Not Home for Christmas: A Day in the Life of the Mighty Eighth.* Brandon, MS: Quail Ridge Press, 2009.

Nichol, John and Rennell, Tony, *Tail-End Charlies—The Last Battles of the Bomber War, 1944-1945.* New York: Thomas Dunn Books, an imprint of St. Martin's Press, 2006.

Paris, John "Pappy," *Pappy's War, A B-17 Gunner's World War II Memoir.* Bennington, VT: Merriam Press, 2004.

Pitt, Barrie, Consulting Editor, *The Military History of World War II.* London: Aerospace Publishing Limited, 1986.

Salmaggi, Cesare and Pallavisini, Cesare, *2194 Days of War.* New York: Barnes & Noble Books, 1977.

Schaffer, Ronald, *Wings of Judgment—American Bombing in World War II.* New York & Oxford: Oxford University Press, 1985.

Shirer, William L., *The Rise and Fall of the Third Reich.* New York: Simon & Schuster, 1960.

Stout, Jay A., *Unsung Eagles: True Stories of America's Citizen Airmen in the Skies of World War II.* Philadelphia & Oxford: Casemate, 2013.

Swanston, Alexander and Swanston, Malcolm, *The Historical Atlas of World War II.* Edison, NJ: Chartwell Books, Inc., 2007.

Vercoe, Tony, *Survival at Stalag IVB: soldiers and airmen remember Germany's largest POW camp of World War II.* Jefferson, NC and London: MacFarland & Company, Inc., 2006.

Ward, Geoffrey C. and Burns, Ken, *The War.* New York: Alfred A. Knopf, 2007.

Wolfe, Tom, *The Right Stuff.* New York: Farrar, Strauss and Giroux, 1979.

Index

A-20 Douglas "Havoc" bomber, 173–174

Abandon ship order *The Wild Hare*, 74–75

African-Americans

At Keesler Field, Biloxi, MS, 29–30, 189, 215

At Tampa, FL, 43–44

Aircraft production statistics 1944, 196

Air Force Magazine article—*The Black March*, 125

Air Medal, 12, 87, 117

Air raids—POW railroad cars, 94–95

Altenbeken, Germany, 17 (map), 69, 71, 74, 85, 114, 213 (drawing)

American heavy bomber strategic policy

Beginning of war until February 3, 1945, 54, 67, 116, 118–119

February 3, 1945 to conclusion of war, 118–121

Anklam, Germany, battle of, 50–51, 148

April 22, 1945—Paul's decision to escape, 15, 167–168

April 24, 1945—Liberation, 125, 175–176

Army Air Forces Cadet Program, Manchester, NH, 24

Army Air Forces Southeast Training Center Pre-Flight School (Pilot) Maxwell Field, AL, 19–23

Arran, Isle of, Scotland (site of 17 B-17 crashes), 46

AT-10 Beech "Wichita" trainer, 27

Attack on *The Wild Hare*, 72–77

Auschwitz Concentration Camp, 116

Aviation Cadet Honor Code, 20

Aviation Cadet Mission Statement, 20

B-17 Boeing "Flying Fortress" bomber described, 32

B-24 Consolidated "Liberator" bomber compared to B-17, 32, 110–112

Balaban, B-17 pilot, 106

Bane, Mark C., Jr., Maj., 22–23, 26

"Bargaining chip" for Hitler then Stalin, 124, 182

B., Mary—letter from, 27

Bartush, Chuck, 41, 86, 164

Bartush, Jack, 41, 82–83, 164

Bartush, J. Addison, Lt.

"Ashamed" comment, 86

First mission—November 25, 1944, 61–67, 114

Map of targets attacked by, 16

Training to become co-pilot, 19–23, 25–28, 32–34

Bartush, Mary A. (Addison's mother) letters from: 84, 117, 155–157, 164–165, 210–211

Bartush, May Cay, 28, 86–87, 117

Bartush, Stephen J., 22, 39, 41–42, 86, 105

Basic flight training, 25–27

Bassingbourn USAAF Air Station, 11–14, 49, 52–53, 55, 57–58, 67, 77, 80, 82, 85–86, 107, 117, 122, 156, 161, 163, 196–197, 199

Bataan Death March, comparison to, 100, 123, 221

Battle of the Bulge, 67, 84–85, 96, 107, 118, 145, 182, 218

"Beaverboard Bomber" expression, 27

Berger, Gottlob, SS General, 151

Berlin mission, February 3, 1945, 62, 113–114, 116, 119–122, 143, 145, 199

Biloxi, MS, 28–29, 44, 189

Biloxi Blues by playwright Neil Simon, 29

Bishop Crew, 35–47, 49, 52–56, 58–59, 66, 69–80, 108–109, 114, 128, 156, 194–195

Bishop, David L., Jr., Lt., first pilot, 13, 35–42, 45–46, 52, 55, 58–59, 66, 69, 75–77, 79–80, 90, 97, 108–109, 156, 190, 193, 202, 206

Bishop, Pearl, letters from, 109

Black March, The

Blanket roll, 126, 128–129, 134, 137

British pharmacist, 127, 129–131, 137, 208

Dysentery, 126, 134,136

Drinking water, 129–134, 137, 169, 208

Dropouts, 129, 131, 133–134, 203

Encouragement from fellow prisoners, 137

Fires at night, 15, 132–133, 136, 170, 172

First week, 123–137

Foot blisters, 128, 131

Frostbite, 132–133

German guards, 127–130, 133, 135, 137, 149–150,152, 168–169, 203, 207, 220

Hershey bars, theft of, 129–130

Hostile encounters with civilians, 149

Misplaced persons, 135

Number of men involved, 125

POW group size, 127, 130

Pneumonia, 136

Shoe and boot problems, 94, 128

Sleeping in barns, 15, 126, 129, 134

SS, encounter with, 150–151

"Thinnest living horse" delivers last food parcels, 153

Tin cup, 128–129, 131

Weather, 126–128, 147–148,151

Blitz, 54–55

Bombach, Aribert, Lt. Col., Luftwaffe, Commandant Stalag Luft IV, 101–103, 126, 132, 206–207

91st Bombardment Group (heavy) Memorial Association website, 8

Bomb run, 43, 53, 63–64, 71–72, 163–164

Boxcars, 40 and 8 (German rail cars), 94

Briefings, pre mission, 61–63, 69–70, 120, 140–141

British heavy bomber strategic policy, 54, 118, 140, 195

Buckingham Army Air Field, Fort Myers, FL (B-17 co-pilot training), 32–33

Buckley Field, CO (enlisted airman training), 30–31

Bucknell, "Bucky," teacher, 24

Bunkroom for flight crew officers, Bassingbourn Air Station, 59, 66, 79

Burgermeister, dead body discovered by escapers, 180–181

"Buzzing" Spartanburg, SC, 39–41, 76

"Cadet widow" expression, 21

Camp Lucky Strike, Le Harve, France, 191

Camouflage Unit—Keesler Field, Biloxi, MS, 30

Caplan, Leslie, M.D., Maj., USAAF flight surgeon, 102–103, 131, 135–136, 209, 220

    Quoted: "It was a march of great hardship," 126

Captured—Paul Lynch, 77

Carpet bombing, 49, 140

Casualties, USAAF airmen in WWII, 80

Catch-22 by author Joseph Heller, 81, 158, 195

Catholic, Roman

    Father Michael Ragan, 13, 57–58, 66, 80, 117, 156, 199, 216

    Nuns in German hospital, 90

Censors, 82, 99, 157, 189

Chaff—"screening force" mission, December 18, 1944, 84, 114

"Cheerful obedience to the will of the leader" (USAAF publication), 26

Chesterfield cigarette wrapper log— Paul's list of German cities:

    Wolin, Stargard, Stettin, Swinemünde, Anklam, Malchin, Waren, Parchim, Uelzen, Hannover, Wittenburg and Halle, 17 (map), 137, 148

Christmas Eve 1944, 85–86

Churchill, Winston, Prime Minister, Great Britain, 107, 195, 223

Civilian death toll from Allied bombings, 104, 142, 195

College Pilot Training Program, 19, 21, 35, 38, 52

Combat Crew Placement Pool, 33

Commissioned status—application for 2nd Lieutenant, 39, 42

Cooke, Alistair, writer, 158

Co-pilot training, 32–33

Cossacks, disappearance of, 188–189

Cowardice, 81, 100

"Cradle of Heroes" expression, 25

Cumings, Charles P., Sgt., 13, 36, 38–41, 69–70, 75–76, 109, 156

Dachau Concentration Camp turned into collection center, 188

"Dawn Patroller" expression, 22, 81

Debriefing, 66, 121, 162

Defectors, 186

Doenitz, Karl, Grand Admiral, German Navy, 149, 204

Dogfight, 63

Dog tags, 76, 93, 175–176

Doolittle, Jimmy, Commanding General, Eighth Air Force, 42, 56, 119

Dresden bombings—13 & 14 February 1945, 12, 108, 113–114, 137, 139–146, 148, 156, 158, 200, 222–223
  91st Bomb Group participation, 139–146
  Civilian casualties, estimates, 142, 144–145
  Nazi reaction, 142, 144–146, 148–149
  RAF pre-briefing, 140–141
  Soviet reaction, 142
  Stars & Stripes news article, 141–142
  Swedish press, 142
Dulag Luft, Frankfurt, Germany, 91–94, 128, 208
"Dumb as a Dodo Bird" expression, 22

Eden, Anthony, British foreign secretary, 187
Elbe River, 145, 148, 151, 153, 168–169, 177, 185–186, 191
Emergency landings, 30, 55, 86, 106, 198
Ersatz "coffee," 129, 134, 147, 152, 183
Escapers:
  Aerial rocket attacks on fuel tanks, 173–174
  Farmhouse, chicken and bonfire, 170
  Fw-190 factory, 170–171
  Mongolian Steppe horse and Red Army scout, 174–175
  Nazi Tiger tanks, 171–172, 174–175
  Red Army patrol, 175–181
  Red Army sergeant with a thumb but no fingers, 176–179, 181–182, 208
  Vodka: "We sure saw them drink it." 15, 176, 181, 184

Execution order recommended by Goebbels, 148–149, 167, 204

Fainting on parade ground, 21, 29
February 3, 1945—*Operation Thunderclap* commences, 113, 118–119, 121
February 6, 1945—*The Black March* commences, 101, 123–130, 222
Ferry trip over Atlantic, 44–47, 49
Flak, 12, 43, 51, 53, 56, 62–65, 71–73, 82–83, 106, 111, 113, 122, 139, 141, 143, 159, 161–163, 197–200
  88mm, 113, 208, 217
  Holing a wing—self sealing tank, 111
  Towers, 113
Fletcher Airfield, Clarksdale, MS, 25–26
Flight Officer/warrant officer designation, 27
Flight surgeons, 79, 81, 101–102, 200
Flint, Robert J., Lt., pilot, 70–71, 73–76
"Flying Boxcar" expression for B-24 "Liberator," 32
"Flying Fortress," capabilities and dimensions, 32
"Fog of war," expression, 121
Fort Devens, MA, 15, 28, 201
Frankfurt, Germany, mission to, 82, 114
Fw-190 Focke-Wulf fighter, 64, 73–74, 171

Gabreski, Francis "Gabby," Maj., 95, 97, 104, 202, 219
Geneva Convention, 43, 89, 93–96,

100–101, 103, 124, 148, 187, 201, 204–206
Chapter 8, "Transfers of Prisoners of War," 95
George Field Army Air Training Center, Lawrenceville, IL, 27
German encounters with Paul
  Friendliness—nuns in hospital and girls in village, 90
  Attractive blonde flirts with Paul, 91
  Conversation with soldier aboard train to Frankfurt, 91
  Luftwaffe interrogator at Dulag Luft, 93
  "Guten Abend"—young girl trades eggs for Ivory soap, 152
German industrial capacity impacted by Allied bombing, 195–196
Gesu Conference—St. Vincent De Paul Society: *Pro Dio; Pro Patria*, 210
Getz, Lowell, author *Pandemonium Over Pilsen*, 159, 163
"Gigs" expression, 23
Goebbels, Joseph, Dr., Reich Minister of Propaganda, 142, 148–149, 167, 204
Goldberg, Marvin, Lt., 58, 157–158
Goose Bay, Labrador, 45, 128
Greatest Generation, attributes and flaws, 158
Greenville Army Air Base, Greenville, MS, 26, 44
Griffin, James, Maj., 14, 200
Gulfport Army Airfield, MS, 13–14, 32–33, 35–36, 38–39, 40–42, 44, 61, 66, 69, 78, 80, 87, 121, 194
Gunnery School, 30–31, 37

H2X airborne radar, 82, 106, 199
"Hanger Queen" expression, 47, 70
Hannover, Germany, bombing of, 151
Harris, Arthur, British Air Marshal, 118
Himmler, Heinrich, SS-Reichsführer, 25
Hiner, Daniel V., Ssgt, 70, 72, 75–76
History Channel—preserving racial balance in Europe, 204
Hitler, Adolf, Führer, Third Reich, 67, 104, 116, 148–149, 151, 160, 167, 179, 181–182, 187, 202–206, 210, 226
  Racist policies, 187, 204
  Unwise military decision-making (invasion of Soviet Union), 179
  Orders use of Allied airmen officer POWs as human shields, 167
  Suicide announced April 30, 1945, 181
"Hollywood Bomber" expression, 32
"Hot pilot" expression, 23, 56

"I ask the questions" –Dulag Luft interrogation, 93
Iceland stop, 45–46
Initial point "I.P.", 63, 160
Interrogations, 91–93
Ireland, Northern—border markings, 45, 47

Japan, 12, 29, 46, 100–101, 123–124, 188, 191
  Treatment of POWs, 100–101
  Soviet Union declares war on, August 9, 1945, 123–124, 188
Jews, 58, 94, 157–158, 175, 204
  Prejudice against, 58, 94, 116, 157–158, 204, 224

Kassel, Germany, mission to, 82, 114

Keesler Field, Biloxi, MS, 29–30, 215

Kendall, John S., Sgt., 13, 36, 69–70, 72–73, 90, 156

Kesselring, Albert, German Field Marshal, 196

Killed in action "KIA", 8, 67, 76, 108, 193, 196–197, 200

King and Queen of England visit Bassingbourn, 49, 53

Klette, Immanuel J., Lt. Col., 55–57, 64, 78, 84, 108, 121, 159, 161–163, 179, 197, 199, 210

Klette's Wild Hares, 108, 197

Knife and fork school, 22

Kohlrabies, root crops, 147, 152, 170, 183, 208

Koniev, Ivan, Marshal of the Soviet Army, 142, 179

"Kriegies," expression, 95, 136, 225

Lagers, 96–97, 103, 127, 202, 209

Lament of a Co-Pilot poem, 32–33

Landers, Barbara A., Leominster High School graduate 1943, 24

Las Vegas Army Field Gunnery School, 30–31, 37

Lattie's "large shawl with fringe," 164

Lebensraum—*Mein Kampf*, 187

Left echelon formation flying position, 157

Leominster High School Year Book, Class of 1943, 23–24

Leominster, MA, 15, 23, 24, 44, 192

Letters from home while serving:
    Addison, 7, 13, 26–27, 39, 59, 80, 83–87, 108–109, 117, 155, 157, 164–165, 211
    Paul, 99

Leuna Werke, I.G. Farben chemical factory, 61–67, 82–83, 114

Lord, Marvin D., Lt. Col., Group Leader, 121, 198–199, 210

Loss of human life by country, 196

Lynch, G. Paul, Sgt.
    Interrogated at Dulag Luft, Frankfurt, Germany, 93
    Map of travels from point of capture to repatriation, 17
    POW at Stalag Luft IV, Tychowo, Poland, 96–104
    Rail travel inside Third Reich, 90–91, 94–96
    Shot down November 26, 1945, 69–77
    Training to become USAAF gunner, 30–31

M2 Browning .50 caliber machine gun, 30–31

4 'M's—good Catholic girls, 11, 27, 80, 83, 155, 165

Maps used by navigators, 113

Marshall, George C., General, Chief of Staff, U.S. Army, 205, 223

Marshalling yard, 61, 82, 106, 108, 118, 120, 144

Massacre at Merseburg—November 2, 1944, 53–54, 63, 196

Maxwell Army Airfield, AL, 19–20, 22, 25

Maxwell, Marion, 155

Me-109 Messerschmitt fighter, 50, 73, 77

Me-262 Messerschmitt fighter jet, 66

Meillerwagen—V-2 mobile launching pad, 107

Mein Kampf, 187

Memphis Belle B-17, 52–53, 163

Merseburg, Germany, 53–54, 61–63, 71, 78, 82, 112, 114, 196–197

Milk run, expression, 70, 81, 106, 143

Miller, Robert J. "JR", Flight Officer, 13, 35–36, 40, 46, 69, 75–76, 79, 80, 97, 122, 156, 190, 193–195, 202

Missing in action: "MIA", 13, 67, 78, 143, 156, 193, 196–197, 200

"Mist, fog, snow, frost, and drizzle," 85

Monkman, Mrs. Gordon, 193–194, 205, 212

Monkman, Owen W., Sgt., 13, 37–38, 40, 69–70, 90, 112, 156, 193–194

Murmansk, Russia—Soviet massacre of defectors, 187–188

"Mr. Dowilly, Mr. Dumbjohn and Mr. Dumbsquat" expressions, 22, 28, 41, 81

Names of some B-17s belonging to 324th Squadron, 108

Name, rank and serial number, 89, 93

Nazi party headquarters, bombing off, 120

New Orleans, LA, trip to, Addison and Paul, 39

New York Times, 189, 207

November 25, 1944, Addison's first mission, 61–67, 114

November 26, 1944
Paul's first and only mission, 69–77, 114
Loss of B-17 *The Wild Hare*, 72–77, 114

Norden bombsight, 14, 42–43, 72, 207, 215

North Ferry Route, 45–46

Nose art, 47, 108

Nuremberg, Court findings and judgments, 89, 204, 226

Observer, Dresden mission, 114, 139–141

"O'clock" enemy fighter positions, 50, 74

Officer's Pay Data Card, 44

Oil Campaign, 61–67

OKH—'Oberkommando des Heeres'—high command German Army, 204–205

Operation Gomorrah—British attack on Hamburg 1943, 118

Operation Millennium—British attack on Cologne 1942, 118

Operation Thunderclap
First U.S. mission to Berlin February 3, 1945, 113–114, 119–122
Rational for 113, 116–119, 121

Osnabruck, Germany, mission to, 69

Our Last Mission by Dawn Trimble Bunyak, quoted, 202–203

Parachuting from *The Wild Hare*, 13, 76–78

Parachute training, 31

Parade ground reviews, 20–21, 29–30

Paris, France, training mission to, 54

Paris, John "Pappy," Sgt.—comment on first week of The Black March, 136–137, 221

P-47 Republic "Thunderbolt" fighter
Crash of on May 15, 1945, 11, 14, 197, 200–201
Dive bombing, witnessed by Paul, 152–153

Park Lane Hotel, Denver, CO, 30

Pathfinder force "PFF", 82–83, 118, 141

Peacock, Raymond C., Flight Officer, 36, 42, 44, 80–81, 87

Pearsall Butter Company, Elgin, Illinois, 105

Pilsen, Czechoslovakia, raid of April 25, 1945
  Attack on airport, 115, 158, 160–161, 163
  Attack on Skoda Armament Plant, 115, 158–160
  Cloud coverage impedes bombing, 161
  Getz, Lowell, 159, 163
  Klette order for second go-around disobeyed, 161
  Newsletter, *Headquarters 1st Air Division* of May 5, 1945, 159
  Operational screw-up—P-51s lost over Prague, 161
  Rhapsody in Red, B-17, 163
  SHAEF announcing the target publicly beforehand, 158–159
  "Some people caught hell"— Addison quote, 162
  324th Squadron position—low and tail-end Charlie, 160
  Planes lost and damaged, 163

Piper Cub, 20

Postkarte, 94

Post-traumatic stress syndrome, 83–84

POWs
  U.S. airmen: 30,000, 43
  French Army, 96

Primary flight training, 23, 25–26

Psychological evaluations of Allied POWs done by Germans, 92

PT-19 Fairchild "Cornell" trainer, 25–26

Racial attitudes in the South, 43–44

Radio beam crossing of Atlantic, 45–46

Ragan, Michael, U.S. Army chaplain, 13, 57–58, 66, 80, 117, 156, 199, 216

Rail trips:
  To Frankfurt, Germany, 90–91
  To Tychowo, Poland, 94–96

RAMPS - Recovered Allied Military Personnel, 191

Red Army
  Approaches Stalag Luft IV, 123
  First Ukrainian Front, 177, 179
  Number of guns, aircraft and tanks and soldiers, 180
  Patrol sweeping for German soldiers near Riesa, 176–181
  "Revenge score"—looting and burning, 180
  V-E Day, 181

Red Cross
  American
    "Nazis Herd U.S. Captives," report of, 124
  International
    Emergency aid from Geneva, truck convoy, 151

Relief tube, B-17, 110

Remagen, Rhine River bridge, capture of, 156

Rhapsody in Red B-17, 108, 121, 163

"Ride the Beam" expression, 20, 22, 45–46, 162

Riesa, Germany
  Collection center for U.S. citizens—technical school

dormitory, 181–182

Paul's arrival—May 12, 1945, 15, 17 (map), 126, 177, 181–182

Paul witness: "I heard screams and often shots." 184

Return to U.S. military control—May 25, 1945, 191

Russian female soldiers—cooks and a medical doctor, 183

Russian major meets Paul, 183–184

U.S. Army chaplains visit—on or about May 18, 1945, 185

U.S. infantry soldiers, 182–183, 185

Robertson, William, Sgt., 37, 79, 193–194

Rochefort, France mission—Addison as first pilot, 115, 157

Roosevelt, Franklin D., U.S. President, 104, 107, 152, 188, 195

Rotary Club of Detroit: "A Tribute," 164

Savannah, Georgia (deployment to Europe from), 44

Schaefer, A.K., 26, 41

Schaffer, Ronald, professor and author, 119, 121

Schweinfurt raid, 50–51

"Seri*ass*" expression, 23, 26, 66, 81, 162

Shedd-Bartush Foods, Inc., 33, 85, 105

Sheen, Earl, Sgt., 37, 79, 108, 121–122, 163, 194

Simon, Neil, playwright, 29

Skunkface III, B-17, 106, 108, 200

Slave labor, 25, 65, 96, 107, 180, 187, 225

Solitary confinement, 92–93, 103

Soviet Union, 9, 29, 103, 116–117, 121, 124, 141–143, 160, 174, 179,

181–182, 186–191, 196

Spaatz, Carl, General, 42, 119–120

Spartanburg, SC, 39–41, 76

Sperry ball turret, 30, 37, 54, 70, 73–75, 110, 112, 193

"Spoony" expression, 22, 81

Squadrons of the 91st BG: 322nd, 323rd, 324th & 401st, 12, 14, 52–56, 73, 79, 81, 93, 106, 108, 121–122, 143, 160–162, 197–198, 200, 210

Squadron operations crew duty sheet, 70

Stalag Luft I, 13, 95, 97, 125, 149, 156, 190, 202

Liberation, 13, 190

Repatriation, 202

Wing commander (POW officer chain-of-command), 97

Stalag Luft III, 123, 202, 206, 222, 226

Stalag Luft IV, 94, 96–104, 123–127, 129, 135, 156, 201–202, 205–206

Abuse of POWs—use of dogs and ear cuffing alleged, 102–103

Barracks, 96–100, 103, 126–127, 222

Black bread, 99

Commandant, 101, 103, 126, 132–133, 206–207

Comparison to Japanese treatment of POWs, 100–101

Electrified barbwire fence, 97

Evacuation, 123–128

Food, 98–99

Formations, 97

Gauntlet run, spring 1944, 102–103

International Red Cross reports—population, accommodation & food, 96, 98

Lagers, 96–98

Mailings; postal matters, 99

POW chain-of-command, 97–98

POW shot and killed—June 1944, 97

Prison life, 96–100

Russian barracks, 103

Short wave radio hidden in a barracks, 99–100

Stealing Red Cross parcels alleged, 103

Warning rail, 97

Stalin, Joseph, Soviet leader, 47, 124, 145, 182, 185–188, 190, 223

Stars and Stripes newspaper, 7, 71, 85, 118, 141

Statler Hotel, Detroit MI, 11–12, 28, 30

Stone, Straffordshire, UK (location for assignment to bomb group), 47

Swinemünde, Germany, 135, 137, 147–148

Tail–end Charlie formation position, 51, 54, 73–74, 158, 160

Tail gunner position, 13, 37, 71, 112, 156

Target classifications or categories, 118

Terry, Henry W., Col, 63, 78–79, 108, 210

The Cadet Rudder (USAAF publication), 26

The Great Escape, 202, 206

The Great Warrior, quoted from, 7, 203, 205, 207

The Right Stuff, by Tom Wolfe, 112

The Wild Hare, B-17, 8, 70–76, 78, 171, 197

The Rise and Fall of the Third Reich by William L. Shirer, 204

Threat of execution of POWs, 148–149

"Thunderbolt," P-47 fighter, 11, 95, 152, 197

Tiger tank, Nazi: size, speed and armament, 171–172, 174–175

Time Life Books:

Anxious Deliverance ("Soviet truculence"), 186

Dresden bombing, 145

General Spaatz quote, "indiscriminately," 120

Stalag Luft III forced march, 222

Tolstoy, Nikolai: *Forced Repatriation to the Soviet Union: The Secret Betrayal,* 9, 186–187, 189

Tomaino, Sam A., Capt., Adjutant, Gulfport Army Airfield, MS, 42

Torgau, Germany—place of link up of U.S. and Red armies, 177

Tour:

Missions requirement, 53, 117, 112, 156

Solo punishment march, 23

Train trips:

To Dulag Luft Frankfurt, 90–91

To Stalag Luft IV Poland, 94–96

Trolley run over Germany after surrender, 163–164

Truman, Harry, U.S. President, 30, 190–191

Twelve O'Clock High, movie, 50

Twenty Missions in Hell, Air Force Magazine article, 62

Uniform, Clothing & Accessory Card—ETO Male Officers, 155

Uniforms supplied to POWs, 92

University of Detroit, 21

University of Pittsburgh, 19, 21, 35, 38, 52

United States, 9, 25, 35, 41–42, 44, 53, 78, 82, 116, 118, 124, 145, 153, 170, 182, 186, 189–190, 196

USCGC Tahoma, 82

V-1 and V-2 rockets, 106–108

Valley, Wales UK, 45, 47

V-E Days—May 8 and 9, 1945, 126, 164, 181, 202

Venereal disease, training, 29

Viaduct, Altenbeken, 17 (map), 69, 71, 74, 85, 89, 114, 213 (drawing)

Vonnegut, Kurt, quoted from *Slaughterhouse 5*, 190

War Crimes and Crimes Against Humanity, 204–205

Warner, John, U.S. Senator, quoted from Congressional Record, 125, 208

Warsaw, Poland—liberation by Red Army 1944, 47

Weight loss, Paul, 14, 191

"West Point of Alabama," 19, 23

Wings of Judgment—American Bombing in World War II, by Schaffer, Ronald, quoted, 119, 121

Wingspan 44-D "blasted into submission," 28

Winter conditions, flying comparison: B-17 versus B-24, 110–111

Wittenberg, Germany, 148, 151–152

Yalta Agreement, 116, 123–124, 153, 182, 185–186, 188–191

Hostile propaganda not permitted (Article 2), 153

"Immediate access" to citizens requirement (Article 2 Section 1), 182

Repatriation of citizens (Article 1), 124, 182, 185, 188

Soviet Union to enter war against Japan, 123–124, 188, 191

Zanotto, Bartolomeo, Ssgt, 70, 73, 75–76

Zeitz raid, 81–82, 114

Zhukov, Georgy, Marshal of the Soviet Army, 179

About the Author

Richard (Dick) Allison is a retired Captain in the United States Naval Reserve Judge Advocate General's Corps, having completed a twenty-six year military career in 1996. During his term of active duty (1968–1971) he served as line officer aboard the aircraft carrier USS Intrepid (CVS-11) and later on an admiral's staff in an administrative capacity. It was during his shipboard years that he developed a keen interest in the subject of military aviation.

As a civilian, Allison worked 35 years as a bank trust-lawyer both in estate and personal trust administration. A lifelong resident of Grosse Pointe Farms, Michigan, Allison served as president of the Rotary Club there and also as chairman of the non-profit Grosse Pointe War Memorial Association. He is married and has a daughter. Retired from both careers now, his interests include skiing, hiking, woodworking, reading military history and writing.

Addison Bartush and the author Sept. 10, 2008 at the Yankee Air Museum Willow Run Airport, Ypsilanti, Michigan.—Richard Allison Collection